Poor relations

Compton Mackenzie

Copyright © BiblioLife, LLC

This book represents a historical reproduction of a work originally published before 1923 that is part of a unique project which provides opportunities for readers, educators and researchers by bringing hard-to-find original publications back into print at reasonable prices. Because this and other works are culturally important, we have made them available as part of our commitment to protecting, preserving and promoting the world's literature. These books are in the "public domain" and were digitized and made available in cooperation with libraries, archives, and open source initiatives around the world dedicated to this important mission.

We believe that when we undertake the difficult task of re-creating these works as attractive, readable and affordable books, we further the goal of sharing these works with a global audience, and preserving a vanishing wealth of human knowledge.

Many historical books were originally published in small fonts, which can make them very difficult to read. Accordingly, in order to improve the reading experience of these books, we have created "enlarged print" versions of our books. Because of font size variation in the original books, some of these may not technically qualify as "large print" books, as that term is generally defined; however, we believe these versions provide an overall improved reading experience for many.

POOR RELATIONS

By COMPTON MACKENZIE
Author of "SYLVIA SCARLETT" "SYLVIA AND MICHAEL" ETC.

HARPER & BROTHERS PUBLISHERS
NEW YORK AND LONDON

Poor Relations

Copyright, 1919, by Harper & Brothers
Printed in the United States of America
Published February, 1920

B-U

THIS THEME IN C MAJOR WITH VARIATIONS IS INSCRIBED TO THE ROMANTIC AND MYSTERIOUS MAJOR C BY ONE WHO WAS PRIVILEGED TO SERVE UNDER HIM DURING MORE THAN TWO YEARS OF WAR

Capri, April 30, 1919.

POOR ❧ ❧
RELATIONS

Poor Relations

CHAPTER I

THERE was nothing to distinguish the departure of the *Murmania* from that of any other big liner leaving New York in October for Liverpool or Southampton. At the crowded gangways there was the usual rain of ultimate kisses, from the quayside the usual gale of speeding handkerchiefs. Ladies in blanket-coats handed over to the arrangement of their table-stewards the expensive bouquets presented by friends who, as the case might be, had been glad or sorry to see them go. Middle-aged gentlemen, who were probably not at all conspicuous on shore, at once made their appearance in caps that they might have felt shy about wearing even during their university prime. Children in the first confusion of settling down ate more chocolates from the gift boxes lying about the cabins than they were likely to be given (or perhaps to want) for some time. Two young women with fresh complexions, short skirts, tam o' shanters, brightly colored jumpers, and big bows to their shoes were already on familiar terms with one of the junior ship's officers, and their laughter (which would soon become one of those unending oceanic accompaniments that make land so pleasant again) was already competing with the noise of the crew. Everybody boasted aloud that they fed you really well on the *Murmania,* and hoped silently that perhaps the sense of being imprisoned in a decaying hot-water bottle (or whatever more or less apt comparison was invented to suggest atmosphere below decks) would pass away in the fresh Atlantic breezes. Indeed it might be said, except in the case of a few ivory-faced ladies already lying back with the professional aloofness of those who are a prey to chronic headaches, that outwardly optimism was rampant.

It was not surprising, therefore, that John Touchwood, the successful romantic playwright and unsuccessful realistic novelist, should on finding himself hemmed in by such invincible cheerfulness surrender to his own pleasant fancies of home. This was one of those moments when he was able to feel that the accusation of sentimentality so persistently laid against his work by superior critics was rebutted out of the very mouth of real life. He looked round at his fellow-passengers as though he would congratulate them on conforming to his later and more profitable theory of art; and if occasionally he could not help seeing a stewardess with a glance of discreet sympathy reveal to an inquirer the ship's provision for human weakness, he did not on this account feel better disposed toward morbid intrusions either upon art or life, partly because he was himself an excellent sailor and partly because after all as a realist he had unquestionably not been a success.

"Time for a shave before lunch, steward?" he inquired heartily.

"The first bugle will go in about twenty minutes, sir."

John paused for an instant at his own cabin to extract from his suitcase the particular outrage upon conventional headgear (it was a deerstalker of Lovat tweed) that he had evolved for this voyage; and presently he was sitting in the barber shop, wondering at first why anybody should be expected to buy any of the miscellaneous articles exposed for sale at such enhanced prices on every hook and in every nook of the little saloon, and soon afterward seriously considering the advantage of a pair of rope-soled shoes upon a heeling deck.

"Very natty things those, sir," said the barber. "I laid in a stock once at Gib., when we did the southern rowt. Shave you close, sir?"

"Once over, please."

"Skin tender?"

"Rather tender."

"Yes, sir. And the beard's a bit strong, sir. Shave yourself, sir?"

"Usually, but I was up rather early this morning."

"Safety razor, sir?"

"If you think such a description justifiable—yes—a safety."

"They're all the go now, and no mistake . . . safety bicycles, safety matches, safety razors . . . they've all come in our time . . . yes, sir, just a little bit to the right —thank you, sir! Not your first crossing, I take it?"

"No, my third."

"Interesting place, America. But I am from Wandsworth myself. Hair's getting rather thin round the temples. Would you like something to brisken up the growth a bit? Another time? Yes, sir. Thank you, sir. Parting on the left's it, I think?"

"No grease," said John as fiercely as he ever spoke. The barber seemed to replace the pot of brilliantine with regret.

"What *would* you like then?" He might have been addressing a spoilt child. "Flowers-and-honey? Eau-de-quinine? Or perhaps a friction? I've got lavingder, carnation, wallflower, vilit, lilerk . . ."

"Bay rum," John declared, firmly.

The barber sighed for such an unadventurous soul; and John, who could not bear to hurt even the most superficial emotions of a barber, changed his mind and threw him into a smiling bustle of gratification.

"Rather strong," John said, half apologetically; for while the friction was being administered the barber had explained in jerks how every time he went ashore in New York or Liverpool he was in the habit of searching about for some novel wash or tonic or pomade, and John did not want to make him feel that his enterprise was unappreciated.

"Strong is it? Well, that's a good fault, sir."

"Yes, I suppose it is."

"What took my fancy was the natural way it smelled."

"Yes, indeed, painfully natural," John agreed.

He stood up and confronted himself in the barber's mirror; regarding the fair, almost florid man, rather under six feet in height, with sanguine blue eyes and full, but clearly cut, lips therein reflected, he came to the comforting conclusion that he did not look his forty-two years and nine months; indeed, while his muffled whistle was shaping rather than uttering the tune of *Nancy Lee,* he nearly asked the barber to guess his age. However, he decided not to risk it, pulled down the lapels of his smoke-colored tweed coat, put on his deerstalker, tipped the barber sufficiently well to secure a parting caress from the brush, promised to meditate the purchase of the rope-soled shoes, and stepped jauntily in the direction of the luncheon bugle. If John Touchwood had not been a successful romantic playwright and an unsuccessful realistic novelist, he might have found in the spectacle of the first lunch of an Atlantic voyage an illustration of human madness and the destructive will of the gods. As it was, his capacity for rapidly covering the domestic offices of the brain with the crimson-ramblers of a lush idealism made him forget the base fabric so prettily if obviously concealed. As it was, he found an exhilaration in all this berserker greed, in the cries of inquisitive children, in the rumpled appearance of women whom the bugle had torn from their unpacking with the urgency of the last trump, in the acrid smell of pickles, and in the persuasive gesture with which the glistening stewards handed the potatoes while they glared angrily at one another over their shoulders. If a cynical realist had in respect of this lunch observed to John that a sow's ear was poor material for a silk purse, he would have contested the universal truth of the proverb, for at this moment he was engaged in chinking the small change of sentimentality in just such a purse.

"How jolly everybody is," he thought, swinging round to his neighbor, a gaunt woman in a kind of draggled mantilla, with an effusion of goodwill that expressed itself in a request to pass her the pickled walnuts. John fancied an impulse to move away her chair when she declined his offer; but of course the chair was fixed, and the only sign of her distaste for pickles or conversation was a faint quiver, which to any one less rosy than John might have suggested abhorrence, but which struck him as merely shyness. It was now that for the first time he became aware of a sickly fragrance that was permeating the atmosphere, a fragrance that other people, too, seemed to be noticing by the way in which they were looking suspiciously at the stewards.

"Rather oppressive, some of these flowers," said John to the gaunt lady.

"I don't see any flowers at our end of the table," she replied.

And then with an emotion that was very nearly horror John realized that, though the barber was responsible, he must pay the penalty in a vicarious mortification. His first impulse was to snatch a napkin and wipe his hair; then he decided to leave the table immediately, because after all nobody *could* suspect him, in these as yet unvexed waters, of anything but repletion; finally, hoping that the much powdered lady opposite swathed in mauve chiffons was getting the discredit of the fragrance, he stayed where he was. Nevertheless, the exhilaration had departed; his neighbors all seemed dull folk; and congratulating himself that after this first confused lunch he might reasonably expect to be put at the captain's table in recognition of the celebrity that he could fairly claim, John took from his pocket a bundle of letters which had arrived just before he had left his hotel and busied himself with them for the rest of the meal.

His success as a romantic playwright and his failure—or, as he would have preferred to think of it in the satisfaction of fixing the guilty fragrance upon the lady in mauve chiffons, his comparative failure—as a realistic novelist had not destroyed John's passion for what he called "being practical in small matters," and it was in pursuit of this that having arranged his letters in two heaps which he mentally labeled as "business" and "pleasure" he began with the former, as a child begins (or ought to begin) his tea with the bread and butter and ends it with the plumcake. In John's case, fresh from what really might be described as a triumphant production in New York, the butter was spread so thickly that "business" was too forbidding a name for such pleasantly nutritious communications. His agent had sent him the returns of the second week; and playing to capacity in one of the largest New York theaters is nearer to a material paradise than anything outside the Mohammedan religion. Then there was an offer from one of the chief film companies to produce his romantic drama of two years ago, that wonderful riot of color and Biblical phraseology, *The Fall of Babylon*. They ventured to think that the cinematograph would do his imagination more justice than the theater, particularly as upon their dramatic ranch in California they now had more than a hundred real camels and eight real elephants. John chuckled at the idea of a few animals compensating for the absence of his words, but nevertheless . . . the entrance of Nebuchadnezzar, yes, it should be wonderfully effective . . . and the great grass-eating scene, yes, that might positively be more impressive on the films . . . with one or two audiences it had trembled for a moment between the sublime and the ridiculous. It was a pity that the offer had not arrived before he was leaving New York, but no doubt he should be able to talk it over with the London representatives of the firm. Hullo here was Janet Bond writing to him . . . charming woman, charming actress. . . . He wandered for a few minutes rather vaguely in the maze of her immense handwriting, but disentangled his comprehension at last and deciphered:

    THE PARTHENON THEATER.
   Sole Proprietress: Miss Janet Bond.
      October 10, 1910.
DEAR MR. TOUCHWOOD,—I wonder if you have forgotten our talk at Sir Herbert's that night? I'm so hoping

not. And your scheme for a real Joan of Arc? *Do* think of me this winter. Your picture of the scene with Gilles de Rais—you see I followed your advice and read him up—has *haunted* me ever since. I can hear the horses' hoofs coming nearer and nearer and the cries of the murdered children. I'm *so* glad you've had a success with *Lucrezia* in New York. I don't *think* it would suit me from what I read about it. You know how *particular* my public is. That's why I'm so anxious to play the Maid. When will *Lucrezia* be produced in London? And where? There are many rumors. Do come and see me when you get back to England, and I'll tell you who I've thought of to play Gilles. I *think* you'll find him *very* intelligent. But of course everything depends on your inclination, or should I say inspiration? And then that wonderful speech to the Bishop! How does it begin? "Bishop, thou hast betrayed thy holy trust." *Do* be a little flattered that I've remembered that line. It needn't *all* be in blank verse, and I think little Truscott would be so good as the Bishop. You see how *enthusiastic* I am and how I *believe* in the idea. All good wishes.

Yours sincerely and hopefully,
JANET BOND.

John certainly was a little flattered that Miss Bond should have remembered the Maid's great speech to the Bishop of Beauvais, and the actress's enthusiasm roused in him an answering flame, so that the cruet before him began to look like the castelated walls of Orleans, and while his gaze was fixed upon the bowl of salad he began to compose *Act II. Scene I—Open country. Enter Joan on horseback. From the summit of a grassy knoll she searches the horizon.* So fixedly was John regarding his heroine on top of the salad that the head steward came over and asked anxiously if there was anything the matter with it. And even when John assured him that there was nothing he took it away and told one of the under-stewards to remove the caterpillar and bring a fresh bowl. Meanwhile, John had picked up the other bundle of letters and begun to read his news from home.

>65 Hill Road,
> St. John's Wood, N.W.,
> *October 10.*

Dear John,—We have just read in the *Telegraph* of your great success and we are both very glad. Edith writes me that she did have a letter from you. I dare say you thought she would send it on to us but she didn't, and of course I understand you're busy only *I* should have liked to have a letter ourselves. James asks me to tell you that he is probably going to do a book on the Cymbalist movement in literature. He says that the time has come to take a final survey of it. He is also writing some articles for the *Fortnightly Review*. We shall all be so glad to welcome you home again.

> Your affectionate sister-in-law,
> Beatrice Touchwood.

"Poor Beatrice," thought John, penitently. "I ought to have sent her a line. She's a good soul. And James . . . what a plucky fellow he is! Always full of schemes for books and articles. Wonderful really, to go on writing for an audience of about twenty people. And I used to grumble because my novels hadn't world-wide circulations. Poor old James . . . a good fellow."

He picked up the next letter; which he found was from his other sister-in-law.

> Halma House,
> 198 Earl's Court Square, S.W.,
> *October 9.*

Dear John,—Well, you've had a hit with *Lucrezia*. Lucky man! If you sent out an Australian company, don't you think I might play lead? I quite understand that you couldn't manage it for me either in London or America, but after all you *are* the author and you surely have *some* say in

the cast. I've got an understudy at the Parthenon, but I can't stand Janet. Such a selfish actress. She literally doesn't think of any one but herself. There's a chance I may get a decent part on tour with Lambton this autumn. George isn't very well, and it's been rather miserable this wet summer in the boarding-house as Bertram and Viola were ill and kept away from school. I would have suggested their going down to Ambles, but Hilda was so very unpleasant when I just hinted at the idea that I preferred to keep them with me in town. Both children ask every day when you're coming home. You're quite the favorite uncle. George was delighted with your success. Poor old boy, he's had another financial disappointment, and your success was quite a consolation.
ELEANOR

"I wish Eleanor was anywhere but on the stage," John sighed. "But she's a plucky woman. I *must* write her a part in my next play. Now for Hilda."

He opened his sister's letter with the most genial anticipation, because it was written from his new country house in Hampshire, that county house which he had coveted for so long and to which the now faintly increasing motion of the *Murmania* reminded him that he was fast returning.

AMBLES,
Wrottesford, Hants,
October 11.

MY DEAR JOHN,—Just a line to congratulate you on your new success. Lots of money in it, I suppose. Dear Harold is quite well and happy at Ambles. Quite the young squire! I had a little coolness with Eleanor—entirely on her side of course, but Bertram is really such a *bad* influence for Harold and so I told her that I did not think you would like her to take possession of your new house before you'd had time to live in it yourself. Besides, so many children all at once would have disturbed poor Mama. Edith drove over with Frida the other day and tells me you wrote to her. I should have liked a letter, too, but you always spoil poor Edith. Poor little Frida looks very peaky. Much love from Harold who is always asking when you're coming home. Mama is very well, I'm glad to say.

> Your affectionate sister,
> HILDA CURTIS.

"She might have told me a little more about the house," John murmured to himself. And then he began to dream about Ambles and to plant old-fashioned flowers along its mellow red-brick garden walls. "I shall be in time to see the coloring of the woods," he thought. The *Murmania* answered his aspiration with a plunge, and several of the rumpled ladies rose hurriedly from table to prostrate themselves for the rest of the voyage. John opened a fourth letter from England.

> THE VICARAGE,
> Newton Candover, Hants,
> *October 7.*

MY DEAREST JOHN,—I was so glad to get your letter, and so glad to hear of your success. Laurence says that if he were not a vicar he should like to be a dramatic author. In fact, he's writing a play now on a Biblical subject, but he fears he will have trouble with the Bishop, as it takes a very broad view of Christianity. You know that Laurence has recently become very broad? He thinks the village people like it, but unfortunately old Mrs. Paxton—you know who I mean—the patroness of the living—is so bigoted that Laurence has had a great deal of trouble with her. I'm sorry to say that dear little Frida is looking thin. We think it's the wet summer. Nothing but rain. Ambles was looking beautiful when we drove over last week, but Harold is a little bumptious and Hilda does not seem to see his faults. Dear Mama was looking *very* well—better than I've seen her for ages. Frida sends such a lot of love to dearest Uncle John. She never stops talking about you. I sometimes get quite jealous for Laurence. Not really, of course, because family affection is the foundation of civil life. Laurence is out in the garden speaking to a man whose pig got into our conservatory this morning. Much love.

Your loving sister,

EDITH.

John put the letter down with a faint sigh: Edith was his favorite sister, but he often wished that she had not married a parson. Then he took up the last letter of the family packet, which was from his housekeeper in Church Row.

39 CHURCH ROW,

Hampstead, N. W.

DEAR SIR,—This is to inform you with the present that everythink is very well at your house and that Maud and Elsa is very well as it leaves me at present. We as heard nothink from Emily since she as gone down to Hambles your other house, and we hope which is Maud, Elsa and myself you wont spend all your time out of London which is looking lovely at present with the leaves beginning to turn and all. With dutiful respects from Maud, Elsa and self, I am,

Your obedient servant,

MARY WORFOLK.

"Dear old Mrs. Worfolk. She's already quite jealous of Ambles . . . charming trait really, for after all it means she appreciates Church Row. Upon my soul, I feel a bit jealous of Ambles myself."

John began to ponder the pleasant heights of Hampstead and to think of the pale blue October sky and of the yellow leaves shuffling and slipping along the quiet alleys in the autumn wind; to think, too, of his library window and of London spread out below in a refulgence of smoke and gold; to think of the chrysanthemums in his little garden and of the sparrows' chirping in the Virginia-creeper that would soon be all aglow like a well banked-up fire against his coming. Five delightful letters really, every one of them full of good wishes and cordial affection! The *Murmania* swooped forward, and there was a faint tingle of glass and cutlery. John gathered up his correspondence to go on deck and bless the Atlantic for being the pathway to home. As he rose from the table he heard a voice say:

"Yes, my dear thing, but I've never been a poor relation yet, and I don't intend to start now."

The saloon was empty except for himself and two women opposite, the climax of whose conversation had come with such a harsh fitness of comment upon the letters he had just been reading. John was angry with himself for the dint so easily made upon the romantic shield he upheld against life's onset; he felt that he had somehow been led into an ambush where all his noblest sentiments had been massacred; five bells sounded upon the empty saloon with an almost funereal gravity; and, when the two women passed out, John, notwithstanding the injured regard of his steward, sat down again and read right through the family letters from a fresh standpoint. The fact of it was that there had turned out to be very few currants in the cake, for the eating of which he had prepared himself with such well-buttered bread. Few currants? There was not a single one, unless Mrs. Worfolk's antagonism to the idea of Ambles might be considered a gritty shred of a currant. John rose at once when he had finished his letters, put them in his pocket, and followed the unconscious disturbers of his hearth on deck. He soon caught sight of them again where, arm in arm, they were pacing the sunlit starboard side and apparently enjoying the gusty southwest wind. John wondered how long it would be before he was given a suitable opportunity to make their acquaintance, and tried to regulate his promenade so that he should always meet them face to face either aft or forward, but never amidships where heavily muffled passengers reclined in critical contemplation of their fellow-travelers over the top of the last popular novel.

"Some men, you know," he told himself, "would join

their walk with a mere remark about the weather. They wouldn't stop to consider if their company was welcome. They'd be so serenely satisfied with themselves that they'd actually succeed . . . yes, confound them . . . they'd bring it off! Yet, after all, I suppose in a way that without vanity I might presume they *would* be rather interested to meet me. Because, of course, there's no doubt that people *are* interested in authors. But, it's no good . . . I can't do that . . . this is really one of those moments when I feel as if I was still seventeen years old . . . shyness, I suppose . . . yet the rest of my family aren't shy."

This took John's thoughts back to his relations, but to a much less complacent point of view of them than before that maliciously apposite remark overheard in the saloon had lighted up the group as abruptly and unbecomingly as a magnesium flash. However inconsistent he might appear, he was afraid that he should be more critical of them in future. He began to long to talk over his affairs with that girl and, looking up at this moment, he caught her eyes, which either because the weather was so gusty or because he was so ready to hang decorations round a simple fact seemed to him like calm moorland pools, deep violet-brown pools in heathery solitudes. Her complexion had the texture of a rose in November, the texture that gains a rare lucency from the grayness and moisture by which one might suppose it would be ruined. She was wearing a coat and skirt of Harris tweed of a shade of misty green, and with her slim figure and fine features she seemed at first glance not more than twenty. But John had not passed her another half-dozen times before he had decided that she was almost a woman of thirty. He looked to see if she was wearing a wedding ring and was already enough interested in her to be glad that she was not. This relief was, of course, not at all due to any vision of himself in a more intimate relationship; but merely because he was glad to find that her personality, of which he was by now more definitely aware than of her beauty (well, not beauty, but charm, and yet perhaps after all he was being too grudging in not awarding her positive beauty) would be her own. There was something distinctly romantic in this beautiful young woman of nearly thirty leading her own life unimpeded by a loud-voiced husband. Of course, the husband might have had a gentle voice, but usually this type of woman seemed a prey to bluffness and bigness, as if to display her atmosphere charms she had need of a rugged landscape for a background. He found himself glibly thinking of her as a type; but with what type could she be classified? Surely she was attracting him by being exceptional rather than typical; and John soothed his alarmed celibacy by insisting that she appealed to him with a hint of virginal wisdom which promised a perfect intercourse, if only their acquaintanceship could be achieved naturally, that is to say, without the least suggestion of an ulterior object. *She had never been a poor relation yet, and she did not intend to start being one now.* Of course, such a woman was still unmarried. But how had she avoided being a poor relation? What was her work? Why was she coming home to England? And who was her companion? He looked at the other woman who walked beside her with a boyish slouch, wore gold pince-nez, and had a tight mouth, not naturally tight, but one that had been tightened by driving and riding. It was absurd to walk up and down forever like this; the acquaintance must be made immediately or not at all; it would never do to hang round them waiting for an opportunity of conversation. John decided to venture a simple remark the next time he met them face to face; but when he arrived at the after end of the promenade deck they had vanished, and the embarrassing thought occurred to him that perhaps having divined his intention they had thus deliberately snubbed him. He went to the rail and leaned over to watch the water undulating past; a sudden gust caught his cap and took it out to sea. He clapped his hand too late to his head; a fragrance of carnations breathed upon the salt windy sunlight; a voice behind him, softly tremulous with laughter, murmured:

"I say, bad luck."

John commended his deerstalker to the care of all the kindly Oceanides and turned round: it was quite easy after all, and he was glad that he had not thought of deliberately letting his cap blow into the sea.

"Look, it's actually floating like a boat," she exclaimed.

"Yes, it was shaped like a boat," John said; he was thinking how absurd it was now to fancy that swiftly vanishing, utterly inappropriate piece of concave tweed should only a few seconds ago have been worn the other way round on a human head.

"But you mustn't catch cold," she added. "Haven't you another cap?"

John did possess another cap, one that just before he left England he had bought about dusk in the Burlington Arcade, one which in the velvety bloom of a July evening had seemed worthy of summer skies and seas, but which in the glare of the following day had seemed more like the shreds of barbaric attire that are brought back by travelers from exotic lands to be taken out of a glass case and shown to visitors when the conversation is flagging on Sunday afternoons in the home counties. Now if John's plays were full of fierce hues, if his novels had been sepia studies of realism which the public considered painful and the critics described as painstaking, his private life had been of a mild uniform pink, a pinkishness that recalled the chaste hospitality of the best spare bedroom. Never yet in that pink life had he let himself go to the extent of wearing a cap, which, even if worn afloat by a colored prizefighter crossing the Atlantic to defend or challenge supremacy, would have created an amused consternation, but which on the head of a well-known romantic playwright must arouse at least dismay and possibly panic. Yet this John (he had reached the point of regarding himself with objective surprise), the pinkishness of whose life, though it might be a protest against cynicism and gloom, was eternally half-way to a blush, went off to his cabin with the intention of putting on that cap. With himself for a while he argued that something must be done to imprison the smell of carnations, that a bowler hat would look absurd, that he really must not catch cold; but all the time this John knew perfectly well that what he really wanted was to give a practical demonstration of his youth. This John did not care a damn about his success as a romantic playwright, but he did care a great deal that these two young women should vote him a suitable companion for the rest of the voyage.

"Why, it's really not so bad," he assured himself, when before the mirror he tried to judge the effect. "I rather think it's better than the other one. Of course, if I had seen when I bought it that the checks were purple and not black I dare say I shouldn't have bought it—but, by Jove, I'm rather glad I didn't notice them. After all, I have a right to be a little eccentric in my costume. What the deuce does it matter to me if people do stare? Let them stare. I shall be the last of the lot to feel seasick, anyway."

John walked defiantly back to the promenade deck, and several people who had not bothered to remark the well groomed florid man before now asked who he was, and followed his progress along the deck with the easily interested gaze of the transatlantic passenger.

For the rest of the voyage John never knew whether the attention his entrance into the saloon always evoked was due to his being the man who wore the unusual cap or to his being the man who had written *The Fall of Babylon;* nor indeed, did he bother to make sure, for he was fortified during the rest of the voyage by the company of Miss Doris Hamilton and Miss Ida Merritt and thoroughly enjoyed himself.

"Now am I attributing to Miss Hamilton more discretion than she's really got?" he asked himself on the last night of the passage, a stormy night off the Irish coast, while he swayed before the mirror in the creaking cabin. John was accustomed, like most men with clear-cut profiles, to take advice from his reflection, and perhaps it was his dramatic instinct that led him usually to talk aloud to this lifelong friend. "Have I in fact been too impulsive in this friendship? Have I? That's the question. I certainly told her a lot about myself, and I think she appreciated my confidence. Yet suppose that she's just an ordinary young woman and goes gossiping all over England about meeting me? I really must remember that I'm no longer a nonentity and that, though Miss Hamilton is not a journalist, her friend is, and, what is more, confessed that the sole object of her visit to America had been to interview distinguished men with the help of Miss Hamilton. The way she spoke about her victims reminded me of the way that fellow in the smoking-saloon talked about the tarpon fishing off Florida . . . famous American statesmen, financiers, and architects existed quite impersonally for her to be caught just like tarpon. Really when I come to think of it I've been at the end of Miss Merritt's rod for five days, and as with all the others the bait was Miss Hamilton."

John's mistrust in the prudence of his behavior during the voyage had been suddenly roused by the prospect of reaching Liverpool next day. The word positively exuded disillusionment; it was as anti-romantic as a notebook of Herbert Spencer. He undressed and got into his bunk; the motion of the ship and the continual opening and shutting of cabin doors all the way along the corridor kept him from sleep, and for a long time he lay awake while the delicious freedom of the seas was gradually enslaved by the sullen, prosaic, puritanical, bilious word—Liverpool. He had come down to his cabin, full of the exhilaration of a last quick stroll up and down the spray-whipped deck; he had come down from a long and pleasant talk all about himself where he and Miss Hamilton had sat in the lee of some part of a ship's furniture the name of which he did not know and did not like to ask, a long and pleasant talk, cozily wrapped in two rugs glistening faintly in the starlight with salty rime; he had come down from a successful elimination of Miss Merritt, his whole personality marinated in freedom, he might say; and now the mere thought of Liverpool was enough to disenchant him and to make him feel rather like a man who was recovering from a brilliant, a too brilliant revelation of himself provoked by champagne. He began to piece together the conversation and search for indiscretions. To begin with, he had certainly talked a great deal too much about himself; it was not dignified for a man in his position to be so prodigally frank with a young woman he had only known for five days. Suppose she had been laughing at him all the time? Suppose that even now she was laughing at him with Miss Merritt? "Good heavens, what an amount I told her," John gasped aloud. "I even told her what my real circulation was when I used to write novels, and I very nearly told her how much I made out of *The Fall of Babylon,* though since that really *was* a good deal, it wouldn't have mattered so much. And what did I say about my family? Well, perhaps that isn't so important. But how much did I tell her of my scheme for *Joan of Arc?* Why, she might have been my confidential secretary by the way I talked. My confidential secretary? And why not? I am entitled to a secretary—in fact my position demands a secretary. But would she accept such a post? Now don't let me be impulsive."

John began to laugh at himself for a quality in which as a matter of fact he was, if anything, deficient. He often used to chaff himself, but, of course, always without the least hint of ill-nature, which is perhaps why he usually selected imaginary characteristics for genial reproof.

"Impulsive dog," he said to himself. "Go to sleep, and don't forget that confidential secretaries afloat and confidential secretaries ashore are very different propositions. Yes, you thought you were being very clever when you bought those rope-soled shoes to keep your balance on a slippery deck, but you ought to have bought a rope-soled cap to keep your head from slipping."

This seemed to John in the easy optimism that prevails upon the borders of sleep an excellent joke, and he passed with a chuckle through the ivory gate.

The next day John behaved helpfully and politely at the Customs, and indeed continued to be helpful and polite until his companions of the voyage were established in a taxi at Euston. He had carefully written down the Hamiltons' address with a view to calling on them one day, but even while he was writing the number of the square in Chelsea he was thinking about Ambles and trying to decide whether he should make a dash across London to Waterloo on the chance of catching the 9:5 P.M. or spend the night at his house in Church Row.

"I think perhaps I'd better stay in town to-night," he said. "Good-by. Most delightful trip across—see you both again soon, I hope. You don't advise me to try for the 9:5?" he asked once more, anxiously.

Miss Hamilton laughed from the depths of the taxi; when she laughed, for the briefest moment John felt an Atlantic breeze sweep through the railway station.

"I recommend a good night's rest," she said.

So John's last thought of her was of a nice practical young woman; but, as he once again told himself, the idea of a secretary was absurd. Besides, did she even know shorthand?

"Do you know shorthand?" he turned round to shout as the taxi buzzed away; he did not hear her answer, if answer there was.

"Of course I can always write," he decided, and without one sigh he busied himself with securing his own taxi for Hampstead.

CHAPTER II

"I'VE got too many caps, Mrs. Worfolk," John proclaimed next morning to his housekeeper. "You can give this one away."

"Yes, sir. Who would you like it given to?"

"Oh, anybody, anybody. Tramps very often ask for old boots, don't they? Some tramp might like it."

"Would you have any erbjections if I give it to my nephew, sir?"

"None whatever."

"It seems almost too perky for a tramp, sir; and my sister's boy—well, he's just at the age when they like to dress theirselves up a bit. He's doing very well, too. His employers is extremely satisfied with the way he's doing. Extremely satisfied, his employers are."

"I'm delighted to hear it."

"Yes, sir. Well, it's been some consolation to my poor sister, I mean to say, after the way her husband behaved hisself, and it's to be hoped Herbert'll take fair warning. Let me see, you *will* be having lunch at home I think you said?"

John winced: this was precisely what he would have avoided by catching the 9:5 at Waterloo last night.

"I shan't be in to lunch for a few days, Mrs. Worfolk, no—er—nor to dinner either as a matter of fact. No—in fact I'll be down in the country. I must see after things there, you know," he added with an attempt to suggest as jovially as possible a real anxiety about his new house.

"The country, oh yes," repeated Mrs. Worfolk grimly; John saw the beech-woods round Ambles blasted by his housekeeper's disapproval.

"You wouldn't care to—er—come down and give a look

round yourself, Mrs. Worfolk? My sister, Mrs. Curtis—"

"Oh, I should prefer not to intrude in any way, sir. But if you insist, why, of course—"

"Oh no, I don't insist," John hurriedly interposed.

"No, sir. Well, we shall all have to get used to being left alone nowadays, and that's all there is to it."

"But I shall be back in a few days, Mrs. Worfolk. I'm a Cockney at heart, you know. Just at first—"

Mrs. Worfolk shook her head and waddled tragically to the door.

"There's nothing else you'll be wanting this morning, sir?" she turned to ask in accents that seemed to convey forgiveness of her master in spite of everything.

"No, thank you, Mrs. Worfolk. Please send Maud up to help me pack. Good heavens," he added to himself when his housekeeper had left the room, "why shouldn't I be allowed a country house? And I suppose the next thing is that James and Beatrice and George and Eleanor will all be offended because I didn't go tearing round to see them the moment I arrived. One's relations never understand that after the production of a play one requires a little rest. Besides, I *must* get on with my new play. I absolutely *must*."

John's tendency to abhor the vacuum of success was corrected by the arrival of Maud, the parlour-maid, whose statuesque anemia and impersonal neatness put something in it. Before leaving for America he had supplemented the rather hasty preliminary furnishing of his new house by ordering from his tailor a variety of country costumes. These Maud, with feminine intuition superimposed on what she would have called her "understanding of valeting," at once produced for his visit to Ambles; John in the prospect of half a dozen unworn peat-perfumed suits of tweed flung behind him any lingering doubt about there being something in success, and with the recapture of his enthusiasm for what he called "jolly things" was anxious that Maud should share in it.

"Do you think these new things are a success, Maud?" he asked, perhaps a little too boisterously. At any rate, the parlor-maid's comprehension of valeting had apparently never been so widely stretched, for a faint coralline blush tinted her waxen cheeks.

"They seem very nice, sir," she murmured, with a slight stress upon the verb.

John felt that he had trespassed too far upon the confines of Maud's humanity and retreated hurriedly. He would have liked to explain that his inquiry had merely been a venture into abstract esthetics and that he had not had the least intention of extracting her opinion about these suits *on him;* but he felt that an attempt at explanation would embarrass her, and he hummed instead over a selection of ties, as a bee hums from flower to flower in a garden, careless of the gardener who close at hand is potting up plants.

"I will take these ties," he announced on the last stave of *A Fine Old English Gentleman.*

Maud noted them gravely.

"And I shall have a few books. Perhaps there won't be room for them?"

"There won't be room for them, not in your dressing-case, sir."

"Oh, I know there won't be room in that," said John, bitterly.

His dressing-case might be considered the medal he had struck in honor of *The Fall of Babylon:* he had passed it every morning on his way to rehearsals and, dreaming of the triumph that might soon be his, had vowed he would buy it were such a triumph granted. It had cost £75, was heavy enough when empty to strain his wrist and when full to break his back, and it contained more parasites of the toilet table and the writing desk than one could have supposed imaginable. These parasites each possessed an abode of such individual shape that leaving them behind made no difference to the number of really useful articles, like pajamas, that could be carried in the cubic space lined with blue corded silk on which they looked down like the inconvenient houses of a fashionable square. Therefore wherever John went, the fittings went too, a glittering worthless mob of cut-glass, pigskin, tortoiseshell and ivory.

"But in my portmanteau," John persisted. "Won't there be room there?"

"I might squeeze them in," Maud admitted. "It depends what boots you're wanting to take with you, sir."

"Never mind," he sighed. "I can make a separate parcel of them."

"There's the basket what we were going to use for the cat, sir."

"No, I should prefer a brown paper parcel," he decided. It would be improper for the books out of which the historical trappings of his *Joan of Arc* were to be manufactured to travel in a lying-in hospital for cats.

John left Maud to finish the packing and went downstairs to his library. This double room of fine proportions was, as one might expect from the library of a popular writer, the core—the veritable omphalos of the house; with its fluted pilasters, cream-colored panels and cherub-haunted ceiling, the expanse of city and sky visible from three sedate windows at the south end and the glimpse of a busy Hampstead street caught from those facing north, not to speak of the prismatic rows of books, it was a room worthy of art's most remunerative triumphs, the nursery of inspiration, and, save for a slight suggestion that the Muses sometimes drank afternoon tea there, the room of an indomitable bachelor. When John stepped upon the wreaths, ribbons, and full-blown roses of the threadbare Aubusson rug that floated like gossamer upon a green carpet of Axminster pile as soft as some historic lawn, he was sure that success was not a vacuum. In his now optimistic mood he hoped ultimately to receive from Ambles the kind of congratulatory benediction that the library at Church Row always bestowed upon his footsteps. Indeed, if he had not had such an ambition for his country house, he could scarcely have endured to quit even for a week this library, where fires were burning in two grates and where the smoke of his Partaga was haunting, like a complacent ghost, the imperturbable air. John possessed another library at Ambles, but he had not yet had time to do more than hurriedly stock it with the standard works that he felt no country house should be without. His library in London was the outcome of historical research preparatory to writing his romantic plays; and since all works of popular historical interest are bound with a much more lavish profusion of color and ornament even than the works of fiction to which they most nearly approximate, John's shelves outwardly resembled rather a collection of armor than a collection of books. There were, of course, many books the insides of which were sufficiently valuable to excuse their dingy exterior; but none of these occupied the line, where romance after romance of exiled queens, confession after confession of morganatic wives, memoir after memoir from above and below stairs, together with catchpenny alliterative gatherings as of rude regents and libidinous landgraves flashed in a gorgeous superficiality of gilt and text. In order to amass the necessary material for a play about Joan of Arc John did not concern himself with original documents. He assumed, perhaps rightly, that a Camembert cheese is more palatable and certainly more portable than a herd of unmilked cows. To dramatize the life of Joan of Arc he took from his shelves *Saints and Sinners of the Fifteenth Century* . . . but a catalogue is unnecessary: enough that when the heap of volumes chosen stood upon his desk it glittered like the Maid herself before the walls of Orleans.

"After all," as John had once pointed out in a moment of exasperation to his brother, James, the critic, "Shakespeare didn't sit all day in the reading-room of the British Museum."

An hour later the playwright, equipped alike for country rambles and poetic excursions, was sitting in a first-class compartment of a London and South-Western railway train;

two hours after that he was sitting in the Wrottesford fly swishing along between high hazel hedges of golden-brown.

"I shall have to see about getting a dog-cart," he exclaimed, when after a five minutes' struggle to let down the window with the aid of a strap that looked like an Anglican stole he had succeeded in opening the door and nearly falling headlong into the lane.

"You have to let down the window *before* you get out," said the driver reproachfully, trying to hammer the frameless window back into place and making such a noise about it that John could not bear to accentuate by argument the outrage that he was offering to this morning of exquisite decline, on which earth seemed to be floating away into a windless infinity like one of her own dead leaves. No, on such a morning controversy was impossible, but he should certainly take immediate steps to acquire a dog-cart.

"For it's like being jolted in a badly made coffin," he thought, when he was once more encased in the fly and, having left the high road behind, was driving under an avenue of sycamores bordered by a small stream, the water of which was stained to the color of sherry by the sunlight glowing down through the arches of tawny leaves overhead. To John this avenue always seemed the entrance to a vast park surrounding his country house; it was indeed an almost unfrequented road, grass-grown in the center and lively with rabbits during most of the day, so that his imagination of ancestral approaches was easily stimulated and he felt like a figure in a painting by Marcus Stone. It was lucky that John's sanguine imagination could so often satisfy his ambition; prosperous playwright though he was, he had not yet made nearly enough money to buy a real park. However, in his present character of an eighteenth-century squire he determined, should the film version of *The Fall of Babylon* turn out successful, to buy a lawny meadow of twenty acres that would add much to the dignity and seclusion of Ambles, the boundaries of which at the back were now overlooked by a herd of fierce Kerry cows who occupied the meadow and during the summer had made John's practice shots with a brassy too much like big-game shooting to be pleasant or safe. After about a mile the avenue came to an end where a narrow curved bridge spanned the stream, which now flowed away to the left along the bottom of a densely wooded hillside. The fly crossed over with an impunity that was surprising in face of a printed warning that extraordinary vehicles should avoid this bridge, and began to climb the slope by a wide diagonal track between bushes of holly, the green of which seemed vivid and glossy against the prevailing brown. The noise of the wheels was deadened by the heavy drift of beech leaves, and the stillness of this russet world, except for the occasional scream of a jay or the flapping of disturbed pigeons, demanded from John's illustrative fancy something more remote and Gothic than the eighteenth century.

"Malory," he said to himself. "Absolute Malory. It's almost impossible not to believe that Sir Gawaine might not come galloping down through this wood."

Eager to put himself still more deeply in accord with the romantic atmosphere, John tried this time to open the door of the fly with the intention of walking meditatively up the hill in its wake; the door remained fast; but he managed to open the window, or rather he broke it.

"I've a jolly good mind to get a motor," he exclaimed, savagely.

Every knight errant's horse in the neighborhood bolted at the thought, and by the time John had reached the top of the hill and emerged upon a wide stretch of common land dotted with ancient hawthorns in full crimson berry he was very much in the present. For there on the other side of the common, flanked by shelving woods of oak and beech and backed by rising downs on which a milky sky ruffled its breast like a huge swan lazily floating, stood Ambles, a solitary, deep-hued, Elizabethan house with dreaming chimney-stacks and tumbled mossy roofs and garden walls rising from the heaped amethysts of innumerable Michaelmas daisies.

"My house," John murmured in a paroxysm of ownership.

The noise of the approaching fly had drawn expectant figures to the gate; John, who had gratified affection, curiosity and ostentation by sending a wireless message from the *Murmania,* a telegram from Liverpool yesterday, and another from Euston last night to announce his swift arrival, had therefore only himself to thank for perceiving in the group the black figure of his brother-in-law, the Reverend Laurence Armitage. He drove away the scarcely formed feeling of depression by supposing that Edith could not by herself have trundled the barrel-shaped vicarage pony all the way from Newton Candover to Ambles, and, finding that the left-hand door of the fly was unexpectedly susceptible to the prompting of its handle, he alighted with such rapidity that not one of his smiling relations could have had any impression but that he was bounding to greet them. The two sisters were so conscious of their rich unmarried brother's impulsive advance that each incited her own child to responsive bounds so that they might meet him half-way along the path to the front door, in the harborage of which Grandma (whose morning nap had been interrupted by a sudden immersion in two shawls, and a rapid swim with Emily, the maid from London, acting as lifebuoy down the billowy passages and stairs of the old house) rocked in breathless anticipation of the filial salute.

"Welcome back, my dear Johnnie," the old lady panted.

"How are you, mother? What, another new cap?"

Old Mrs. Touchwood patted her head complacently.

"We bought it at Threadgale's in Galton. The ribbons are the new hollyhock red."

"Delightful!" John exclaimed. "And who helped you to choose it? Little Frida here?"

"Nobody *helped* me, Johnnie. Hilda accompanied me into Galton; but she wanted to buy a sardine-opener for the house."

John had not for a moment imagined that his mother had

wanted any advice about a cap; but inasmuch as Frida, in what was intended to be a demonstrative welcome, prompted by her mother, was rubbing her head against his ribs like a calf against a fence, he had felt he ought to hook her to the conversation somehow. John's concern about Frida was solved by the others' gathering round him for greetings.

First Hilda offered her sallow cheek, patting while he kissed it her brother on the back with one hand, and with the other manipulating Harold in such a way as to give John the impression that his nephew was being forced into his waistcoat pocket.

"He feels you're his father now," whispered Hilda with a look that was meant to express the tender resignation of widowhood, but which only succeeded in suggesting a covetous maternity. John doubted if Harold felt anything but a desire to escape from being sandwiched between his mother's crape and his uncle's watch chain, and he turned to embrace Edith, whose cheeks, soft and pink as a toy balloon, were floating tremulously expectant upon the glinting autumn air.

"We've been so anxious about you," Edith murmured. "And Laurence has such a lot to talk over with you."

John, with a slight sinking that was not altogether due to its being past his usual luncheon hour, turned to be welcomed by his brother-in-law.

The vicar of Newton Candover's serenity if he had not been a tall and handsome man might have been mistaken for smugness; as it was, his personality enveloped the scene with a ceremonious dignity that was not less than archidiaconal, and except for his comparative youthfulness (he was the same age as John) might well have been considered archiepiscopal.

"Edith has been anxious about you. Indeed, we have all been anxious about you," he intoned, offering his hand to John, for whom the sweet damp odors of autumn became a whiff of pious women's veils, while the leaves fluttering gently down from the tulip tree in the middle of the lawn lisped like the India-paper of prayer-books.

"I've got an air-gun, Uncle John," ejaculated Harold, who having for some time been inhaling the necessary breath now expelled the sentence in a burst as if he had been an air-gun himself. John hailed the announcement almost effusively; it reached him with the kind of relief with which in childhood he had heard the number of the final hymn announced; and a robin piping his delicate tune from the garden wall was welcome as birdsong in a churchyard had been after service on Sundays handicapped by the litany.

"Would you like to see me shoot at something?" Harold went on, hastily cramming his mouth with slugs.

"Not now, dear," said Hilda, hastily. "Uncle John is tired. And don't eat sweets just before lunch."

"Well, it wouldn't tire him to see me shoot at something. And I'm not eating sweets. I'm getting ready to load."

"Let the poor child shoot if he wants to," Grandma put in.

Harold beamed ferociously through his spectacles, took a slug from his mouth, fitted it into the air-gun, and fired, bringing down two leaves from an espalier pear. Everybody applauded him, because everybody felt glad that it had not been a window or perhaps even himself; the robin cocked his tail contemptuously and flew away.

"And now I must go and get ready for lunch," said John, who thought a second shot might be less innocuous, and was moreover really hungry. His bedroom, dimity draped, had a pleasant rustic simplicity, but he decided that it wanted living in: the atmosphere at present was too much that of a well-recommended country inn.

"Yes, it wants living in," said John to himself. "I shall put in a good month here and break the back of Joan of Arc."

"What skin is this, Uncle John?" a serious voice at his elbow inquired. John started; he had not observed Harold's scout-like entrance.

"What skin is that, my boy?" he repeated in what he thought was the right tone of avuncular jocularity and looking down at Harold, who was examining with myopic intensity the dressing-case. "That is the skin of a white elephant."

"But it's brown," Harold objected.

John rashly decided to extend his facetiousness.

"Yes, well, white elephants turn brown when they're shot, just as lobsters turn red when they're boiled."

"Who shot it?"

"Oh, I don't know—probably some friend of the gentleman who keeps the shop where I bought it."

"When?"

"Well, I can't exactly say when—but probably about three years ago."

"Father used to shoot elephants, didn't he?"

"Yes, my boy, your father used to shoot elephants."

"Perhaps he shot this one."

"Perhaps he did."

"Was he a friend of the gentleman who keeps the shop where you bought it?"

"I shouldn't be surprised," said John.

"Wouldn't you?" said Harold, skeptically. "My father was an asplorer. When I'm big I'm going to be an asplorer, too; but I sha'n't be friends with shopkeepers."

"Confounded little snob," John thought, and began to look for his nailbrush, the address of whose palatial residence of pigskin only Maud knew.

"What are you looking for, Uncle John?" Harold asked.

"I'm looking for my nailbrush, Harold."

"Why?"

"To clean my nails."

"Are they dirty?"

"Well, they're just a little grubby after the railway journey."

"Mine aren't," Harold affirmed in a lofty tone. Then

after a minute he added: "I thought perhaps you were looking for the present you brought me from America."

John turned pale and made up his mind to creep unobserved after lunch into the market town of Galton and visit the local toyshop. It would be an infernal nuisance, but it served him right for omitting to bring presents either for his nephew or his niece.

"You're too smart," he said nervously to Harold. "Present time will be after tea." The sentence sounded contradictory somehow, and he changed it to "the time for presents will be five o'clock."

"Why?" Harold asked.

John was saved from answering by a tap at the door, followed by the entrance of Mrs. Curtis.

"Oh, Harold's with you?" she exclaimed, as if it were the most surprising juxtaposition in the world.

"Yes, Harold's with me," John agreed.

"You mustn't let him bother you, but he's been so looking forward to your arrival. *When* is Uncle coming, he kept asking."

"Did he ask *why* I was coming?"

Hilda looked at her brother blankly, and John made up his mind to try that look on Harold some time.

"Have you got everything you want?" she asked, solicitously.

"He hasn't got his nailbrush," said Harold.

Hilda assumed an expression of exaggerated alarm.

"Oh dear, I hope it hasn't been lost."

"No, no, no, it'll turn up in one of the glass bottles. I was just telling Harold that I haven't really begun my unpacking yet."

"Uncle John's brought me a present from America," Harold proclaimed in accents of greedy pride.

Hilda seized her brother's hand affectionately.

"Now you oughtn't to have done that. It's spoiling him. It really is. Harold never expects presents."

"What a liar," thought John. "But not a bigger one than I am myself," he supplemented, and then he announced aloud that he must go into Galton after lunch and send off an important telegram to his agent.

"I wonder . . ." Hilda began, but with an arch look she paused and seemed to thrust aside temptation.

"What?" John weakly asked.

"Why . . . but no, he might bore you by walking too slowly. Harold," she added, seriously, "if Uncle John is kind enough to take you into Galton with him, will you be a good boy and leave your butterfly net at home?"

"If I may take my air-gun," Harold agreed.

John rapidly went over in his mind the various places where Harold might be successfully detained while he was in the toyshop, decided that the risk would be too great, pulled himself together, and declined the pleasure of his nephew's company on the ground that he must think over very carefully the phrasing of the telegram he had to send, a mental process, he explained, that Harold might distract.

"Another day, darling," said Hilda, consolingly.

"And then I'll be able to take my fishing-rod," said Harold.

"He *is* so like his poor father," Hilda murmured.

John was thinking sympathetically of the distant Amazonian tribe that had murdered Daniel Curtis, when there was another tap at the door, and Frida crackling loudly in a clean pinafore came in to say that the bell for lunch was just going to ring.

"Yes, dear," said her aunt. "Uncle John knows already. Don't bother him now. He's tired after his journey. Come along, Harold."

"He can have my nailbrush if he likes," Harold offered.

"Run, darling, and get it quickly then."

Harold rushed out of the room and could be heard hustling his cousin all down the corridor, evoking complaints of "Don't, Harold, you rough boy, you're crumpling my frock."

The bell for lunch sounded gratefully at this moment,

and John, without even washing his hands, hurried downstairs trying to look like a hungry ogre, so anxious was he to avoid using Harold's nailbrush.

The dining-room at Ambles was a long low room with a large open fireplace and paneled walls; from the window-seats bundles of drying lavender competed pleasantly with the smell of hot kidney-beans upon the table, at the head of which John took his rightful place; opposite to him, placid as an untouched pudding, sat Grandmama. Laurence said grace without being invited after standing up for a moment with an expression of pained interrogation; Edith accompanied his words by making with her forefinger and thumb a minute cruciform incision between two of the bones of her stays, and inclined her head solemnly toward Frida in a mute exhortation to follow her mother's example. Harold flashed his spectacles upon every dish in turn; Emily's waiting was during this meal of reunion colored with human affection.

"Well, I'm glad to be back in England," said John, heartily.

An encouraging murmur rippled round the table from his relations.

"Are these French beans from our own garden?" John asked presently.

"Scarlet-runners," Hilda corrected. "Yes, of course. We never trouble the greengrocer. The frosts have been so light . . ."

"I haven't got a bean left," said Laurence.

John nearly gave a visible jump; there was something terribly suggestive in that simple horticultural disclaimer.

"Our beans are quite over," added Edith in the astonished voice of one who has tumbled upon a secret of nature. She had a habit of echoing many of her husband's remarks like this; perhaps "echoing" is a bad description of her method, for she seldom repeated literally and often not immediately. Sometimes indeed she would wait as long as half an hour before she reissued in the garb of a personal philosophical discovery or of an exegitical gloss the most casual remark of Laurence, a habit which irritated him and embarrassed other people, who would look away from Edith and mutter a hurried agreement or ask for the salt to be passed.

"I remember," said old Mrs. Touchwood, "that beans were a favorite dish of poor Papa, though I myself always liked peas better."

"I like peas," Harold proclaimed.

"I like peas, too," cried Frida excitedly.

"Frida," said her father, pulling out with a click one of the graver tenor stops in his voice, "we do not talk at table about our likes and dislikes."

Edith indorsed this opinion with a grave nod at Frida, or rather with a solemn inclination of the head as if she were bowing to an altar.

"But I like new potatoes best of all," continued Harold. "My gosh, all buttery!"

Laurence screwed up his eye in a disgusted wince, looked down his nose at his plate, and drew a shocked cork from his throat.

"Hush," said Hilda. "Didn't you hear what Uncle Laurence said, darling?"

She spoke as one speaks to children in church when the organ begins; one felt that she was inspired by social tact rather than by any real reverence for the clergyman.

"Well, I do like new potatoes, and I like asparagus."

Frida was just going to declare for asparagus, too, when she caught her father's eye and choked.

"Evidently the vegetable that Frida likes best," said John, riding buoyantly upon the gale of Frida's convulsions, "is an artichoke."

It is perhaps lucky for professional comedians that rich uncles and judges rarely go on the stage; their occupation might be even more arduous if they had to face such competitors. Anyway, John had enough success with his joke to feel much more hopeful of being able to find suitable presents in Galton for Harold and Frida; and in the silence of exhaustion that succeeded the laughter he broke the news of his having to go into town and dispatch an urgent telegram that very afternoon, mentioning incidentally that he might see about a dog-cart, and, of course, at the same time a horse. Everybody applauded his resolve except his brother-in-law who looked distinctly put out.

"But you won't be gone before I get back?" John asked.

Laurence and Edith exchanged glances fraught with the unuttered solemnities of conjugal comprehension.

"Well, I *had* wanted to have a talk over things with you after lunch," Laurence explained. "In fact, I have a good deal to talk over. I should suggest driving you in to Galton, but I find it impossible to talk freely while driving. Even our poor old pony has been known to shy. Yes, indeed, poor old Primrose often shies."

John mentally blessed the aged animal's youthful heart, and said, to cover his relief, that old maids were often more skittish than young ones.

"Why?" asked Harold.

Everybody felt that Harold's question was one that should not be answered.

"You wouldn't understand, darling," said his mother; and the dining-room became tense with mystery.

"Of course, if we could have dinner put forward half an hour," said Laurence, dragging the conversation out of the slough of sex, "we could avail ourselves of the moon."

"Yes, you see," Edith put in eagerly, "it wouldn't be so dark with the moon."

Laurence knitted his brow at this and his wife hastened to add that an earlier dinner would bring Frida's bed-time much nearer to its normal hour.

"The point is that I have a great deal to talk over with John," Laurence irritably explained, "and that," he looked as if he would have liked to add "Frida's bed-time can go to the devil," but he swallowed the impious dedication and crumbled his bread.

Finally, notwithstanding that everybody felt very full of roast beef and scarlet-runners, it was decided to dine at half-past six instead of half-past seven.

"Poor Papa, I remember," said old Mrs. Touchwood, "always liked to dine at half-past three. That gave him a nice long morning for his patients and time to smoke his cigar after dinner before he opened the dispensary in the evening. Supper was generally cold unless he anticipated a night call, in which case we had soup."

All were glad that the twentieth century had arrived, and they smiled sympathetically at the old lady, who, feeling that her anecdote had scored a hit, embarked upon another about being taken to the Great Exhibition when she was eleven years old, which lasted right through the pudding, perhaps because it was trifle, and Harold did not feel inclined to lose a mouthful by rash interruptions.

After lunch John was taken all over the house and all round the garden and congratulated time after time upon the wisdom he had shown in buying Ambles: he was made to feel that property set him apart from other men even more definitely than dramatic success.

"Of course, Daniel was famous in his way," Hilda said. "But what did he leave me?"

John, remembering the £120 a year in the bank and the collection of stuffed humming birds at the pantechnicon, the importation of which to Ambles he was always dreading, felt that Hilda was not being ungratefully rhetorical.

"And of course," Laurence contributed, "a vicar feels that his glebe—the value of which by the way has just gone down another £2 an acre—is not his own."

"Yes, you see," Edith put in, "if anything horrid happened to Laurence it would belong to the next vicar."

Again the glances of husband and wife played together in mid-air like butterflies.

"And so," Laurence went on, "when you tell us that you hope to buy this twenty-acre field we all realize that in doing so you would most emphatically be consolidating your property."

"Oh, I'm sure you're wise to buy," said Hilda, weightily.

"It would make Ambles so much larger, wouldn't it?" suggested Edith. "Twenty acres, you see . . . well, really, I suppose twenty acres would be as big as from . . ."

"Come, Edith," said her husband. "Don't worry poor John with comparative acres—we are all looking at the twenty-acre field now."

The fierce little Kerry cows eyed the prospective owner peacefully, until Harold hit one of them with a slug from his air-gun, when they all began to career about the field, kicking up their heels and waving their tails.

"Don't do that, my boy," John said, crossly—for him very crossly.

A short cut to Galton lay across this field, which John, though even when they were quiet he never felt on really intimate terms with cows, had just decided to follow

"Darling, that's such a cruel thing to do," Hilda expostulated. "The poor cow wasn't hurting you."

"It was looking at me," Harold protested.

"There is a legend about Francis of Assisi, Harold," his Uncle Laurence began, "which will interest you and at the same time . . ."

"Sorry to interrupt," John broke in, "but I must be getting along. This telegram . . . I'll be back for tea."

He hurried off and when everybody called out to remind him of the short cut across the twenty-arce field he waved back cheerfully, as if he thought he was being wished a jolly walk; but he took the long way round.

It was a good five miles to Galton in the opposite direction from the road by which he had driven up that morning; but on this fine autumn afternoon, going down hill nearly all the way through a foreground of golden woods with prospects of blue distances beyond, John enjoyed the walk, and not less because even at the beginning of it he stopped once or twice to think how jolly it would be to see Miss Hamilton and Miss Merritt coming round the next bend in the road. Later on, he did not bother to include Miss Merritt, and finally he discovered his fancy so steadily fixed upon Miss Hamilton that he was forced to remind himself that Miss Hamilton in such a setting would demand a much higher standard of criticism than Miss Hamilton on the promenade deck of the *Murmania*. Nevertheless, John continued to think of her; and so pleasantly did her semblance walk beside him and so exceptionally mild was the afternoon for the season of the year that he must have strolled along the greater part of the way. At any rate, when he saw the tower of Galton church he was shocked to find that it was already four o'clock.

CHAPTER III

THE selection of presents for children is never easy, because in order to extract real pleasure from the purchase it is necessary to find something that excites the donor as much as it is likely to excite the recipient. In John's case this difficulty was quadrupled by having to find toys with an American air about them, and on top of that by the narrowly restricted choice in the Galton shops. He felt that it would be ridiculous, even insulting, to produce for Frida as typical of New York's luxurious catering for the young that doll, the roses of whose cheeks had withered in the sunlight of five Hampshire summers, and whose smile had failed to allure as little girls those who were now marriageable young women. Nor did he think that Harold would accept as worthy of American enterprise those more conspicuous portions of a diminutive Uhlan's uniform fastened to a dog's-eared sheet of cardboard, the sword belonging to which was rusting in the scabbard and the gilt lancehead of which no longer gave the least illusion of being metal. Finally, however, just as the clock was striking five he unearthed from a remote corner of the large ironmonger's shop, to which he had turned in despair from the toys offered him by the two stationers, a toboggan, and not merely a toboggan but a Canadian toboggan stamped with the image of a Red Indian.

"It was ordered for a customer in 1895," the ironmonger explained. "There was heavy snow that year, you may remember."

If it had been ordered by Methuselah when he was still in his 'teens John would not have hesitated.

"Well, would you—er—wrap it up," he said, putting down the money.

"Hadn't the carrier better bring it, sir?" suggested the

ironmonger. "He'll be going Wrottesford way to-morrow morning."

Obviously John could not carry the toboggan five miles, but just as obviously he must get the toboggan back to Ambles that night: so he declined the carrier, and asked the ironmonger to order him a fly while he made a last desperate search for Frida's present. In the end, with twilight falling fast, he bought for his niece twenty-nine small china animals, which the stationer assured him would enchant any child between nine and eleven, though perhaps less likely to appeal to ages outside that period. A younger child, for instance, might be tempted to put them in its mouth, even to swallow them if not carefully watched, while an older child might tread on them. Another advantage was that when the young lady for whom they were intended grew out of them, they could be put away and revived to adorn her mantelpiece when she had reached an age to appreciate the possibilities of a mantelpiece. John did not feel as happy about these animals as he did about the toboggan: there was not a single buffalo among them, and not one looked in the least distinctively American, but the stationer was so reassuring and time was going by so rapidly that he decided to risk the purchase. And really when they were deposited in a cardboard box among cotton-wool they did not look so dull, and perhaps Frida would enjoy guessing how many there were before she unpacked them.

"Better than a Noah's Ark," said John, hopefully.

"Oh yes, much better, sir. A much more suitable present for a young lady. In fact Noah's Arks are considered all right for village treats, but they're in very little demand among the gentry nowadays."

When John was within a quarter of a mile from Ambles he told the driver of the fly to stop. Somehow he must creep into the house and up to his room with the toboggan and the china animals; it was after six, and the children would have been looking out for his return since five. Perhaps the cows would have gone home by now and he should not excite their nocturnal apprehensions by dragging the toboggan across the twenty-acre field. Meanwhile, he should tell the fly to wait five minutes before driving slowly up to the house, which would draw the scent and enable him with Emily's help to reach his room unperceived by the backstairs. A heavy mist hung upon the meadow, and the paper wrapped round the toboggan, which was just too wide to be carried under his arm like a portfolio, began to peel off in the dew with a swishing sound that would inevitably attract the curiosity of the cows were they still at large; moreover, several of the china animals were now chinking together and, John could not help feeling with some anxiety, probably chipping off their noses.

"I must look like a broken-down Santa Claus with this vehicle," he said to himself. "Where's the path got to now? I wonder why people wiggle so when they make a path? Hullo! What's that?"

The munching of cattle was audible close at hand, a munching that was sometimes interrupted by awful snorts.

"Perhaps it's only the mist that makes them do that," John tried to assure himself. "It seems very imprudent to leave valuable cows out of doors on a damp night like this."

There was a sound of heavy bodies moving suddenly in unison.

"They've heard me," thought John, hopelessly. "I wish to goodness I knew something about cows. I really must get the subject up. Of course, they *may* be frightened of *me*. Good heavens, they're all snorting now. Probably the best thing to do is to keep on calmly walking; most animals are susceptible to human indifference. What a little fool that nephew of mine was to shoot at them this afternoon. I'm hanged if he deserves his toboggan."

The lights of Ambles stained the mist in front; John ran the last fifty yards, threw himself over the iron railings, and stood panting upon his own lawn. In the distance could be heard the confused thudding of hoofs dying away toward the far end of the twenty-acre meadow.

"I evidently frightened them," John thought.

A few minutes later he was calling down from the landing outside his bedroom that it was time for presents. In the first brief moment of intoxication that had succeeded his defeat of the cattle John had seriously contemplated tobogganing downstairs himself in order to "surprise the kids" as he put it. But from his landing the staircase looked all wrong for such an experiment and he walked the toboggan down, which lamplight appeared to him a typical product of the bear-haunted mountains of Canada.

Everybody was waiting for him in the drawing-room; everybody was flatteringly enthusiastic about the toboggan and seemed anxious to make it at home in such strange surroundings; nobody failed to point out to the lucky boy the extreme kindness of his uncle in bringing back such a wonderful present all the way from America—indeed one almost had the impression that John must often have had to wake up and feed it in the night.

"The trouble you must have taken," Hilda exclaimed.

"Yes, I did take a good deal of trouble," John admitted. After all, so he had—a damned sight more trouble than any one there suspected.

"When will it snow?" Harold asked. "To-morrow?"

"I hope not—I mean, it might," said John. He must keep up Harold's spirits, if only to balance Frida's depression, about whose present he was beginning to feel very doubtful when he saw her eyes glittering with feverish anticipation while he was undoing the string. He hoped she would not faint or scream with disappointment when it was opened, and he took off the lid of the box with the kind of flourish to which waiters often treat dish-covers when they wish to promote an appetite among the guests.

"How sweet," Edith murmured.

John looked gratefully at his sister; if he had made his will that night she would have inherited Ambles.

"Ah, a collection of small china animals," said Laurence, choosing a cat to set delicately upon the table for general admiration. John wished he had not chosen the cat that seemed to suffer with a tumor in the region of the tail and disinclined in consequence to sit still.

"Yes, I was anxious to get her a Noah's Ark," John volunteered, seeming to suggest by his tone how appropriate such a gift would have been to the atmosphere of a vicarage. "But they've practically given up making Noah's Arks in America, and you see, these china animals will serve as toys now, and later on, when Frida is grown-up, they'll look jolly on the mantelpiece. Those that are not broken, of course."

The animals had all been taken out of their box by now, but a few paws and ears were still adhering to the cotton-wool.

"Frida is always very light on her toys," said Edith, proudly.

"Not likely to put them in her mouth," said John, heartily. "That was the only thing that made me hesitate when I first saw them in Fifth Avenue. But they don't look quite so edible here."

"Frida never puts anything in her mouth," Edith generalized, primly. "And she's given up biting her nails since Uncle John came home, haven't you, dear?"

"That's a good girl," John applauded; he did not believe in Frida's sudden conquest of autophagy, but he was anxious to encourage her in every way at the moment.

Yes, the gift-horses had shown off their paces better than he had expected, he decided. To be sure, Frida did not appear beside herself with joy, but at any rate she had not burst into tears—she had not thrust the present from her sight with loathing and begged to be taken home. And then Harold, who had been staring at the animals through his glasses, like the horrid little naturalist that he was, said:

"I've seen some animals like them in Mr. Goodman's shop."

John hoped a blizzard would blow to-morrow, that Harold would toboggan recklessly down the steepest slope of the downs behind Ambles, and that he would hit an oak tree at the bottom and break his glasses. However, none of these dark thoughts obscured the remote brightness with which he answered:

"Really, Harold. Very likely. There is a considerable exportation of china animals from America nowadays. In fact I was very lucky to find any left in America."

"Let's go into Galton to-morrow and look at Mr. Goodman's animals," Harold suggested.

John had never suspected that one day he should feel grateful to his brother-in-law; but when the dinner-bell went at half-past six instead of half-past seven solely on his account, John felt inclined to shake him by the hand. Nor would he have ever supposed that he should one day welcome the prospect of one of Laurence's long confidential talks. Yet when the ladies departed after dessert and Laurence took the chair next to himself as solemnly as if it were a faldstool, he encouraged him with a smile.

"We might have our little talk now," and when Laurence cleared his throat John felt that the conversation had been opened as successfully as a local bazaar. Not merely did John smile encouragingly, but he actually went so far as to invite him to go ahead.

Laurence sighed, and poured himself out a second glass of port.

"I find myself in a position of considerable difficulty," he announced, "and should like your advice."

John's mind went rapidly to the balance in his pass-book instead of to the treasure of worldly experience from which he might have drawn.

"Perhaps before we begin our little talk," said Laurence, "it would be as well if I were to remind you of some of the outstanding events and influences in my life. You will then be in a better position to give me the advice and help—ah—the moral help, of which I stand in need—ah—in sore need."

"He keeps calling it a little talk," John thought, "but by

Jove, it's lucky we did have dinner early. At this rate he won't get back to his vicarage before cock-crow."

John was not deceived by his brother-in-law's minification of their talk, and he exchanged the trim Henry Clay he had already clipped for a very large Upman that would smoke for a good hour.

"Won't you light up before you begin?" he asked, pushing a box of commonplace Murillos toward his brother-in-law, whose habit of biting off the end of a cigar, of letting it go out, of continually knocking off the ash, of forgetting to remove the band till it was smoldering, and of playing miserable little tunes with it on the rim of a coffee-cup, in fact of doing everything with it except smoke it appreciatively, made it impossible for John, so far as Laurence was concerned, to be generous with his cigars.

"I think you'll find these not bad."

This was true; the Murillos were not actually bad.

"Thanks, I will avail myself of your offer. But to come back to what I was saying," Laurence went on, lighting his cigar with as little expression of anticipated pleasure as might be discovered in the countenance of a lodging-house servant lighting a fire. "I do not propose to occupy your time by an account of my spiritual struggles at the University."

"You ought to write a novel," said John, cheerfully.

Laurence looked puzzled.

"I am now occupied with the writing of a play, but I shall come to that presently. Novels, however . . ."

"I was only joking," said John. "It would take too long to explain the joke. Sorry I interrupted you. Cigar gone out? Don't take another. It doesn't really matter how often those Murillos go out."

"Where am I?" Laurence asked in a bewildered voice.

"You'd just left Oxford," John answered, quickly.

"Ah, yes, I was at Oxford. Well, as I was saying, I shall not detain you with an account of my spiritual struggles there. . . . I think I may almost without presumption refer to them as my spiritual progress . . . let it suffice that I found myself on the vigil of my ordination after a year at Cuddesdon Theological College a convinced High Churchman. This must not be taken to mean that I belonged to the more advanced or what I should prefer to call the Italian party in the Church of England. I did not."

Laurence here paused and looked at John earnestly; since John had not the remotest idea what the Italian party meant and was anxious to avoid being told, he said in accents that sought to convey relief at hearing his brother-in-law's personal contradiction of a charge that had for long been whispered against him:

"Oh, you didn't?"

"No, I did not. I was not prepared to go one jot or one tittle beyond the Five Points."

"Of the compass, you mean," said John, wisely. "Quite so."

Then seeing that Laurence seemed rather indignant, he added quickly, "Did I say the compass? How idiotic! Of course, I meant the law."

"The Five Points are the Eastward Position . . ."

"It was the compass after all," John thought. "What a fool I was to hedge."

"The Mixed Chalice, Lights, Wafer Bread, and Vestments, but *not* the ceremonial use of Incense."

"And those are the Five Points?"

Laurence inclined his head.

"Which you were not prepared to go beyond, I think you said?" John gravely continued, flattering himself that he was re-established as an intelligent listener.

"In adhering to these Five Points," Laurence proceeded, "I found that I was able to claim the support of a number of authoritative English divines. I need only mention Bishop Ken and Bishop Andrews for you to appreciate my position."

"Eastward, I think you said," John put in; for his brother-in-law had paused again, and he was evidently intended to say something.

"I perceive that you are not acquainted with the divergences of opinion that unhappily exist in our national Church."

"Well, to tell you the truth—and I know you'll excuse my frankness—I haven't been to church since I was a boy," John admitted. "But I know I used to dislike the litany very much, and of course I had my favorite hymns—we most of us have—and really I think that's as far as I got. However, I have to get up the subject of religion very shortly. My next play will deal with Joan of Arc, and, as you may imagine, religion plays an important part in such a theme—a very important part. In addition to the vision that Joan will have of St. Michael in the first act, one of my chief unsympathetic characters is a bishop. I hope I'm not hurting your feelings in telling you this, my dear fellow. Have another cigar, won't you? I think you've dipped the end of that one in the coffee-lees."

Laurence assured John bitterly that he had no reason to be particularly fond of bishops. "In fact," he went on, "I'm having a very painful discussion with the Bishop of Silchester at this moment, but I shall come to that presently. What I am anxious, however, to impress upon you at this stage in our little talk is the fact that on the vigil of my ordination I had arrived at a definite theory of what I could and could not accept. Well, I was ordained deacon by the Bishop of St. Albans and licensed to a curacy in Plaistow—one of the poorest districts in the East End of London. Here I worked for three years, and it was here that fourteen years ago I first met Edith."

"Yes, I seem to remember. Wasn't she working at a girls' club or something? I know I always thought that there must be a secondary attraction."

"At that time my financial position was not such as to warrant my embarking upon matrimony. Moreover, I had in a moment of what I should now call boyish exaltation registered a vow of perpetual celibacy. Edith, however, with that devotion which neither then nor at any crisis since has failed me expressed her willingness to consent to an indefinite engagement, and I remember with gratitude that it was just this consent of hers which was the means of widening the narrow—ah—the all too narrow path which at that time I was treading in religion. My vicar and I had a painful dispute upon some insignificant doctrinal point; I felt bound to resign my curacy, and take another under a man who could appreciate and allow for my speculative temperament. I became curate to St. Thomas's, Kensington, and had hopes of ultimately being preferred to a living. I realized in fact that the East End was a cul-de-sac for a young and—if I may so describe myself without being misunderstood—ambitious curate. For three years I remained at St. Thomas's and obtained a considerable reputation as a preacher. You may or may not remember that some Advent Addresses of mine were reprinted in one of the more tolerant religious weeklies and obtained what I do not hesitate to call the honor of being singled out for malicious abuse by the *Church Times*. Eleven years ago my dear father died and by leaving me an independence of £417 a year enabled me not merely to marry Edith, but very soon afterwards to accept the living of Newton Candover. I will not detain you with the history of my financial losses, which I hope I have always welcomed in the true spirit of resignation. Let it suffice that within a few years owing to my own misplaced charity and some bad advice from a relative of mine on the Stock Exchange my private income dwindled to £152, while at the same time the gross income of Newton Candover from £298 sank to the abominably low nett income of £102—a serious reflection, I think you will agree, upon the shocking financial system of our national Church. It may surprise you, my dear John, to learn that such blows from fate not only did not cast me down into a state of spiritual despair and intellectual atrophy, but that they actually had the effect of inciting me to still greater efforts."

John had been fumbling with his check book when Laurence began to talk about his income; but the unexpected turn of the narrative quietened him, and the Upman was going well.

"You may or may not come across a little series of devotional meditations for the Man in the Street entitled Lampposts. They have a certain vogue, and I may tell you in confidence that under the pseudonym of The Lamplighter I wrote them. The actual financial return they brought me was slight. Barabbas, you know, was a publisher. Ha-ha! No, although I made nothing, or rather practically nothing out of them for my own purse, by leading me to browse among many modern works of theology and philosophy I began to realize that there was a great deal of reason for modern indifference and skepticism. In other words, I discovered that, in order to keep the man in the street a Christian, Christianity must adapt itself to his needs. Filled with a reverent enthusiasm and perhaps half-consciously led along such a path by your conspicuous example of success, I have sought to embody my theories in a play, the protagonist of which is the apostle Thomas, whom when you read the play you will easily recognize as the prototype of the man in the street. And this brings me to the reason for which I have asked you for this little talk. The fact of the matter is that in pursuing my studies of the apostle Thomas I have actually gone beyond his simple rugged agnosticism, and I now at forty-two years of age after eighteen years as a minister of religion find myself unable longer to accept in any literal sense of the term whatever the Virgin Birth."

Laurence poured himself out a third glass of port and waited for John to recover from his stupefaction.

"But I don't think I'm a very good person to talk to about these abstruse divine obstetrics," John protested. "I really haven't considered the question. I know of course to what you refer, but I think this is essentially an occasion for professional advice."

"I do not ask for advice upon my beliefs," Laurence explained. "I recognize that nobody is able to do anything for them except myself. What I want you to do is to let Edith, myself, and little Frida stay with you at Ambles—of course we should be paying guests and you could use our pony and trap and any of the vicarage furniture that you thought suitable—until it has been decided whether I am likely or not to have any success as a dramatist. I do not ask you to undertake the Quixotic task of trying to obtain a public representation of my play about the apostle Thomas. I know that Biblical subjects are forbidden by the Lord Chamberlain, surely a monstrous piece of flunkeyism. But I have many other ideas for plays, and I'm convinced that you will sympathize with my anxiety to be able to work undisturbed and, if I may say so, in close propinquity to another playwright who is already famous."

"But why do you want to leave your own vicarage?" John gasped.

"My dear fellow, owing to what I can only call the poisonous behavior of Mrs. Paxton, my patron, to whom while still a curate at St. Thomas's, Kensington, I gave an abundance of spiritual consolation when she suffered the loss of her husband, owing as I say to her poisonous behavior following upon a trifling quarrel about some alterations I made in the fabric of *my* church without consulting her, I have been subject to ceaseless inquisition and persecution. There has been an outcry in the more bigoted religious press about my doctrine, and in short I have thought it best and most dignified to resign my living. I am therefore, to use a colloquialism,—ah—at a loose end."

"And Edith?" John asked.

"My poor wife still clings with feminine loyalty to those accretions to faith from which I have cut myself free. In most things she is at one with me, but I have steadily resisted the temptation to intrude upon the sanctity of her intimate beliefs. She sees my point of view. Of her sympathy I can only speak with gratitude. But she is still an old-fashioned believer. And indeed I am glad, for I should not like to think of her tossed upon the stormy seas of doubt and exposed to the—ah—hurricanes of speculation that surge through my own brains."

"And when do you want to move in to Ambles?"

"Well, if it would be convenient, we should like to begin gradually to-morrow. I have informed the Bishop that I will—ah—be out in a fortnight."

"But what about Hilda?" John asked, doubtfully. "She is really looking after Ambles for me, you know."

"While we have been having our little talk in the dining-room Edith has been having her little talk with Hilda in the drawing-room, and I think I hear them coming now."

John looked up quickly to see the effect of that other little talk, and determined to avoid for that night at least anything in the nature of little talks with anybody.

"Laurence dear," said Edith mildly, "isn't it time we were going?"

John knew that not Hilda herself could have phrased more aptly what she was feeling; he was sure that in her opinion it was indeed high time that Edith and Laurence were going.

Laurence went over to the window and pulled aside the curtains to examine the moon.

"Yes, my dear, I think we might have Primrose harnessed. Where is Frida?"

"She is watching Harold arrange the animals that John gave her. They are playing at visiting the Natural History Museum."

John was aware that he had not yet expressed his own willingness for the Armitage family to move into Ambles; he was equally aware that Hilda was trying to catch his eye with a questioning and indignant glance and that he had already referred the decision to her. At the same time he could not bring himself to exalt Hilda above Edith who was the younger and he was bound to admit the favorite of his two sisters; moreover, Hilda was the mother of Harold, and if Harold was to be considered tolerable in the same house as himself, he could not deny as much of his forbearance to Laurence.

"Well, I suppose you two girls have settled it between you?" he said.

Hilda, who did not seem either surprised or elated at being called a girl, observed coldly that naturally it was for John to decide, but that if the vicarage family was going to occupy Ambles extra furniture would be required immediately.

"My dear," said Laurence. "Didn't you make it clear to Hilda that as much of the vicarage furniture as is required can be sent here immediately? John and I had supposed that you were settling all these little domestic details during your little talk together."

"No, dear," Edith said, "we settled nothing. Hilda felt, and of course I can't help agreeing with her, that it is really asking too much of John. She reminded me that he has come down here to work."

The last icicle of opposition melted from John's heart; he could not bear to think of Edith's being lectured all the way home by her husband under the light of a setting moor. "I dare say we can manage," he said, "and really, you know Hilda, it will do the rooms good to be lived in. I noticed this afternoon a slight smell of damp coming from the unfurnished part of the house."

"Apples, not damp," Hilda snapped. "I had the apples stored in one of the disused rooms."

"All these problems will solve themselves," said Laurence, grandly. "And I'm sure that John cannot wish to attempt them to-night. Let us all remember that he may be tired. Come along, Edith. We have a long day before us to-morrow. Let us say good-night to Mama."

Edith started: it was the first time in eleven years of married life that her husband had adopted the Touchwood style of addressing or referring to their mother, and it seemed to set a seal upon his more intimate association with her family in the future. If any doubts still lingered about the forthcoming immigration of the vicarage party to Ambles they were presently disposed of once and for all by Laurence.

"What are you carrying?" he asked Frida, when they were gathered in the hall before starting.

"Uncle John's present," she replied.

"Do not bother. Uncle John has invited us to stay here, and you do not want to expose your little animals to the risk of being chipped. No doubt Harold will look after them for you in the interim—the short interim. Come, Edith, the moon is not going to wait for us, you know. I have the reins. Gee-up, Primrose!"

"Fond as I am of Edith," Hilda said, when the vicarage family was out of hearing. "Fond as I am of Edith," she repeated without any trace of affection in accent or expression, "I do think this invasion is an imposition upon your kindness. But clergymen are all alike; they all become dictatorial and obtuse; they're too fond of the sound of their own voices."

"Laurence is perhaps a little heavy," John agreed, "a little suave and heavy like a cornflour shape, but we ought to do what we can for Edith."

He tactfully offered Hilda a share in his own benevolence, in which she ensconced herself without hesitation.

"Well, I suppose we shall have to make the best of it. Indeed the only thing that *really* worries me is what we are to do with the apples."

"Oh, Harold will soon eat them up," said John; though he had not the slightest intention of being sarcastic, Hilda was so much annoyed by this that she abandoned all discussion of the vicarage and talked so long about Harold's inside and with such a passionate insistence upon what he required of sweet and sour to prevent him from dropping before her very eyes, that John was able fairly soon to plead that the hour was late and that he must go to bed.

In his bedroom, which was sharp-scented with autumnal airs and made him disinclined for sleep, John became sentimental over Edith and began to weave out of her troubles a fine robe for his own good-nature in which his sentimentality was able to show itself off. He assured himself of Edith's luck in having Ambles as a refuge in the difficult time through which she was passing and began to visualize her past life as nothing but a stormy prelude to a more tranquil present in which he should be her pilot. That Laurence would be included in his beneficence was certainly a flaw in the emerald of his bounty, a fly in the amber of his self-satisfaction; but, after all, so long as Edith was secure and happy such blemishes were hardly perceptible. He ought to think himself lucky that he was in a position to help his relations; the power of doing kind actions was surely the greatest privilege accorded to the successful man. And what right had Hilda to object? Good gracious, as if she herself were not dependent enough upon him! But there had always been visible in Hilda this wretched spirit of competition. It had been in just the same spirit that she had married Daniel Curtis; she had not been able to endure her younger sister's engagement to the tall handsome curate and had snatched at the middle-aged explorer in order to be married simultaneously and secure the best wedding presents for herself. But what had Daniel Curtis seen in Hilda? What had that myopic and taciturn man found in Hilda to gladden a short visit to England between his life on the Orinoco and his intended life at the back of the uncharted Amazons? And had his short experience of her made him so reckless that nothing but his spectacles were found by the rescuers? What mad impulse to perpetuate his name beyond the numerous beetles, flowers, monkeys, and butterflies to which it was already attached by many learned societies had led him to bequeath Harold to humanity? Was not his collection of humming birds enough?

"I'm really very glad that Edith is coming to Ambles," John murmured. "Very glad indeed. It will serve Hilda right." He began to wonder if he actually disliked Hilda and to realize that he had never really forgiven her for refusing to be interested in his first published story. How well he remembered that occasion—twenty years ago almost to a day. It had been a dreary November in the time when

London really did have fogs, and when the sense of his father's approaching death had added to the general gloom. James had been acting as his father's partner for more than a year and had already nearly ruined the practice by his inexperience and want of affability. George and himself were both in the city offices—George in wool, himself in dogbiscuits. George did not seem to mind the soul-destroying existence and was full of financial ambition; but himself had loathed it and cared for nothing but literature. How he had pleaded with that dry old father, whose cynical tormented face on its pillow smeared with cigar ash even now vividly haunted his memory; but the fierce old man had refused him the least temporary help and had actually chuckled with delight amidst all his pain at the thought of how his family would have to work for a living when he should mercifully be dead. Was it surprising, when that morning he had found at the office a communication from a syndicate of provincial papers to inform him of his story's being accepted, that he should have arrived home in the fog, full of hope and enthusiasm? And then he had been met with whispering voices and the news of his father's death. Of course he had been shocked and grieved, even disappointed that it was too late to announce his success to the old man; but he had not been able to resist telling Hilda, a gawky, pale-faced girl of eighteen, that his story had been taken. He could recall her expression in that befogged gaslight even now, her expression of utter lack of interest, faintly colored with surprise at his own bad taste. Then he had gone upstairs to see his mother, who was bathed in tears, though she had been warned at least six months ago that her husband might die at any moment. He had ventured after a few formal words of sympathy to lighten the burden of her grief by taking the auspicious communication from his pocket, where it had been cracking nervously between his fingers, and reading it to her. He had been sure that she would be interested because she was a great reader of stories and must surely derive a grateful wonder from the contemplation of her own son as an author.

But she was evidently too much overcome by the insistency of grief and by the prospect of monetary difficulties in the near future to grasp what he was telling her; it had struck him that she had actually never realized that the stories she enjoyed were written by men and women any more than it might have struck another person that advertisements were all written by human beings with their own histories of love and hate.

"You mustn't neglect your office work, Johnnie," was what she had said. "We shall want every halfpenny now that Papa is gone. James does his best, but the patients were more used to Papa."

After these two rebuffs John had not felt inclined to break his good news to James, who would be sure to sneer, or to George, who would only laugh; so he had wandered upstairs to the old schoolroom, where he had found Edith sitting by a dull fire and dissuading little Hugh from throwing coals at the cat. As soon as he had told Edith what had happened she had made a hero of him, and ever afterwards treated him with admiration as well as affection. Had she not prophesied even that he would be another Dickens? That was something like sisterly love, and he had volunteered to read her the original rough copy, which, notwithstanding Hugh's whining interruptions, she had enjoyed as much as he had enjoyed it himself. Certainly Edith must come to Ambles; twenty years were not enough to obliterate the memory of that warm-hearted girl of fifteen and of her welcome praise.

But Hugh? What malign spirit had brought Hugh to his mind at a moment when he was already just faintly disturbed by the prospect of his relations' increasing demands upon his attention? Hugh was only twenty-seven now and much too conspicuously for his own good the youngest of the family; like all children that arrive unexpectedly after a long interval, he had seemed the pledge of his parents' renewed youth on the very threshold of old age, and had been spoiled, even by his cross-grained old father, in consequence:

as for his mother, though it was out of her power to spoil him extravagantly with money, she gave him all that she did not spend on caps for herself. John determined to make inquiries about Hugh to-morrow. Not another penny should he have from him, not another farthing. If he could not live on what he earned in the office of Stephen Crutchley, who had accepted the young spendthrift out of regard for their lifelong friendship, if he could not become a decent, well-behaved architect, why, he could starve. Not another penny . . . and the rest of his relations agreed with John on this point, for if to him Hugh was a skeleton in the family cupboard, to them he was a skeleton at the family feast.

John expelled from his mind all misgivings about Hugh, hoped it would be a fine day to-morrow so that he could really look round the garden and see what plants wanted ordering, tried to remember the name of an ornamental shrub recommended by Miss Hamilton, turned over on his side, and went to sleep.

CHAPTER IV

EARLY next morning John dreamed that he was buying calico in an immense shop and that in a dreamlike inconsequence the people there, customers and shopmen alike, were abruptly seized with a frenzy of destruction so violent that they began to tear up all the material upon which they could lay their hands; indeed, so loud was the noise of rent cloth that John woke up with the sound of it still in his ears. Gradually it was borne in upon a brain wrestling with actuality that the noise might have emanated from the direction of a small casement in his bedroom looking eastward into the garden across a steep penthouse which ran down to within two feet of the ground. Although the noise had stopped some time before John had precisely located its whereabouts and really before he was perfectly convinced that he was awake, he jumped out of bed and hurried across the chilly boards to ascertain if after all it had only been a relic of his dream. No active cause was visible; but the moss, the stonecrop and the tiles upon the penthouse had been clawed from top to bottom as if by some mighty tropical cat, and John for a brief instant savored that elated perplexity which generally occurs to heroes in the opening paragraphs of a sensational novel.

"It's a very old house," he thought, hopefully, and began to grade his reason to a condition of sycophantic credulity. "And, of course, anything like a ghost at seven o'clock in the morning is rare—very rare. The evidence would be unassailable . . ."

After toadying to the marvelous for a while, he sought a natural explanation of the phenomenon and honestly tried not to want it to prove inexplicable. The noise began again overhead; a fleeting object darkened the casement like the swift passage of a bird and struck the penthouse below; there was a slow grinding shriek, a clatter of broken tiles and leaden piping; a small figure stuck all over with feathers emerged from the herbaceous border and smiled up at him.

"Good heavens, my boy, what in creation are you trying to do?" John shouted, sternly.

"I'm learning to toboggan, Uncle John."

"But didn't I explain to you that tobogganing can only be carried out after a heavy snowfall?"

"Well, it hasn't snowed yet," Harold pointed out in an offended voice.

"Listen to me. If it snows for a month without stopping, you're never to toboggan down a roof. What's the good of having all those jolly hills at the back of the house if you don't use them?"

John spoke as if he had brought back the hills from America at the same time as he was supposed to have brought back the toboggan.

"There's a river, too," Harold observed.

"You can't toboggan down a river—unless, of course, it gets frozen over."

"I don't want to toboggan down the river, but if I had a Canadian canoe for the river I could wait for the snow quite easily."

John, after a brief vision of a canoe being towed across the Atlantic by the *Murmania,* felt that he was being subjected to the lawless exactions of a brigand, but could think of nothing more novel in the way of defiance than:

"Go away now and be a good boy."

"Can't I . . ." Harold began.

"No, you can't. If those chickens' feathers . . ."

"They're pigeons' feathers," his nephew corrected him.

"If those feathers stuck in your hair are intended to convey an impression that you're a Red Indian chief, go and sit in your wigwam till breakfast and smoke the pipe of peace."

"Mother said I wasn't to smoke till I was twenty-one."

"Not literally, you young ass. Why, good heavens, in my

young days such an allusion to Mayne Reid would have been eagerly taken up by any boy."

Something was going wrong with this conversation, John felt, and he added, lamely:

"Anyway, go away now."

"But, Uncle John, I . . ."

"Don't Uncle John me. I don't feel like an uncle this morning. Suppose I'd been shaving when you started that fool's game. I might have cut my head off."

"But, Uncle John, I've left my spectacles on one of the chimneys. Mother said that whenever I was playing a rough game I was to take off my spectacles first."

"You'll have to do without your spectacles, that's all. The gardener will get them for you after breakfast. Anyway, a Red Indian chief in spectacles is unnatural."

"Well, I'm not a Red Indian any longer."

"You can't chop and change like that. You'll have to be a Red Indian now till after breakfast. Don't argue any more, because I'm standing here in bare feet. Go and do some weeding in the garden. You've pulled up all the plants on the roof."

"I can't read without my spectacles."

"Weed, not read!"

"Well, I can't weed, either. I can't do anything without my spectacles."

"Then go away and do nothing."

Harold shuffled off disconsolately, and John rang for his shaving water.

At breakfast Hilda asked anxiously after her son's whereabouts; and John, the last vestige of whose irritation had vanished in the smell of fried bacon and eggs, related the story of the morning's escapade as a good joke.

"But he can't see anything without his spectacles," Hilda exclaimed.

"Oh, he'll find his way to the breakfast table all right," John prophesied.

"These bachelors," murmured Hilda, turning to her

mother with a wry little laugh. "Hark! isn't that Harold calling?"

"No, no, no, it's the pigeons," John laughed. "They're probably fretting for their feathers."

"It's to be hoped," said old Mrs. Touchwood, "that he's not fallen into the well by leaving off his spectacles like this. I never could abide wells. And I hate to think of people leaving things off suddenly. It's always a mistake. I remember little Hughie once left off his woollen vests in May and caught a most terrible cold that wouldn't go away—it simply wouldn't go."

"How is Hugh, by the way?" John asked.

"The same as ever," Hilda put in with cold disapproval. She was able to forget Harold's myopic wanderings in the pleasure of crabbing her youngest brother.

"Ah, you're all very hard on poor Hughie," sighed the old lady. "But he's always been very fond of his poor mother."

"He's very fond of what he can get out of you," Hilda sneered.

"And it's little enough he can, poor boy. Goodness knows I've little enough to spare for him. I wish you could have seen your way to do something for Hughie, Johnnie," the old lady went on.

"John has done quite enough for him," Hilda snapped, which was perfectly true.

"He's had to leave his rooms in Earl's Court," Mrs. Touchwood lamented.

"What for? Getting drunk, I suppose?" John inquired, sternly.

"No, it was the drains. He's staying with his friend, Aubrey Fenton, whom I cannot pretend to like. He seems to me a sad scapegrace. Poor little Hughie. I wish everything wasn't against him. It's to be hoped he won't go and get married, poor boy, for I'm sure his wife wouldn't understand him."

"Surely he's not thinking of getting married," exclaimed John in dismay.

"Why no, of course not," said the old lady. "How you do take anybody up, Johnnie. I said it's to be hoped he *won't* get married."

At this moment Emily came in to announce that Master Harold was up on the roof shouting for dear life. "Such a turn as it give Cook and I, mum," she said, "to hear that garshly voice coming down the chimney. Cook was nearly took with the convolsions, and if it had of been after dark, mum, she says she's shaw she doesn't know what she wouldn't of done, she wouldn't, she's that frightened of howls. That's the one thing she can't ever be really comfortable for in the country, she says, the howls and the hearwigs."

"I'm under the impression," John declared, solemnly, "that I forbade Harold to go near the roof. If he has disobeyed my express commands he must suffer for it by the loss of his breakfast. He has chosen to go back on the roof: on the roof he shall stay."

"But his breakfast?" Hilda almost whispered. She was so much awed by her brother's unusually pompous phraseology that he began to be impressed by it himself and to feel the first faint intimations of the pleasures of tyranny: he began to visualize himself as the unbending ruler of all his relations.

"His breakfast can be sent up to him, and I hope it will attract every wasp in the neighborhood."

This to John seemed the most savage aspiration he could have uttered: autumnal wasps disturbed him as much as dragons used to disturb princesses.

"Harold likes wasps," said Hilda. "He observes their habits."

This revelation of his nephew's tastes took away John's last belief in his humanity, and the only retort he could think of was a suggestion that he should go at once to a boarding-school.

"Likes wasps?" he repeated. "The child must be mad. You'll tell me next that he likes black beetles."

"He trained a black beetle once to eat something. I forget

what it was now. But the poor boy was so happy about his little triumph. You ought to remember, John, that he takes after his father."

John made up his mind at this moment that Daniel Curtis must have married Hilda in a spirit of the purest empirical science.

"Well, he's not to go training insects in my house," John said, firmly. "And if I see any insects anywhere about Ambles that show the slightest sign of having been encouraged to suppose themselves on an equal with mankind I shall tread on them."

"I'm afraid the crossing must have upset you, Johnnie," said old Mrs. Touchwood, sympathetically. "You seem quite out of sorts this morning. And I don't like the idea of poor little Harold's balancing himself all alone on a chimney. It was never any pleasure to me to watch tight-rope dancers or acrobats. Indeed, except for the clowns, I never could abide circuses."

Hilda quickly took up the appeal and begged John to let the gardener rescue her son.

"Oh, very well," he assented. "But, once for all, it must be clearly understood that I've come down to Ambles to write a new play and that some arrangement must be concluded by which I have my mornings completely undisturbed."

"Of course," said Hilda, brightening at the prospect of Harold's release.

"Of course," John echoed, sardonically, within himself. He did not feel that the sight of Harold's ravening after his breakfast would induce in him the right mood for Joan of Arc. So he left the breakfast table and went upstairs to his library. Here he found that some "illiterate oaf," as he characterized the person responsible, had put in upside down upon the shelves the standard works he had hastily amassed. Instead of setting his ideas in order, he had to set his books in order: and after a hot and dusty morning with the rows of unreadable classics he came downstairs to find that the vicarage party had arrived just in time for lunch, bringing with them as the advance guard of their occupation a large clothes basket filled with what Laurence described as "necessary odds and ends that might be overlooked later."

"It's my theory of moving," he added. "The small things first."

He enunciated this theory so reverently that his action acquired from his tone a momentous gravity like the captain of a ship's when he orders the women and children into the boats first.

The moving of the vicarage party lasted over a fortnight, during which John found it impossible to settle down to Joan of Arc. No sooner would he have worked himself up to a suitable frame of mind in which he might express dramatically and poetically the maid's reception of her heavenly visitants than a very hot man wearing a green baize apron would appear in the doorway of the library and announce that a chest of drawers had hopelessly involved some vital knot in the domestic communications. It was no good for John to ask Hilda to do anything: his sister had taken up the attitude that it was all John's fault, that she had done her best to preserve his peace, that her advice had been ignored, and that for the rest of her life she intended to efface herself.

"I'm a mere cipher," she kept repeating.

On one occasion when a bureau of sham ebony that looked like a blind man's dream of Cologne Cathedral had managed to wedge all its pinnacles into the lintel of the front door, John observed to Laurence he had understood that only such furniture from the vicarage as was required to supplement the Ambles furniture would be brought there.

"I thought this bureau would appeal to you," Laurence replied. "It seemed to me in keeping with much of your work."

John looked up sharply to see if he was being chaffed; but his brother-in-law's expression was earnest, and the intended compliment struck more hardly at John's self-confidence than the most malicious review.

"Does my work really seem like gimcrack gothic?" he asked himself.

In a fit of exasperation he threw himself so vigorously into the business of forcing the bureau into the house that when it was inside it looked like a ruined abbey on the afternoon of a Bank Holiday.

"It had better be taken up into the garrets for the present," he said, grimly. "It can be mended later on."

The comparison of his work to that bureau haunted John at his own writing-table for the rest of the morning; thinking of the Bishop of Silchester's objection to Laurence, he found it hard to make the various bishops in his play as unsympathetic as they ought to be for dramatic contrast; then he remembered that after all it had been due to the Bishop of Silchester's strong action that Laurence had come to Ambles: the stream of insulting epithets for bishops flowed as strongly as ever, and he worked in a justifiable pun upon the name of Pierre Cauchon, his chief episcopal villain.

"I wonder, if I were allowed to, whether I would condemn Laurence to be burnt alive. Wasn't there a Saint Laurence who was grilled? I really believe I would almost grill him, I really do. There's something exceptionally irritating to me about that man's whole personality. And I'm not at all sure I approve of a clergyman's giving up his beliefs. One might get a line out of that, by the way—something about a weathercock and a church steeple. I don't think a clergyman ought to surrender so easily. It's his business not to be influenced by modern thought. This passion for realism is everywhere. . . . Thank goodness, I've been through it and got over it and put it behind me forever. It's a most unprofitable creed. What was my circulation as a realist? I once reached four thousand. What's four thousand? Why, it isn't half the population of Galton. And now Laurence Armitage takes up with it after being a vicar for ten years. Idiot! Religion isn't realistic: it never was realistic. Religion is the entertainment of man's spirituality just as the romantic drama is the entertainment of his mentality. I don't read Anatole France for my representation of Joan of Arc. What business has Laurence to muddle his head with—what's his name—Colonel Ingoldsby—Ingersoll—when he ought to be thinking about his Harvest Festival? And then he has the effrontery to compare my work with that bureau! If that's all his religion meant to him—that ridiculous piece of gimcrack gothic, no wonder it wouldn't hold together. Why, the green fumed oak of a sentimental rationalism would be better than that. Confound Laurence! I knew this would happen when he came. He's taken my mind completely off my own work. I can't write a word this morning."

John rushed away from his manuscript and weeded furiously down a secluded border until the gardener told him he had weeded away the autumn-sown sweet-peas that were coming along nicely and standing the early frosts a treat.

"I'm not even allowed to weed my own garden now," John thought, burking the point at issue; and his disillusionment became so profound that he actually invited Harold to go for a walk with him.

"Can I bring my blow-pipe?" asked the young naturalist, gleefully.

"You don't want to load yourself up with soap and water," said John. "Keep that till you come in."

"My South American blow-pipe, Uncle John. It's a real one which father sent home. It belonged to a little Indian boy, but the darts aren't poisoned, father told mother."

"Don't you be too sure," John advised him. "Explorers will say anything."

"Well, can I bring it?"

"No, we'll take a non-murderous walk for a change. I'm tired of being shunned by the common objects of the countryside."

"Well, shall I bring *Ants, Bees, and Wasps?*"

"Certainly not. We don't want to go trailing about Hampshire like two jam sandwiches."

"I mean the book."

"No, if you want to carry something, you can carry my cleek and six golf balls."

"Oh, yes, and then I'll practice bringing eggs down in my mouth from very high trees."

John liked this form of exercise, because at the trifling cost of making one ball intolerably sticky it kept Harold from asking questions; for about two hundred yards he enjoyed this walk more than any he had ever taken with his nephew.

"But birds' nesting time won't come till the spring," Harold sighed.

"No," said John, regretfully: there were many lofty trees round Ambles, and with his mouth full of eggs anything might happen to Harold.

The transference of the vicarage family was at last complete, and John was penitently astonished to find that Laurence really did intend to pay for their board; in fact, the ex-vicar presented him with a check for two months on account calculated at a guinea a week each. John was so much moved by this event—the manner in which Laurence offered the check gave it the character of a testimonial and thereby added to John's sense of obligation—that he was even embarrassed by the notion of accepting it. At the same time a faint echo of his own realistic beginnings tinkled in his ear a warning not to refuse it, both for his own sake and for the sake of his brother-in-law. He therefore escaped from the imputation of avarice by suggesting that the check should be handed to Hilda, who, as housekeeper, would know how to employ it best. John secretly hoped that Hilda, through being able to extract what he thought of as "a little pin money for herself" out of it, might discard the martyr's halo that was at present pinching her brains tightly enough, if one might judge by her constricted expression.

"There will undoubtedly be a small profit," he told himself, "for if Laurence has a rather monkish appetite, Edith and Frida eat very little."

Perhaps Hilda did manage to make a small profit; at any rate, she seemed reconciled to the presence of the Armitages and gave up declaring that she was a cipher. The fatigue of moving in had made Laurence's company, while he was suffering from the reaction, almost bearable. Frida, apart from a habit she had of whispering at great length in her mother's ear, was a nice uninquisitive child, and Edith, when she was not whispering back to Frida or echoing Laurence, was still able to rouse in her brother's heart feelings of warm affection. Old Mrs. Touchwood had acquired from some caller a new game of Patience, which kept her gently simmering in the lamplight every evening; Harold had discovered among the odds and ends of salvage from the move a sixpenny encyclopedia that, though it made him unpleasantly informative, at any rate kept him from being interrogative, which John found, on the whole, a slight advantage. Janet Bond had written again most seriously about Joan of Arc, and the film company had given excellent terms for *The Fall of Babylon*. Really, except for two huffy letters from his sisters-in-law in London, John was able to contemplate with much less misgivings a prospect of spending all the winter at Ambles. Beside, he had secured his dog-cart with a dashing chestnut mare, and was negotiating for the twenty-acre field.

Yes, everything was very jolly, and he might even aim at finishing the first draft of the second act before Christmas. It would be jolly to do that and jolly to invite James and Beatrice and George and Eleanor, but not Hugh—no, in no circumstances should Hugh be included in the yuletide armistice—down to Ambles for an uproarious jolly week. Then January should be devoted to the first draft of the third act—really it should be possible to write to Janet Bond presently and assure her of a production next autumn. John was feeling particularly optimistic. For three days in succession the feet of the first act had been moving as rhythmically and regularly toward the curtain as the feet of guardsmen move along the Buckingham Palace Road. It was a fine frosty morning, and even so early in the day John was tapping his second egg to the metrical apostrophes of Uncle Laxart's speech offering to take his niece, Joan, to interview Robert de Baudricourt. Suddenly he noticed that Laurence had not yet put in his appearance. This was strange behavior for one who still preserved from the habit of many early services an excited punctuality for his breakfast, and lightly he asked Edith what had become of her husband.

"He hopes to begin working again at his play this morning. Seeing you working so hard makes him feel lazy." Edith laughed faintly and fearfully, as if she would deprecate her own profanity in referring to so gross a quality as laziness in connection with Laurence, and perhaps for the first time in her life she proclaimed that her opinion was only an echo of Laurence's own by adding, "*he* says that it makes him feel lazy. So he's going to begin at once."

John, whose mind kept reverting iambically and trochaically to the curtain of his first act, merely replied, without any trace of awe, that he was glad Laurence felt in the vein.

"But he hasn't decided yet," Edith continued, "which room he's going to work in."

For the first time a puff of apprehension twitched the little straw that might be going to break the camel's back.

"I'm afraid I can't offer him the library," John said quickly. "*And you shall see the King of France to-day,*" he went on composing in his head. "No—*And you shall see King Charles*—no—*and you shall see the King of France at once*—no—*and you shall see the King of France forthwith. Sensation among the villagers standing round. Forthwith* is weak at the end of a line. *I swear that you shall see the King of France. Sensation.* Yes, that's it."

The top of John's egg was by this time so completely cracked by his metronomic spoon that a good deal of the shell was driven down into the egg· it did not matter, however, because appetite and inspiration were both disposed of by the arrival of Laurence.

"I wish you could have managed to help me with some of these things," he was muttering reproachfully to his wife.

The things consisted of six or seven books, a quantity of foolscap, an inkpot dangerously brimming, a paper-knife made of olive wood from Gethsemane, several pens and pencils, and a roll of blotting paper as white as the snow upon the summit of Mont Blanc, and so fat that John thought at first it was a tablecloth and wondered what his brother-in-law meant to do with it. He was even chilled by a brief and horrible suspicion that he was going to hold a communion service. Edith rose hastily from the table to help her husband unload himself.

"I'm so sorry, dear, why didn't you ring?"

"My dear, how could I ring without letting my materials drop?" Laurence asked, patiently.

"Or call?"

"My chin was too much occupied for calling. But it doesn't matter, Edith. As you see, I've managed to bring everything down quite safely."

"I'm so sorry," Edith went on. "I'd no idea . . ."

"I told you that I was going to begin work this morning."

"Yes, how stupid of me . . . I'm so sorry . . ."

"Going to work, are you?" interrupted John, who was anxious to stop Edith's conjugal amenity. "That's capital."

"Yes, I'm really only waiting now to choose my room."

"I'm sorry I can't offer you mine . . . but I must be alone. I find . . ."

"Of course," Laurence agreed with a nod of sympathetic knowingness. "Of course, my dear fellow, I shouldn't dream of trespassing. I, though indeed I've no right to compare myself with you, also like to work alone. In fact I consider that a secure solitude provides the ideal setting for dramatic composition. I have a habit—perhaps it comes from preparing my sermons with my eye always upon the spoken rather than upon the written word—I have a habit of declaiming many of my pages aloud to myself. That necessitates my being alone—absolutely alone."

"Yes, you see," Edith said, "if you're alone you're not disturbed."

John who was still sensitive to Edith's truisms tried to cover her last by incorporating Hilda in the conversation with a "What room do you advise?"

"Why not the dining-room? I'll tell Emily to clear away the breakfast things at once."

"Clear away?" Laurence repeated.

"And they won't be laying for lunch till a quarter-to-one."

"Laying for lunch?" Laurence gasped. "My dear Hilda! I don't wish to attribute to my—ah—work an importance which perhaps as a hitherto unacted playwright I have no right to attribute, but I think John at any rate will appreciate my objection to working with—ah—the breadknife suspended over my head like the proverbial sword of Damocles. No, I'm afraid I must rule out the dining-room as a practicable environment."

"And Mama likes to sit in the drawing-room," said Hilda.

"In any case," Laurence said, indulgently, "I shouldn't feel at ease in the drawing-room. So I shall not disturb Mama. I had thought of suggesting that the children should be given another room in which to play, but to tell the truth I'm tired of moving furniture about. The fact is I miss my vicarage study: it was my own."

"Yes, nobody at the vicarage ever thought of interrupting him, you see," Edith explained.

"Well," said John, roused by the necessity of getting Joan started upon her journey to interview Robert de Baudricourt, "there are several empty bedrooms upstairs. One of them could be transformed into a study for Laurence."

"That means more arranging of furniture," Laurence objected.

"Then there's the garret," said John. "You'd find your bureau up there."

Laurence smiled in order to show how well he understood that the suggestion was only playfulness on John's side and how little he minded the good-natured joke.

"There is one room which might be made—ah—conducive to good work, though at present it is occupied by a quantity of apples; they, however, could easily be moved."

"But I moved them in there from what is now your room," Hilda protested.

"It is good for apples to be frequently moved," said Laurence, kindly. "In fact, the oftener they are moved, the better. And this holds good equally for pippins, codlins, and russets. On the other hand it means I shall lose half a day's work, because even if I *could* make a temporary beginning anywhere else, I should have to superintend the arrangement of the furniture."

"But I thought you didn't want to have any more furniture arranging to do," Hilda contested, acrimoniously. "There are two quite empty rooms at the other end of the passage."

"Yes, but I like the room in which the apples are. John will appreciate my desire for a sympathetic milieu."

"Come, come, we will move the apples," John promised, hurriedly.

Better that the apples should roll from room to room eternally than that he should be driven into offering Laurence a corner of the library, for he suspected that notwithstanding the disclaimer this was his brother-in-law's real objective.

"It doesn't say anything about apples in the encyclopedia," muttered Harold in an aggrieved voice. "*Apoplexy treatment of, Apothecaries measure, Appetite loss of. This may be due to general debility, irregularity in meals, overwork, want of exercise, constipation, and many other* . . ."

"Goodness gracious me, whatever has the boy got hold of?" exclaimed his grandmother.

"Grandmama, if you mix Lanoline with an equal quantity of Sulphur you can cure Itch," Harold went on with his spectacles glued to the page. "And, oh, Grandmama, you know you told me not to make a noise the other day because your heart was weak. Well, you're suffering from flatulence.

The encyclopedia says that many people who are suffering from flatulence think they have heart disease."

"Will no one stop the child?" Grandmama pleaded.

Laurence snatched away the book from his nephew and put it in his pocket.

"That book is mine, I believe, Harold," he said, firmly, and not even Hilda dared protest, so majestic was Laurence and so much fluttered was poor Grandmama.

John seized the opportunity to make his escape; but when he was at last seated before his table the feet of the first act limped pitiably; Laurence had trodden with all his might upon their toes; his work that morning was chiropody, not composition, and bungling chiropody at that. After lunch Laurence was solemnly inducted to his new study, and he may have been conscious of an ecclesiastical parallel in the manner of his taking possession, for he made a grave joke about it.

"Let us hope that I shall not be driven out of my new living by being too—ah—broad."

His wife did not realize that he was being droll and had drawn down her lips to an expression of pained sympathy, when she saw the others all laughing and Laurence smiling his acknowledgments; her desperate effort to change the contours of her face before Laurence noticed her failure to respond sensibly gave the impression that she had nearly swallowed a loose tooth.

"Perhaps you'd like me to bring up your tea, dear, so that you won't be disturbed?" she suggested.

"Ah, tea . . ." murmured Laurence. "Let me see. It's now a quarter-past two. Tea is at half-past four. I will come down for half an hour. That will give me a clear two hours before dinner. If I allow a quarter of an hour for arranging my table, that will give me four hours in all. Perhaps considering my strenuous morning four hours will be enough for the first day. I don't like the notion of working after dinner," he added to John.

"No?" queried John, doubtfully. He had hoped that his

brother-in-law would feel inspired by the port: it was easy enough to avoid him in the afternoon, especially since on the first occasion that he had been taken for a drive in the new dogcart he had evidently been imbued with a detestation of driving that would probably last for the remainder of his life; in fact he was talking already of wanting to sell Primrose and the vicarage chaise.

"Though of course on some evenings I may not be able to help it," added Laurence. "I may *have* to work."

"Of course you may," John assented, encouragingly. "I dare say there'll be evenings when the mere idea of waiting even for coffee will make you fidgety. You mustn't lose the mood, you know."

"No, of course, I appreciate that."

"There's nothing so easily lost as the creative gift, Balzac said."

"Did he?" Laurence murmured, anxiously. "But I promise you I shall let nothing interfere with me *if*—" the conjunction fizzed from his mouth like soda from a syphon, "*if* I'm in the—ah—mood. The mood—yes—ah—precisely." His brow began to lower; the mood was upon him; and everybody stole quietly from the room. They had scarcely reached the head of the stairs when the door opened again and Laurence called after Edith: "I should prefer that whoever brings me news of tea merely knocks without coming in. I shall assume that a knock upon my door means tea. But I don't wish anybody to come in."

Laurence disappeared. He seemed under the influence of a strong mental aphrodisiac and was evidently guaranteeing himself against being discovered in an embarrassing situation with his Muse.

"This is very good for me," thought John. "It has taught me how easily a man may make a confounded ass of himself without anybody's raising a finger to warn him. I hope I didn't give that sort of impression to those two women on board. I shall have to watch myself very carefully in future."

At this moment Emily announced that Lawyer Deacle was waiting to see Mr. Touchwood, which meant that the twenty-acre field was at last his. The legal formalities were complete; that very afternoon John had the pleasure of watching the fierce little Kerry cows munch the last grass they would ever munch in his field. But it was nearly dusk when they were driven home, and John lost five balls in celebrating his triumph with a brassy.

Laurence appeared at tea in a velveteen coat, which probably provided the topic for the longest whisper that even Frida had ever been known to utter.

"Come, come, Frida," said her father. "You won't disturb us by saying aloud what you want to say." He had leaned over majestically to emphasize his rebuke and in doing so brushed with his sleeve Grandmama's wrist.

"Goodness, it's a cat," the old lady cried, with a shudder. "I shall have to go away from here, Johnnie, if you have a cat in the house. I'd rather have mice all over me than one of those horrid cats. Ugh! the nasty thing!"

She was not at all convinced of her mistake even when persuaded to stroke her son-in-law's coat.

"I hope it's been properly shooed out. Harold, please look well under all the chairs, there's a good boy."

During the next few days John felt that he was being in some indefinable way ousted by Laurence from the spiritual mastery of his own house. John was averse from according to his brother-in-law a greater forcefulness of character than he could ascribe to himself; if he had to admit that he really was being supplanted somehow, he preferred to search for the explanation in the years of theocratic prestige that gave a background to the all-pervasiveness of that sacerdotal personality. Yet ultimately the impression of his own relegation to a secondary place remained elusive and incommunicable. He could not for instance grumble that the times of the meals were being altered nor complain that in the smallest detail the domestic mechanism was being geared up or down to suit Laurence; the whole sensation was essentially of a spiritual eviction, and the nearest he could get to formulating his resentment (though perhaps resentment was too definite a word for this vague uneasiness) was his own gradually growing opinion that of all those at present under the Ambles roof Laurence was the most important. This loss of importance was bad for John's work, upon which it soon began to exert a discouraging influence, because he became doubtful of his own position, hypercritical of his talent, and timid about his social ability. He began to meditate the long line of failures to dramatize the immortal tale of Joan of Arc immortally, to see himself dangling at the end of this long line of ineptitudes and to ask himself whether bearing in mind the vastness of even our own solar system it was really worth while writing at all. It could not be due to anything or anybody but Laurence, this sense of his own futility; not even when a few years ago he had reached the conclusion that as a realistic novelist he was a failure had he been so profoundly conscious of his own insignificance in time and space.

"I shall have to go away if I'm ever to get on with this play," he told himself.

Yet still so indefinite was his sense of subordinacy at Ambles that he accused his liver (an honest one that did not deserve the reproach) and bent over his table again with all the determination he could muster. The concrete fact was still missing; his capacity for self-deception was still robust enough to persuade him that it was all a passing fancy, and he might have gone plodding on at Ambles for the rest of the winter if one morning about a week after Laurence had begun to write, the door of his own library had not opened to the usurper, manuscript in hand.

"I don't like to interrupt you, my dear fellow. . . . I know you have your own work to consider . . . but I'm anxious for your opinion—in fact I should like to read you my first act."

It was useless to resist: if it were not now, it would be later.

"With pleasure," said John. Then he made one effort. "Though I prefer reading to myself."

"That would involve waiting for the typewriter. Yes, my screed is—ah—difficult to make out. And I've indulged in a good many erasures and insertions. No, I think you'd better let me read it to you."

John indicated a chair and looked out of the window longingly at the birds, as patients in the hands of a dentist regard longingly the sparrows in the dingy evergreens of the dentist's back garden.

"When we had our little talk the other day," Laurence began, "you will remember that I spoke of a drama I had already written, of which the disciple Thomas was the protagonist. This drama notwithstanding the probably obstructive attitude of the Lord Chamberlain I have rewritten, or rather I have rewritten the first act. I call the play—ah—*Thomas*."

"It sounds a little trivial for such a serious subject, don't you think?" John suggested. "I mean, Thomas has come to be associated in so many people's minds with footmen. Wouldn't *Saint Thomas* be better, and really rather more respectful? Many people still have a great feeling of reverence for apostles."

"No, no, *Thomas* it is: *Thomas* it must remain. You have forgotten perhaps that I told you he was the prototype of the man in the street. It is the simplicity, the unpretentiousness of the title that for me gives it a value. Well, to resume. *Thomas. A play in four acts. By Laurence Armytage.* By the way, I'm going to spell my name with a *y* in future. Poetic license. Ha-ha! I shall not advertise the change in the *Times*. But I think it looks more literary with a *y*. *Act the First. Scene the First. The shore of the Sea of Galilee.* I say nothing else. I don't attempt to describe it. That is what I have learnt from Shakespeare. This modern passion for description can only injure the greatness of the theme. *Enter from the left the Virgin Mary*."

"Enter who?" asked John in amazement.

"The Virgin Mary. The mother . . ."

"Yes, I know who she is, but . . . well, I'm not a religious man, Laurence, in fact I've not been to church since I was a boy . . . but . . . no, no, you can't do that."

"Why not?"

"It will offend people."

"I want to offend people," Laurence intoned. "If thy eye offend thee, pluck it out."

"Well, you did," said John. "You put in a *y* instead."

"I'm not jesting, my dear fellow."

"Nor am I," said John. "What I want you to understand is that you can't bring the Virgin Mary on the stage. Why, I'm even doubtful about Joan of Arc's vision of the Archangel Michael. Some people may object, though I'm counting on his being generally taken for St. George."

"I know that you are writing a play about Joan of Arc, but—and I hope you'll not take unkindly what I'm going to say—but Joan of Arc can never be more than a pretty piece of mediævalism, whereas Thomas . . ."

John gave up, and the next morning he told the household that he was called back to London on business.

"Perhaps I shall have some peace here," he sighed, looking round at his dignified Church Row library.

"Mrs. James called earlier this morning, sir, and said not to disturb you, but she hoped you'd had a comfortable journey and left these flowers, and Mrs. George has telephoned from the theater to say she'll be here almost directly."

"Thank you, Mrs. Worfolk," John said. "Perhaps Mrs. George will be taking lunch."

"Yes, sir, I expect she will," said his housekeeper.

CHAPTER V

MRS. GEORGE TOUCHWOOD—or as she was known on the stage, Miss Eleanor Cartright—was big-boned, handsome, and hawklike, with the hungry look of the ambitious actress who is drawing near to forty—she was in fact thirty-seven—and realizes that the disappointed adventuresses of what are called strong plays are as near as she will ever get to the tragedy queens of youthful aspiration. Such an one accustomed to flash her dark eyes in defiance of a morally but not esthetically hostile gallery and to have the whole of a stage for the display of what well-disposed critics hailed as vitality and cavaliers condemned as lack of repose, such an one in John's tranquil library was, as Mrs. Worfolk put it, "rather too much of a good thing and no mistake"; and when Eleanor was there, John experienced as much malaise as he would have experienced from being shut up in a housemaid's closet with a large gramophone and the housemaid. This claustrophobia, however, was the smallest strain that his sister-in-law inflicted upon him; she affected his heart and his conscience more acutely, because he could never meet her without a sensation of guilt on account of his not yet having found a part for her in any of his plays, to which was added the fear he always felt in her presence that soon or late he should from sheer inability to hold out longer award her the leading part in his play. George had often seriously annoyed him by his unwillingness to help himself; but at the thought of being married for thirteen years to Eleanor he had always excused his brother's flaccid dependence.

"George is a bit of a sponge," James had once said, "but Eleanor! Eleanor is the roughest and toughest loofah that was ever known. She is irritant and absorbent at the same time, and by gad, she has the appearance of a loofah."

The prospect of Eleanor's company at lunch on the morning after his return to town gave John a sensation of having escaped the devil to fall into the deep sea, of having jumped from the frying-pan into the fire, in fact of illustrating every known proverbial attempt to express the distinction without the difference.

"It's a great pity that Eleanor didn't marry Laurence," he thought. "Each would have kept the other well under, and she could have played Mary Magdalene in that insane play of his. And, by Jove, if they *had* married, neither of them would have been a relation! Moreover, if Laurence had been caught by Eleanor, Edith might never have married at all and could have kept house for me. And if Edith hadn't married, Hilda mightn't have married, and then Harold would never have been born."

John's hard pruning of his family-tree was interrupted by a sense of the house's having been attacked by an angry mob—an illusion that he had learnt to connect with his sister-in-law's arrival. To make sure, however, he went out on the landing and called down to know if anything was the matter.

"Mrs. George is having some trouble with the taxi-man, sir," explained Maud, who was holding the front-door open and looking apprehensively at the pictures that were clattering on the walls in the wind.

"Why does she take taxis?" John muttered, irritably. "She can't afford them, and there's no excuse for such extravagance when the tube is so handy."

At this moment Eleanor reached the door, on the threshold of which she turned like Medea upon Jason to have the last word with the taxi-driver before the curtain fell.

"Did Mr. Touchwood get my message?" she was asking.

"Yes, yes," John called down. "I'm expecting you to lunch."

When he watched Eleanor all befurred coming upstairs, he felt not much less nervous than a hunter of big game face to face with his first tiger; the landing seemed to wobble like a howdah; now he had fired and missed, and she was embracing him as usual. How many times at how many meetings with Eleanor had he tried unsuccessfully to dodge that kiss—which always seemed improper whether because her lips were too red, or too full, he could never decide, though he always felt when he was released that he ought to beg her husband's pardon.

"You were an old beast not to come and see us when you got back from America; but never mind, I'm awfully glad to see you, all the same."

"Thank you very much, Eleanor. Why are you glad?"

"Oh, you sarcastic old bear!"

This perpetual suggestion of his senility was another trick of Eleanor's that he deplored; dash it, he was two years younger than George, whom she called Georgieboy.

"No, seriously," Eleanor went on. "I was just going to wire and ask if I could send the kiddies down to the country. Lambton wants me for a six weeks' tour before Xmas, and I can't leave them with Georgie. You see, if this piece catches on, it means a good shop for me in the new year."

"Yes, I quite understand your point of view," John said. "But what I don't understand is why Bertram and Viola can't stay with their father."

"But George is ill. Surely you got my letter?"

"I didn't realize that the presence of his children might prove fatal. However, send them down to Ambles by all means."

"Oh, but I'd much rather not after the way Hilda wrote to me, and now that you've come back there's no need."

"I don't quite understand."

"Well, you won't mind having them here for a short visit? Then they can go down to Ambles for the Christmas holidays."

"But the Christmas holidays won't begin for at least six weeks."

"I know."

"But you don't propose that Bertram and Viola should spend six weeks here?"

"They'll be no bother, you old crosspatch. Bertram will be at school all day, and I suppose that Maud or Elsa will always be available to take Viola to her dancing-lessons. You remember the dancing-lessons you arranged for?"

"I remember that I accepted the arrangement," said John.

"Well, she's getting on divinely, and it would be a shame to interrupt them just now, especially as she's in the middle of a Spanish series. Her *cachucha* is . . ." Eleanor could only blow a kiss to express what Viola's *cachucha* was. "But then, of course, I had a Spanish grandmother."

When John regarded her barbaric personality he could have credited her with being the granddaughter of a cannibal queen.

"So I thought that her governess could come here every morning just as easily as to Earl's Court. In fact, it will be more convenient, or at any rate, equally convenient for her, because she lives at Kilburn."

"I dare say it will be equally convenient for the governess," said John, sardonically.

"And I thought," Eleanor continued, "that it would be a good opportunity for Viola to have French lessons every afternoon. You won't want to have her all the time with you, and the French governess can give the children their tea. That will be good for Bertram's accent."

"I don't doubt that it will be superb for Bertram's accent, but I absolutely decline to have a French governess bobbing in and out of my house. It's bound to make trouble with the servants who always think that French governesses are designing and licentious, and I don't want to create a false impression."

"Well, aren't you an old prude? Who would ever think that you had any sort of connection with the stage? By the way, you haven't told me if there'll be anything for me in your next."

"Well, at present the subject of my next play is a secret . . . and as for the cast . . ."

John was so nearly on the verge of offering Eleanor the part of Mary of Anjou, for which she would be as suitable as a giraffe, that in order to effect an immediate diversion he asked her when the children were to arrive.

"Let me see, to-day's Saturday. To-morrow I go down to Bristol, where we open. They'd better come to-night, because to-morrow being Sunday they'll have no lessons, which will give them time to settle down. Georgie will be glad to know they're with you."

"I've no doubt he'll be enchanted," John agreed.

The bell sounded for lunch, and they went downstairs.

"I've got to be back at the theater by two," Eleanor announced, looking at the horridly distorted watch upon her wrist. "I wonder if we mightn't ask Maud to open half-a-bottle of champagne? I'm dreadfully tired."

John ordered a bottle to be opened; he felt rather tired himself.

"Let us be quite clear about this arrangement," he began, when after three glasses of wine he felt less appalled by the prospect, and had concluded that after all Bertram and Viola would not together be as bad as Laurence with his play, not to mention Harold with his spectacles and entomology, his interrogativeness and his greed. "The English governess will arrive every morning for Viola. What is her name?"

"Miss Coldwell."

"Miss Coldwell then will be responsible for Viola all the morning. The French governess is canceled, and I shall come to an arrangement with Miss Coldwell by which she will add to her salary by undertaking all responsibility for Viola until Viola is in bed. Bertram will go to school, and I shall rely upon Miss Coldwell to keep an eye on his behavior at home."

"And don't forget the dancing-lessons."

"No, I had Madame What's-her-name's account last week."

"I mean, don't forget to arrange for Viola to go."

"That pilgrimage will, I hope, form a part of what Miss Coldwell would probably call 'extras.' And after all perhaps George will soon be fit."

"The poor old boy has been awfully seedy all the summer."

"What's he suffering from? Infantile paralysis?"

"It's all very well for you to joke about it, but you don't live in a wretched boarding-house in Earl's Court. You mustn't let success spoil you, John. It's so easy when everything comes your way to forget the less fortunate people. Look at me. I'm thirty-four, you know."

"Are you really? I should never have thought it."

"I don't mind your laughing at me, you old crab. But I don't like you to laugh at Georgie."

"I never do," John said. "I don't suppose that there's anybody alive who takes George as seriously as I do."

Eleanor brushed away a tear and said she must get back to the rehearsal.

When she was gone John felt that he had been unkind, and he reproached himself for letting Laurence make him cynical.

"The fact is," he told himself, "that ever since I heard Doris Hamilton make that remark in the saloon of the *Murmania,* I've become suspicious of my family. She began it, and then by ill luck I was thrown too much with Laurence, who clinched it. Eleanor is right: I *am* letting myself be spoilt by success. After all, there's no reason why those two children shouldn't come here. *They* won't be writing plays about apostles. I'll send George a box of cigars to show that I didn't mean to sneer at him. And why didn't I offer to pay for Eleanor's taxi? Yes, I am getting spoilt. I must watch myself. And I ought not to have joked about Eleanor's age."

Luckily his sister-in-law had finished the champagne, for if John had drunk another glass he might have offered her the part of the Maid herself.

The actual arrival of Bertram and Viola passed off more

successfully. They were both presentable, and John was almost flattered when Mrs. Worfolk commented on their likeness to him, remembering what a nightmare it had always seemed when Hilda used to excavate points of resemblance between him and Harold. Mrs. Worfolk herself was so much pleased to have him back from Ambles that she was in the best of good humours, and even the statuesque Maud flushed with life like some Galatea.

"I think Maud's a darling, don't you, Uncle John?" exclaimed Viola.

"We all appreciate Maud's—er—capabilities," John hemmed.

He felt that it was a silly answer, but inasmuch as Maud was present at the time he could not, either for his sake or for hers give an unconditional affirmative.

"I swopped four blood-allys for an Indian in the break," Bertram announced.

"With an Indian, my boy, I suppose you mean."

"No, I don't. I mean for an Indian—an Indian marble. And I swopped four Guatemalas for two Nicaraguas."

"You ought to be at the Foreign Office."

"But the ripping thing is, Uncle John, that two of the Guatemalas are fudges."

"Such a doubtful coup would not debar you from a diplomatic career."

"And I say, what is the Foreign Office? We've got a French chap in my class."

"You ask for an explanation of the Foreign Office. That, my boy, might puzzle the omniscience of the Creator."

"I say, I don't twig very well what you're talking about."

"The attributes of the Foreign Office, my boy, are rigidity where there should be suppleness, weakness where there should be firmness, and for intelligence the substitution of hair brushed back from the forehead."

"I say, you're ragging me, aren't you? No, really, what is the Foreign Office?"

"It is the ultimate preserve of a privileged imbecility."

Bertram surrendered, and John congratulated himself upon the possession of a nephew whose perseverance and curiosity had been sapped by a scholastic education.

"Harold would have tackled me word by word during one of our walks. I shall enter into negotiations with Hilda at Christmas to provide for his mental training on condition that I choose the school. Perhaps I shall hear of a good one in the Shetland Islands."

When Mrs. Worfolk visited John as usual at ten o'clock to wish him good-night, she was enthusiastic about Bertram and Viola.

"Well, really, sir, if yaul pardon the liberty, I must say I wouldn't never of believed that Mrs. George's children *could* be so quiet and nice-behaved. They haven't given a bit of trouble, and I've never heard Maud speak so highly of anyone as of Miss Viola. 'That child's a regular little angel, Mrs. Worfolk,' she said to me. Well, sir, I'm bound to say that children does brighten up a house. I'm sure I've done my best what with putting flowers in all the vawses and one thing and another, but really, well I'm quite taken with your little nephew and niece, and I've had some experience of them, I mean to say, what with my poor sister's Herbert and all. I *have* put the tantalus ready. Good-night, sir."

"The fact of the matter is," John assured himself, "that when I'm alone with them I can manage children perfectly. I only hope that Miss Coldwell will fall in with my ideas. If she does, I see no reason why we shouldn't spend an extremely pleasant time all together."

Unfortunately for John's hope of a satisfactory coalition with the governess he received a hurried note by messenger from his sister-in-law next morning to say that Miss Coldwell was laid up: the precise disease was illegible in Eleanor's communication, but it was serious enough to keep Miss Coldwell at home for three weeks. *"Meanwhile,"* Eleanor wrote, *"she is trying to get her sister to come down from"*—the abode of the sister was equally illegible. *"But the most important thing is,"* Eleanor went on, *"that little V. shouldn't miss her dancing-lessons. So will you arrange for Maud to take her every Tuesday and Friday? And, of course, if there's anything you want to know, there's always George."*

Of George's eternal being John had no doubts; of his knowledge he was less sanguine: the only thing that George had ever known really well was the moment to lead trumps.

"However," said John, in consultation with his housekeeper, "I dare say we shall get along."

"Oh, certainly we shall, sir," Mrs. Worfolk confidently proclaimed, "well, I mean to say, I've been married myself."

John bowed his appreciation of this fact.

"And though I never had the happiness to have any little toddlers of my own, anyone being married gets used to the idea of having children. There's always the chance, as you might say. It isn't like as if I was an old maid, though, of course, my husband died in Jubilee year."

"Did he, Mrs. Worfolk, did he?"

"Yes, sir, he planed off his thumb when he was working on one of the benches for the stands through him looking round at a black fellow in a turban covered in jewelry who was driving to Buckingham Palace. One of the new arrivals, it was; and his arm got blood poisoning. That's how I remember it was Jubilee year, though usually I'm a terror for knowing when anything did occur. He wouldn't of minded so much, he said, only he was told it was the Char of Persia and that made him mad."

"Why? What had he got against the Shah?"

"He hadn't got nothing against the Char. But it wasn't the Char; and if he'd of known it wasn't the Char he never wouldn't of turned round so quick, and there's no saying he wouldn't of been alive to this day. No, sir, don't you worry about this governess. I dare say if she'd of come she'd only of caused a bit of unpleasantness all round."

At the same time, John thought, when he sent for the

children in order to make the announcement of Miss Coldwell's desertion, notwithstanding Mrs. Worfolk's optimism it was a pity that the first day of their visit should be a Sunday.

"I'm sorry to say, Viola, and, of course, Bertram, this applies equally to you, that poor Miss Coldwell has been taken very ill."

That strange expression upon the children's faces might be an awkward attempt to express their youthful sympathy, but it more ominously resembled a kind of gloating ecstacy, as they stood like two cherubs outside the gates of paradise, or two children outside a bunshop.

"Very ill," John went on, "so ill indeed that it is feared she will not be able to come for a few days, and so . . ."

Whatever more John would have said was lost in the riotous acclamations with which Bertram and Viola greeted the sad news. After the first cries and leaps of joy had subsided to a chanted duet, which ran somehow like this:

"Oh, oh, Miss Coldwell,
She can't come to Hampstead,
Hurrah, hurrah, hurrah,
Miss Coldwell's not coming:"

John ventured to rebuke the singers for their insensibility to human suffering.

"For she may be dangerously ill," he protested.

"How fizzing," Bertram shouted.

"She might die."

The prospect that this opened before Bertram was apparently too beautiful for any verbal utterance, and he remained open-mouthed in a mute and exquisite anticipation of liberty.

"What and never come to us ever again?" Viola breathed, her blue eyes aglow with visions of a larger life.

John shook his head, gravely.

"Oh, Uncle John," she cried, "wouldn't that be glorious?"

Bertram's heart was too full for words: he simply turned head over heels.

"But you hard-hearted little beasts," their uncle expostulated.

"She's most frightfully strict," Viola explained.

"Yes, we shouldn't have been able to do anything decent if she'd come," Bertram added.

A poignant regret for that unknown governess suffering from her illegible complaint pierced John's mind. But perhaps she would recover, in which case she should spend her convalescence at Ambles with Harold; for if when in good health she was strict, after a severe illness she might be ferocious.

"Well, I'm not at all pleased with your attitude," John declared. "And you'll find me twice as strict as Miss Coldwell."

"Oh, no, we shan't," said Bertram with a smile of jovial incredulity.

John let this contradiction pass: it seemed an imprudent subject for debate. "And now, to-day being Sunday, you'd better get ready for church."

"Oh, but we always dress up on Sunday," Viola said.

"So does everybody," John replied. "Go and get ready."

The children left the room, and he rang for Mrs. Worfolk.

"Master Bertram and Miss Viola will shortly be going to church, and I want you to arrange for somebody to take them."

Mrs. Worfolk hesitated.

"Who was you thinking of, sir?"

"I wasn't thinking of anybody in particular, but I suppose Maud could go."

"Maud has her rooms to do."

"Well, Elsa."

"Elsa has her dinner to get."

"Well, then, perhaps you would . . ."

"Yaul pardon the liberty, sir, but I never go to church except of an evening *sometimes*; I never could abide being stared at."

"Oh, very well," said John, fretfully, as Mrs. Worfolk retired. "Though I'm hanged if *I'm* going to take them," he added to himself, "at any rate without a rehearsal."

The two children soon came back in a condition of complete preparation and insisted so loudly upon their uncle's company that he yielded; though when he found himself with a child on either side of him in the sabbath calm of the Hampstead streets footfall-haunted, he was appalled at his rashness. There was a church close to his own house, but with an instinct to avoid anything like a domestic scandal he had told his nephew and niece that it was not a suitable church for children, and had led them further afield through the ghostly November sunlight.

"But look here," Bertram objected, "we can't go through any slums, you know, because the cads will bung things at my topper."

"Not if you're with me," John argued. "I am wearing a top-hat myself."

"Well, they did when I went for a walk with Father once on Sunday."

"The slums round Earl's Court are probably much fiercer than the slums round Hampstead," John suggested. "And anyway here we are."

He had caught a glimpse of an ecclesiastical building, which unfortunately turned out to be a Jewish tabernacle and not open: a few minutes later, however, an indubitably Anglican place of worship invited their attendance, and John trying not to look as bewildered as he felt let himself be conducted by a sidesman to the very front pew.

"I wonder if he thinks I'm a member of parliament. But I wish to goodness he'd put us in the second row. I shall be absolutely lost where I am."

John looked round to catch the sidesman's eye and plead for a less conspicuous position, but even as he turned his head a terrific crash from the organ proclaimed that it was too late and that the service had begun.

By relying upon the memories of youthful worship John might have been able to cope successfully with Morning Prayer, even with that florid variation of it which is generally known as Mattins. Unluckily the church he had chosen for the spiritual encouragement of his nephew and niece was to the church of his recollections as Mount Everest to a molehill. As a simple spectator without encumbrances he might have enjoyed the service and derived considerable inspiration from it for the decorative ecclesiasticism of his new play; as an uncle it alarmed and confused him. The lace-hung acolytes, the candles, the chrysanthemums, the purple vestments and the ticking of the thurible affected him neither with Protestant disgust nor with Catholic devoutness, but much more deeply as nothing but incentives to the unanswerable inquiries of Bertram and Viola.

"What are they doing?" whispered his nephew.

"Hush!" he whispered back in what he tried to feel was the right intonation of pious reproof.

"What's that little boy doing with a spoon?" whispered his niece.

"Hush!" John blew forth again. "Attend to the service."

"But it isn't a real service, is it?" she persisted.

Luckily the congregation knelt at this point, and John plunged down with a delighted sense of taking cover. Presently he began to be afraid that his attitude of devotional self-abasement might be seeming a little ostentatious, and he peered cautiously round over the top of the pew; to his dismay he perceived that Bertram and Viola were still standing up.

"Kneel down at once," he commanded in what he hoped would be an authoritative whisper, but which was in the result an agonized croak.

"I want to see what they're doing," both children protested.

Bertram's Etons appeared too much attentuated for a sharp tug, nor did John feel courageous enough in the front row to jerk Viola down upon her knees by pulling her petticoats, which might come off. He therefore covered his face with his hands in what was intended to look like a spasm of acute reverence and growled at them both to kneel down, unless they wanted to be sent back instantly to Earl's Court. Evidently impressed by this threat the children knelt down; but they were no sooner upon their knees than the perverse congregation rose to its feet, the concerted movement taking John so completely unawares that he was left below and felt when he did rise like a naughty boy who has been discovered hiding under a table. He was not put at ease by Viola's asking him to find her place in the prayer-book; it seemed to him terrible to discern the signs of a vindictive spirit in one so young.

"Hush," he whispered. "You must remember that we're in the front row and must be careful not to disturb the—" he hesitated at the word "performers" and decided to envelop whatever they were in a cough.

There were no more questions for a while, nothing indeed but tiptoe fidgetings until two acolytes advanced with lighted candles to a position on each side of the deacon who was preparing to read the gospel.

"Why can't he see to read?" Bertram asked. "It's not dark."

"Hush," John whispered. "This is the gospel."

He knew he was safe in affirming so much, because the announcement that he was about to read the gospel had been audibly given out by the deacon. At this point the congregation crossed its innumerable features three times, and Bertram began to giggle; immediately afterward fumes poured from the swung censer, and Viola began to choke. John felt that it was impossible to interrupt what was presumably considered the *pièce de resistance* of the service by leading the two children out along the whole length of the church; yet he was convinced that if he did not lead them out their gigglings and snortings would have a disastrous effect upon the soloist. Then he had a brilliant idea: Viola was obviously much upset by the incense and he would escort her out into fresh air with the solicitude that one gives to a sick person: Bertram he should leave behind to giggle alone. He watched his nephew bending lower and lower to contain his mirth; then with a quick propulsive gesture he hurried Viola into the aisle. Unfortunately when with a sigh of relief he stood upon the steps outside and put on his hat he found that in his confusion he had brought out Bertram's hat, which on his intellectual head felt like a precariously balanced inkpot; and though he longed to abandon Bertram to his well merited fate he could not bring himself to walk up Fitzjohn's Avenue in Bertram's hat, nor could he even contemplate with equanimity the notion of Bertram's walking up under his. Had it been a week-day either of them might have passed for an eccentric advertisement, but on a Sunday. . . .

"And if I stand on the steps of a church holding this minute hat in my hand," he thought, "people will think I'm collecting for some charity. Confound that boy! And I can't pretend that I'm feeling too hot in the middle of November. Dash that boy! And I certainly can't wear it. A Japanese juggler wouldn't be able to wear it. Damn that boy!"

Yet John would rather have gone home in a baby's bonnet than enter the church again, and the best that could be hoped was that Bertram dismayed at finding himself alone would soon emerge. Bertram, however, did not emerge, and John had a sudden fear lest in his embarrassment he might have escaped by another door and was even now rushing blindly home. Blindly was the right adverb indeed, for he would certainly be unable to see anything from under his uncle's hat. Viola, having recovered from her choking fit, began to cry at this point, and an old lady who must have noted with tender approval John's exit came out with a bottle of smelling-salts, which she begged him to make use of. Before he could decline she had gone back inside the church leaving him with the bottle. If he could have forced the contents down Viola's throat without attracting more attention he would have done so, but by this time one or two passers-by had stopped to stare at the scene, and he heard one of them tell his companion that it was a street conjurer just going to perform.

"Will anything make you stop crying?" he asked his niece in despair.

"I want Bertram," she wailed.

And at that moment Bertram appeared, led out by two sidesmen.

"Your little boy doesn't know how to behave himself in church," one of them informed John, severely.

"I was only looking for my hat," Bertram explained. "I thought it had rolled into the next pew. Let go of my arm. I slipped off the hassock. I couldn't help making a little noise, Uncle John."

John was grateful to Bertram for thus exonerating him publicly from the responsibility of having begotten him, and he inquired almost kindly what had happened.

"The hassock slipped, and I fell into the next pew."

"I'm sorry my nephew made a noise," said John to the sidesman. "My niece was taken ill, and he was left behind by accident. Thank you for showing him the way out, yes. Come along, Bertram, I've got your hat. Where's mine?"

Bertram looked blankly at his uncle.

"Do you mean to say—" John began, and then he saw a passing taxi to which he shouted.

"Those smelling-salts belong to an old lady," he explained hurriedly and quite inadequately to the bewildered sidesman into whose hands he had thrust the bottle. "Come along," he urged the children, and when they were scrambling into the taxi he called back to the sidesmen, "You can give to the jumble sale any hat that is swept up after the service."

Inside the taxi John turned to the children.

"One would think you'd never been inside a church before," he said, reproachfully.

"Bertram," said Viola, in bland oblivion of all that her

uncle had endured, "when we dress up to-day shall we act going to church, or finish Robinson Crusoe?"

"Wait till we see what we can find for dressing up," Bertram advised.

John displayed a little anxiety.

"Dressing up?" he repeated.

"We always dress up every Sunday," the children burst forth in unison.

"Oh, I see—it's a kind of habit. Well, I dare say Mrs. Worfolk will be able to find you an old duster or something."

"Duster," echoed Viola, scornfully. "That's not enough for dressing up."

"I didn't suggest a duster as anything but a supplement to your ordinary costume. I didn't anticipate that you were going to rely entirely upon the duster."

"I say, V, can you twig what Uncle John says?"

Viola shook her head.

"Nor more can I," said Bertram, sympathetically.

Before the taxi reached Church Row, John found himself adopting a positively deferential manner towards his nephew and his niece, and when they were once again back in the quiet house, the hall of which was faintly savoury with the maturing lunch he asked them if they would mind amusing themselves for an hour while he wrote some letters.

"For I take it you won't want to dress up immediately," he added as an excuse for attending to his own business.

The children confirmed his supposition, but went on to inform him that the domenical régime at Earl's Court prescribed a walk after church.

"Owing to the accident to my hat I'm afraid I must ask you to let me off this morning."

"Right-o," Bertram agreed, cheerfully. "But I vote we come up and sit with you while you write your letters. I think letters are a beastly fag, don't you?"

John felt that the boy was proffering his own and his sister's company in a spirit of altruism, and he could not muster enough gracelessness to decline the proposal. So upstairs they all went.

"I think this is rather a ripping room, don't you, V?"

"The carpet's very old," said Viola.

"Have you got any decent books?" Bertram inquired, looking round at the shelves. "Any Henty's, I mean, or anything?"

"No, I'm afraid I haven't," said John, apologetically.

"Or bound up Boys Own Papers?"

John shook his head.

"But I'll tell you what I have got," he added with a sudden inspiration. "Kingsley's *Heroes*."

"Is that a pi book?" asked Bertram, suspiciously.

"Not at all. It's about Greek gods and goddesses, essentially broad-minded divinities."

"Right-o. I'll have a squint at it, if you like," Bertram volunteered. "Come on, V, don't start showing off your rotten dancing. Come and look at this book. It's got some spiffing pictures."

"Lunch won't be very long," John announced in order to propitiate any impatience at what they might consider the boring entertainment he was offering.

Presently the two children left their uncle alone, and he observed with pride that they took with them the book. He little thought that so mild a dose of romance as could be extracted from Kingsley's *Heroes* would before the twilight of that November day run through 36 Church Row like fire. But then John did not know that there was a calf's head for dinner that night; he had not realized the scenic capacity of the cistern cupboard at the top of the house; and most of all he had not associated with dressing up on Sunday afternoon the histrionic force that Bertram and Viola inherited from their mother.

"Is it Androméda or Andrómeda?" Bertram asked at lunch.

"Andrómeda, my boy," John answered. "Perseus and Andromeda."

"I think it would make a jolly good play, don't you?" Bertram went on.

Really, thought John, this nephew was a great improvement upon that spectacled inquisitor at Ambles.

"A capital play," he agreed, heartily. "Are you thinking of writing it?"

"V and I thought we'd do it instead of finishing Robinson Crusoe. Well, you see, you haven't got any decent fur rugs, and V's awfully stupid about having her face blacked."

"It's my turn not to be a savage," Viola pleaded in defense of her squeamishness.

"I said you could be Will Atkins as well. I know I'd jolly well like to be Will Atkins myself."

"All right," Viola offered. "You can, and I'll be Robinson."

"You can't change like that in the middle of a play," her brother argued.

John, who appreciated both Viola's dislike of burnt-cork and Bertram's esthetic objection to changing parts in the middle of a piece, strongly recommended Perseus and Andromeda.

"Of course, you got the idea from Kingsley? Bravo, Bertram," he said, beaming with cordial patronage.

"And I suppose," his nephew went on, "that you'd rather we played at the top of the house. I expect it would be quieter, if you're writing letters. Mother said you often liked to be quiet." He alluded to this desire rather shamefully, as if it were a secret vice of his uncle, who hurriedly approved the choice of the top landing for the scene of the classic drama.

"Then would you please tell Mrs. Worfolk that we *can* have the calf's head?"

"The what?"

"V found a calf's head in the larder, and it would make a fizzing Gorgon's head, but Mrs. Worfolk wouldn't let us have it."

John was so much delighted with the trend of Bertram's

ingenuity that he sent for Mrs. Worfolk and told her that the calf's head might be borrowed for the play.

"I'll take no responsibility for your dinner," said his housekeeper, warningly.

"That's all right, Mrs. Worfolk. If anything happens to the head I shan't grumble. There'll always be the cold beef, won't there?"

Mrs. Worfolk turned up her eyes to heaven and left the room.

"Well, I think I've arranged that for you successfully."

"Thank you, Uncle John," said Bertram.

"Thank you, Uncle John," said Viola.

What nice quiet well-mannered children they were, after all; and he by no means ought to blame them for the fiasco of the churchgoing; the setting had of course been utterly unfamiliar; these ritualistic places of worship were a mistake in an unexcitable country like England. John retired to his library and lit a Corona with a sense that he thoroughly deserved a good cigar.

"Children are not difficult," he said to himself, "if one tries to put oneself in their place. That request for the calf's head undoubtedly showed a rare combination of adaptiveness with for a schoolboy what was almost a poetic fancy. Harold would have wanted to know how much the head weighed, and whether in life it preferred to browse on buttercups or daisies; but when finally it was cooked he would have eaten twice as much as anybody else. I prefer Bertram's attitude; though naturally I can appreciate a housekeeper's feelings. These cigars are in capital condition. Really, Bertram's example is infectious, and by gad, I feel quite like a couple of hours with Joan. Yes, it's a pity Laurence hasn't got Bertram's dramatic sense. A great pity."

The sabbath afternoon wore on, and though John did not accumulate enough energy to seat himself at his table, he dreamed a good deal of wonderful situations in the fourth act, puffing away at his cigar and hearing from time to time distant shouts and scamperings; these, however, did not keep him from falling into a gentle doze, from which he was abruptly wakened by the opening of the library door.

"Ah, is that tea?" he asked cheerfully in that tone with which the roused sleeper always implies his uninterrupted attention to time and space.

"No, sir, it's me," a grim voice replied. "And if you don't want us all to be drowned where we stand, it being a Sunday afternoon, and not a plumber to be got, and Maud in the hysterics, and those two young Tartars screaming like Bedlamites, and your dinner ruined and done for, and the feathers gone from Elsa's new hat, per-raps you could come upstairs, Mr. Touchwood. Gordon's head indeed, and the boy as naked as a stitch!"

John jumped to his feet and hurried out on the landing; at the same moment Bertram with nothing to cover him except a pudding-shape on his head, a tea-tray on his arm, a Turkish scimitar at his waist, and the pinions of a blue and green bird tied round his ankles leapt six stairs of the flight above and alighting at his uncle's feet, thrust the calf's head into his face.

"You're turned to stone, Phineus," he yelled. "You can't move. You've seen the Gorgon."

"There he goes again with his Gordon and his Gladstone," said Mrs. Worfolk. "How dare you be so daring?"

"The Gorgon's sister," cried Bertram lunging at her with the scimitar. "Beware, I am invisible."

Whereupon he enveloped the calf's head in a napkin, held the tea-tray before his face, and darted away upstairs.

"I'm afraid he's a little over-excited," said John, doubtfully.

At this moment a stream of water began to flow past his feet and pour down upon him from the landing above.

"Why, the house is full of water," he gasped.

"It's what I'm trying to tell you, sir," Mrs. Worfolk fumed. "He's done something with that there cistern and burst it. *I* can't stop the water."

John followed Perseus on his wild flight up the stairs down which every moment water was flowing more freely. When he reached the cistern cupboard he discovered Maud bound fast to the disordered cistern, while Viola holding in her mouth a large ivory paper-knife and wearing what looked like Mrs. Worfolk's sealskin jacket that John had given her last Christmas was splashing at full length in a puddle on the floor and clawing at Maud's skirts with ferocious growls and grunts.

"You dare try to undress me again, Master Bertram," the statuesque Maud was screaming.

"Well, Andromeda's got practically nothing on in the book, and you said you'd rather not be the sea-monster," Bertram was arguing. "Andromeda," he cried seeing by the manner of his uncle's advance that the curtain must now be rung down upon the play, "I have turned the monster to stone. Go on, V, you can't move from now on."

Viola stiffened and without a twitch let the stream of water pour down upon her, while Bertram planting his foot in the small of her back waved triumphantly the Gorgon's head, both of whose ears gave way under the strain, so that John's dinner was soon as wet as he was.

The cistern emptied itself at last; Maud was released; Bertram and Viola were led downstairs to be dried and on Mrs. Worfolk's recommendation sent instantly to bed.

"I told you," said Bertram, "that if Miss Coldwell had come, we couldn't have done anything decent."

What woman, John wondered, might serve as a comparable deterrent? The fantastic idea of appealing for aid to Doris Hamilton flashed through his mind, but on second thoughts he felt that there would be something undignified in asking her to come at such a moment. Then he remembered how often he had heard his sister-in-law Beatrice lament her childlessness. Why should he not visit James and Beatrice this very evening? He owed them a visit, and his domestics were all obviously too much agitated even to contemplate the preparation of dinner. Mrs. Worfolk would perhaps be in a better temper when he got back and he would explain to her that the seal was a marine animal, the skin of which would not be injured by water.

"I think I'll ask Mrs. James to give us a helping hand this week," John suggested. "I shall be rather busy myself."

"Yes, sir, and so shall I, trying to get the house straight again which it looks more like Shooting the Chutes at Earl's Court than a gentleman's house, I'm bound to say."

"Still it might have been worse, Mrs. Worfolk. They might have played with another element. Fire, for instance. That would have been much more awkward."

"And it's thanks to me the house isn't on fire as well," Mrs. Worfolk shrilled in her indignation. "For if that young Turk didn't come charging down into the kitchen and trying to tell me that the kitchen-fire was a serpent and start attacking it tooth and nail. And there was poor Elsa shut up in the coal-cellar and hollering fit to break anyone's heart. 'She's Daniel in a tower of brass,' he says as bold as a tower of brass himself."

"And what were you, Mrs. Worfolk?" John asked.

"Oh, his lordship had the nerve to say I was an atlas. 'Yes,' I said, 'my lord, you let me catch hold of you and I'll make your behind look like an atlas before I've done with it.'"

"Do you think that Mrs. James could control them?" John asked.

"I wouldn't say as the Lord Mayor himself could control them, but it's not for me to give advice when good food can be turned into Gordon's heads. And whatever give them the idea, I don't know, for I'm sure General Gordon was a very handsome man to look at. Yaul excuse me, sir, but if you don't want to catch your death, you'd better change *your* things."

John followed Mrs. Worfolk's advice, and an hour later he was walking through the misty November night in the direction of St. John's Wood.

CHAPTER VI

IF a taxi had lurked in any of the melancholy streets through which John was making his way to Hill Road he would have taken refuge in it gratefully, for there was no atmosphere that preyed upon his mind with such a sense of desolation as the hour of evening prayer in a respectable Northern suburb. The occasional footsteps of uninspired lovers dying away into by-streets; the occasional sounds of stuffy worship proceeding from church or chapel; the occasional bark of a dog trying to obtain admittance to an empty house; the occasional tread of a morose policeman; the occasional hoot of a distant motor-horn; the occasional whiff of privet-shrubberies and of damp rusty railings; the occasional effusions of chlorotic gaslight upon the raw air, half fog, half drizzle; the occasional shadows that quivered upon the dimly luminous blinds of upper windows; the occasional mutterings of housemaids in basements—not even John's buoyant spirit could rise above such a weight of depressing adjuncts to the influential Sabbath gloom. He began to accuse himself of having been too hasty in his treatment of Bertram and Viola; the scene at Church Row viewed in retrospect seemed to him cheerful and, if the water had not reached his Aubusson rug, perfectly harmless. No doubt, in the boarding-house at Earl's Court such behavior had been considered impossible. Had not the children talked of finishing Robinson Crusoe and alluded to his own lack of suitable fur rugs? Evidently last week the drama had been interrupted by the landlady because they had been spoiling her fur rugs. John was on the point of going back to Church Row and inviting the children to celebrate his return in a jolly impromptu supper, when he remembered that there were at least five more Sundays before Christmas. Next Sunday they would probably decide to revive the Argonauts, a story that, so far as he could recall the incidents, offered many opportunities for destructive ingenuity. Then, the Sunday after, there would be Theseus and the Minotaur; if there were another calf's head in the larder, Bertram might easily try to compel Mrs. Worfolk to be the Minotaur and *wear* it, which might mean Mrs. Worfolk's resignation from his service, a prospect that could not be faced with equanimity. But would the presence of Beatrice exercise an effective control upon this dressing up, and could he stand Beatrice for six weeks at a stretch? He might, of course, engage her to protect him and his property during the first few days, and after that to come for every week end. Suppose he did invite Doris Hamilton, but, of course, that was absurd—suppose he did invite Beatrice, would Doris Hamilton—would Beatrice come? Could it possibly be held to be one of the duties of a confidential secretary to assist her employer in checking the exuberance of his juvenile relations? Would not Miss Hamilton decide that her post approximated too nearly to that of a governess? Obviously such a woman had never contemplated the notion of becoming a governess. But had she ever contemplated the notion of becoming a confidential secretary? No, no, the plan was fantastic, unreal . . . he must trust to Beatrice and hope that Miss Coldwell would presently recover, or that Eleanor's tour would come to a sudden end, or that George would have paid what he owed his landlady and feel better able to withstand her criticism of his children. If all these hopes proved unfounded, a schoolboy, like the rest of human nature, had his price—his noiselessness could be bought in youth like his silence later on. John was turning into Hill Road when he made this reflection; he was within the area of James' cynical operations.

John's eldest brother was at forty-six an outwardly rather improved, an inwardly much debased replica of their father. The old man had not possessed a winning personality, but his energy and genuine powers of accomplishment had made him a successful general practitioner, because people overlooked his rudeness in the confidence he gave them and forgave his lack of sympathy on account of his obvious devotion to their welfare. He with his skeptical and curious mind, his passion for mathematics and hatred of idealism, and his unaffected contempt for the human race could not conceive a worse hell in eternity than a general practice offered him in life; but having married a vain, beautiful, lazy and conventional woman, he could not bring himself to spoil his honesty by blaming for the foolish act anything more tangible than the scheme of creation; and having made himself a damned uncomfortable bed with a pretty quilt, as he used to say, he had decided that he must lie on it. No doubt, many general practitioners go through life with the conviction that they were intended to devote themselves to original research; but Dr. Robert Touchwood from what those who were qualified to judge used to say of him had reason to feel angry with his fate.

James, who as a boy had shown considerable talent, was chosen by his father to inherit the practice. It was typical of the old gentleman that he did not assume this succession as the right of the eldest son, but that he deliberately awarded it to James as the most apparently adequate of his offspring. Unfortunately James, who was dyspeptic even at school, chose to imitate his father's mannerisms while he was still a student at Guy's and helping at odd hours in the dispensary. Soon after he had taken his finals and had seen his name engraved upon the brass plate underneath his father's, old Dr. Touchwood fell ill of an incurable disease and James found himself in full charge of the practice, which he proceeded to ruin, so that not long after his father's death he was compelled to sell it for a much smaller sum than it would have fetched a few years before. For a time he played alternately with the plan of setting up as a specialist in Harley Street or of burying himself in the country to write a monograph on British dragon-flies—for some reason these fierce and brilliant insects touched a responsive chord in James. He finally decided upon the dragon-flies and went down to Ockham Common in Surrey to search for *Sympetrum Fonscolombii,* a rare migrant that was reported from that locality in 1892. He could not prove that it was any more indigenous than himself to the sophisticated county, but in the course of his observations he met Beatrice Pyrke, the daughter of a prosperous inn-keeper in a neighboring town, and married her. Nothwithstanding such a catch—he used to vow that she was more resplendent than even *Anax Imperator*—he continued to take an interest in dragon-flies, until his monograph was unluckily forestalled a few years later. It was owing to an article of his in one of the entomological journals that he encountered Daniel Curtis—a meeting which led to Hilda's marriage. In those days—John had not yet made a financial success of literature—this result had seemed to the embittered odonatist a complete justification of the many hours he had wasted in preparing for his never-to-be written monograph, because his sister's future had for some time been presenting a disagreeable and insoluble problem. Besides observing dragon-flies, James spent one year in making a clock out of fishbones, and another year in perfecting a method of applying gold lacquer to poker-work.

A more important hobby, however, that finally displaced all the others was foreign literature, in the criticism of which he frequently occupied pages in the expensive reviews, pages that gradually grew numerous enough to make first one book and then another. James' articles on foreign literature were always signed; but he also wrote many criticisms of English literature that were not signed. This hack-work exasperated him so much that he gradually came to despising the whole of English literature after the eighteenth century with the exception of the novels of George Meredith. These he used to read aloud to his wife when he was feeling particularly bilious and derive from her nervous bewilderment a savage satisfaction. In her the critic possessed a perpetual incarnation of the British public that he so deeply scorned, and he treated his wife in the same way as he fancied he treated the larger entity: without either of them he would have been intellectually at a loose end. For all his admiration of French literature James spoke the language with a hideous British accent. Once on a joint holiday John, who for the whole of a channel-crossing had been listening to his brother's tirades against the rottenness of modern English literature and his pæans on behalf of modern French literature, had been much consoled when they reached Calais to find that James could not make himself intelligible even to a porter.

"But," as John had said with a chuckle, "perhaps Meredith couldn't have made himself intelligible to an English porter."

"It's the porter's fault," James had replied, sourly.

For some years now the critic with his wife and a fawn-coloured bulldog had lived in furnished apartments at 65 Hill Road, a creeper-matted house of the early 'seventies which James characterized as quiet and Beatrice as handy; in point of fact it was neither, being exposed to barrel-organs and remote from busses. A good deal of the original furniture still incommoded the rooms; but James had his own chair, Beatrice had her own footstool, and Henri Beyle the bulldog his own basket. The fire-place was crowned by an overmantel of six decorative panels, all that was left of James' method of applying gold lacquer to poker-work. There were also three or four family portraits, which John for some reason coveted for his own library, and a drawer-cabinet of faded and decrepit dragon-flies. Some bookshelves filled with yellow French novels gave an exotic look to the drab room, which, whenever James was not smoking his unusually foul pipes, smelt of gravy and malt vinegar except near the window, where the predominant perfume was of ferns and oilcloth. Between the living-room and the bedroom were double-doors hidden by brown plush curtains, which if opened quickly revealed nothing but a bleak expanse of bed and a gray window fringed with ragged creepers.

When a visitor entered this room to wash his hands he used to look at James' fishbone clock under its bell-glass on a high chest of drawers and shiver in the dampness, the fireplace was covered by a large wardrobe, and one of Beatrice's hats was often on the bed, the counterpane of which was stenciled with Beyle's paws. John, who loathed this bedroom, always said he did not want to wash his hands, when he took a meal at Hill Road.

The depression of his Sunday evening walk had made John less critical than he usually was of James' rooms, and he heard the gate of the front-garden swing back behind him with a sense of pleasurable expectation.

"There will be cold mutton for supper," he said to himself, thinking rather guiltily of the calf's head that he might have eaten and to partake of which he had not invited his brother and Beatrice. "Cold mutton and a very wet salad, with either tinned pears or tinned pineapple to follow—or perhaps stewed figs."

When John entered, James was deep in his armchair with Beyle snoring on his lap, where he served as a rest for the large book that his master was reading.

"Hullo," the critic exclaimed without attempting to rise. "You *are* back in town then?"

"Yes, I came back on Friday."

"I thought you wouldn't be able to stand the country for long. Remember what Horry Walpole said about the country?"

"Yes," said John, quickly. He had not the least idea really, but he had long ago ceased to have any scruples about preventing James first of all from trying to remember a quotation, secondly from trying to find it, thirdly from asking Beatrice where she had hidden the book in which it was to be found, and finally from not only reading it when the book was found, but also from reading page after page of irrelevant matter in the context. "Though Ambles is really very jolly," he added. "I'm expecting you and Beatrice to spend Christmas with me, you know."

James grunted.

"Well, we'll see about that. I don't belong to the Dickens Fellowship and I shall be pretty busy. You popular authors soon forget what it means to be busy. So you've had another success? Who was it this time—Lucretia Borgia, eh?" he laughed, bitterly. "Good lord, it's incredible, isn't it? But the English drama's in a sick state—a very sick state."

"All contemporary art is in a sick state according to the critics," John observed. "Critics are like doctors; they are not prejudiced in favor of general good-health."

"Well, isn't it in a sick state?" James demanded, truculently.

"I don't know that I think it is. However, don't let's begin an argument before supper. Where's Beatrice?"

"She bought a new hat yesterday and has gone to demonstrate its becomingness to God and woman."

"I suppose you mean she's gone to church? I went to church myself this morning."

"What for? Copy?"

"No, no, no. I took George's children."

"You don't mean to say that you've got *them* with you?"

John nodded, and his brother exploded with an uproarious laugh.

"Well, I was fool enough to marry before I was thirty," he bellowed. "But at any rate I wasn't fool enough to have any children. So you're going to sup with us. I ought to warn you it's cold mutton to-night."

"Really? Capital! There's nothing I like better than cold mutton."

"Upon my soul, Johnnie, I'll say this for you. You may write stale romantic plays about the past, but you manage to keep plenty of romantic sauce for the present. Yes, you're a born optimist. Look at your skin—pink as a baby's. Look at mine—yellow as a horse's tooth. Have you heard my new name for your habit of mind? Rosification. Rather good, eh? And you can rosify anything from Lucretia Borgia to cold mutton. Now don't look angry with me, Johnnie; you must rosify my ill-humor. With so many roses you can't expect not to have a few thorns as well, and I'm one of them. No, seriously, I congratulate you on your success. And I always try to remember that you write with your tongue in your cheek."

"On the contrary I believe I write as well as I can," said John, earnestly. "I admit that I gave up writing realistic novels, but that was because they didn't suit my temperament."

"No, by gad, they didn't! And, anyway, no Englishman *can* write a realistic novel—or any other kind of a novel if it comes to that. My lord, the English novel!"

"Look here," John protested. "I do not want to argue about either plays or novels to-night. But if you must talk about books, talk about your own, not mine. Beatrice wrote to me that you had something coming along about the French Symbolists. I shouldn't have thought that they would have appealed to you."

"They don't. I hate them."

"Well, why write a book about them? Their day has been over a long time."

"To smash them. To prove that they were a pretentious set of epileptic humbugs."

"Sort of Max Nordau business?"

"Max Nordau! I hope you aren't going to compare me with that flat-footed bus-conductor. No, no, Johnnie, the rascals took themselves seriously and I'm going to smash them on their own estimate of their own importance. I'm going to prove that they were on the wrong track and led nowhere."

"It's consoling to learn that even French literature can go off the lines sometimes."

"Of course it can, because it runs on lines. English literature on the contrary never had any lines on which to run, though in the eighteenth century it followed a fairly decent coaching-road. Modern English literature, however, is like a rogue elephant trampling down the jungle that its predecessors made some attempt to cultivate."

"I never knew that even moral elephants had taken up agriculture seriously."

James blew all the ashes of his pipe over Beyle in a gust of contempt, and rose from his chair.

"The smirk!" he cried. "The traditional British smirk! The gerumky-gerum horse-laugh! British humor! Ha-ha! Begotten by Punch out of Mrs. Grundy with the Spectator for godfather. *'Go to, you have made me mad.'*"

"It's a pity you can't tell me about your new book without flying into a rage," John said, mildly. "You haven't told me yet when it's to appear."

"My fourteen readers aren't languishing. But to repay politeness by politeness, my book will come out in March."

"I'm looking forward to it," John declared. "Have you got good terms from Worrall?"

"As good terms as a consumptive bankrupt might expect from Shylock. What does the British public care for criticism? You should hear me reading the proofs to Beatrice. You should really have the pleasure of watching her face, and listening to her comments. Do you know why Beatrice goes to church? I'll tell you. She goes to indulge in a debauch of the accumulated yawns of the week."

"Hush, here she is," John warned him.

James laughed again.

"Johnnie, you're *impayable*. Your sensitiveness to Beatrice betrays the fount of your success. You treat the British public with just the same gentlemanly gurgle. And above all you're a good salesman. That's where George failed when he tried whisky on commission."

"I don't believe you're half the misanthropist you make yourself out."

"Of course, I'm not. I love human nature. Didn't I marry Beatrice, and didn't I spend a year in making a clock out of fishbones to amuse my landlady's children, and wasn't I a doctor of medicine without once using my knowledge of poisons? I love mankind—but dragon-flies were more complex and dogs are more admirable. Well, Beatrice, did you enjoy the sermon?"

His wife had come in and was greeting John broadly and effusively, for when she was excited her loud contralto voice recaptured many rustic inflections of her youth. She was a tall woman, gaudily handsome, conserving in clothes and coiffure the fashions of her prime as queens do and barmaids who become the wives of publicans. On Sundays she wore a lilac broadcloth with a floriated bodice cut close to the figure; but she was just as proud of her waist on weekdays and discreet about her legs, which she wrapped up in a number of petticoats. She was as real or as unreal as a cabinet-photograph of the last decade of the nineteenth century: it depended on the attitude of the observer. Although there was too much of her for the apartments, it could not be said that she appeared out of place in them; in fact she was rather like a daughter of the house who had come home for the holidays.

"Why, it's John," she expanded in a voice rich with welcome. "How are you, little stranger?"

"Thank you very much for the flowers, Beatrice. They were much appreciated."

"I wanted you to know that we were still in the land of the livin'. You're goin' to stay to supper, of course? But you'll have to be content with cold mutton, don't you know."

There was a tradition among novelists that well-bred people leave out their final "g's"; so Beatrice saved on these consonants what she squandered upon aspirates.

"And how do you think Jimmie's lookin'?" she went on. "I suppose he's told you about his new book. Comin' out in March, don't you know. I feel awfully up in French poitry since he read it out to me. Don't light another pipe now, dear. The girl's gettin' the supper at once. I think you're lookin' very well, Johnnie, I do indeed. Don't you think he's lookin' very well, Jimmie? Has Bill Bailey been out for his run?" This was Beatrice's affectionate diminutive for Henri Beyle, the dog.

"No, I won't bother about my hands," John put in hastily to forestall Beatrice's next suggestion.

"We had such a dull sermon," she sighed.

Her husband grunted a request to spare them the details.

"Well, don't you know, it's a dull time for sermons now before Christmas. But it didn't matter, as what I really wanted was a puff of fresh air. Yes, I'd begun to think you'd forgotten all about us," she rambled on, turning archly to John. "I know we must be dull company, but all work and no play, don't you know . . . yours is all plays and no work. Jimmie, I made a joke," she laughed, twitching her husband's sleeve to secure his attention. "Did you hear?"

"Yes, I heard," he growled.

"I thought it was rather good, didn't you, Johnnie?"

"Very good indeed," he assented, warmly. "Though I do work occasionally."

"Oh, of course, you silly thing, I wasn't bein' serious. I told you it was a joke. I know you must work a bit. Here comes the girl with supper. You'll excuse me, Johnnie, while I go and titivate myself. I sha'n't be a minute."

Beatrice retired to the bedroom whence she could be heard humming over her beautification.

"You're not meditating marriage, are you?" James mocked.

The bachelor shook his head.

"At the same time," he protested, stoutly, "I don't think you're entitled to sneer at Beatrice. Considering—" he was about to say "everything," but feeling that this would include his brother too pointedly he substituted, "the weather, she's wonderfully cheerful. And you know I've always insisted that these rooms are cramped."

"Yes, well, when a popular success oils my palm, John, we'll move next door to you in Church Row."

John wished that James would not always harp upon their respective fortunes: it made him feel uncomfortable, especially when he was sitting down to cold mutton. Besides, it was unfair; had he not once advised James to abandon criticism and take up—he had been going to suggest "anything except literature," but he had noticed James' angry dismay and had substituted "creative work." What had been the result? An outburst of contemptuous abuse, a violent renunciation of anything that approximated to his own work. If James despised his romantic plays, why could he not be consistent and despise equally the wealth they brought him? He honored his brother's intellectual sincerity, why could not his brother do as much for his?

"What beats me," James had once exclaimed, "is how a man like you who professes to admire—no, I believe you're honest—who does admire Stendhal, Turgenev, Flaubert and Merimée, who recognizes the perfection of *Manon Lescaut* and *Adolphe,* who in a word has taste, can bring himself to eructate the *Fall of Babylon.*"

"It's all a matter of knowing one's own limitations," John had replied. "I tried to write realistic novels. But my temperament is not realistic."

"No, if it were," James had murmured, "you wouldn't stand my affectation of superiority."

It was this way James had of once in a very long while putting himself in the wrong that used always to heal John's wounded generosity. But these occasional lapses—as he supposed his cynical brother would call them—were becoming less and less frequent, and John had no longer much excuse for clinging to his romantic reverence for the unlucky head of his family.

During the first half of supper Beatrice delivered a kind of lecture on housekeeping in London on two pounds twelve shillings and sixpence a week, including bones for the dog; by the time that the stewed figs were put on the table this monologue had reduced both brothers to such a state of gloom by striking at James' experience and John's imagination, that the sourness of the cream came as a natural corollary; anything but sour cream would have seemed an obtrusive reminder of housekeeping on more than two pounds twelve shillings and sixpence a week, including bones for the dog. John was convinced by his sister-in-law's mood that she would enjoy a short rest from speculating upon the comparative versatility of mutton and beef, and by James' reception of her remarks that he would appreciate her housekeeping all the more after being compelled to regard for a while the long procession of chops that his landlady would inevitably marshal for him while his wife was away. The moment seemed propitious to the unfolding of his plan.

"I want to ask you both a favor," he began. "No, no, Beatrice, I disagree with you. I don't think the cream is really sour. I find it delicious, but I daren't ever eat more than a few figs. The cream, however, is particularly delicious. In fact I was on the point of inquiring the name of your dairy."

"If we have cream on Sundays," Beatrice explained, "Jimmie has to put up with custard-powder on Wednesdays. But if we don't have cream on Sundays, I can spare enough eggs on Wednesdays for real custard."

"That's very ingenious of you," John declared. "But you didn't hear what I was saying when I broke off in defense of the cream, *which* is delicious. I said that I wanted to ask a favor of you both."

"King Cophetua and the Beggar Maid," James chuckled. "Or were you going to suggest to Beatrice that next time you have supper with us she should experiment not only with fresh cream, but also with some rare dish like nightingales' tongues—or even veal, for instance?"

"Now, Jimmie, you're always puttin' hits in at me about veal; but if I get veal, it throws me out for the whole week."

John made another effort to wrench the conversation free from the topic of food:

"No, no, James. I was going to ask you to let Beatrice come and give me a hand with our nephew and our niece." He slightly accentuated the pronoun of plural possession. "Of course, that is to say, if Beatrice would be so kind."

"What do you want her to do? Beat them?" James asked.

"No, no, no, James. I'm not joking. As I explained to you, I've got these two children—er—staying with me. It appears that George is too overstrained, too ill, that is, to manage them during the few weeks that Eleanor will be away on tour, and I thought that if Beatrice could be my guest for a week or two until the governess has re-created her nervous system, which I understand will take about a month, I should feel a great weight off my mind. A bachelor household, you know, is not primarily constructed to withstand an invasion by children. You'd find them very difficult here, James, if you hadn't got Beatrice."

"Oh, Johnnie, I should love it," his sister-in-law cried. "That is if Jimmie could spare me."

"Of course, I could. You'd better take her back with you to-night."

"No, really?" said John. "Why that would be splendid. I'm immensely obliged to you both."

"He's quite anxious to get rid of me," Beatrice laughed, happily. "I sha'n't be long packin'. Fancy lookin' after Eleanor's two youngsters. I've often thought I *would* rather like to see if I couldn't bring up children."

"Now's your chance," John jovially offered.

"Jimmie didn't ever care much for youngsters," Beatrice explained.

Her husband laughed bitterly.

"Quite enough people hate me, as it is," he sneered, "without deliberately creating a child of my own to add to the number."

"Oh, no, of course, dear, I know we're better off as we are," Beatrice said with a soothing pat for her husband's round shoulders. "Only the idea comes into my head now and again that I'd just like to see if I couldn't manage them, that's all, dear. I'm not complaining."

"I don't want to hurry you away," James muttered. "But I've got some work to do."

"We'd better send the servant out to look for a taxi at once," John suggested. "It's Sunday night, you know."

Twenty minutes later, Beatrice looking quite fashionable now in her excitement—so many years had it obliterated—was seated in the taxi; John was half-way along the garden path on his way to join her, when his brother called him back.

"Oh, by the way, Johnnie," he said in gruff embarrassment, "I've got an article on Alfred de Vigny coming out soon in *The Nineteenth Century*. It can't bring me in less than fifteen guineas, but it might not be published for another three months. I can show you the editor's letter, if you like. I wonder if you could advance me ten guineas? I'm a little bothered just at the moment. There was a vet's bill for the dog and . . ."

"Of course, of course, my dear fellow. I'll send you a check to-night. Thanks very much for—er—releasing Beatrice, I mean—helping me out of a difficulty with Beatrice. Very good of you. Good-night. I'll send the check at once."

"Don't cross it," said James.

On the way back to Hampstead in the dank murkiness of the cab, Beatrice became confidential.

"Jimmie always hated me to pass remarks about havin' children, don't you know, but it's my belief that he feels it as much as anyone. Look at the fuss he makes of poor old Bill Bailey. And bein' the eldest son and havin' the pictures of his grandfather and grandmother, I'm sure there are times when he'd give a lot to explain to a youngster of his own who they really were. It isn't so interestin' to explain to me, don't you know, because they aren't my relations, except, of course, by marriage. I always feel myself that Jimmie for an eldest son has been very unlucky. Well, there's you, for instance. I don't mean to say he's jealous, because he's not; but still I dare say he sometimes thinks that he ought to be where you are, though, of course, that doesn't mean to say that he'd like you to be where he is. But a person can't help feelin' that there's no reason why you shouldn't both have been where you are. The trouble with Jimmie was that he wasted a lot of time when he was young, and sometimes, though I wouldn't say this to anybody but you, sometimes I do wonder if he doesn't think he married too much in a hurry. Then there were his dragon-flies. There they all are falling to pieces from want of interest. I don't suppose anybody in England has taken so much trouble as Jimmie over dragon-flies, but what *is* a dragon-fly? They'll never be popular with the general public, because though they don't sting, people think they do. And then that fellow—who is it—it begins with an M—oh dear, my memory is something chronic! Well, anyway, he wrote a book about bees, and it's tremendously popular. Why? Because a bee is well-known. Certainly they sting too, but then they have honey and people keep them. If people kept dragon-flies, it would be different. No, my opinion is that for an eldest son Jimmie has been very unlucky."

The next day Bertram disappeared to school at an hour of the morning which John remembered did exist in his youth, but which he had for long regarded as a portion of the great backward and abysm of time. Beatrice tactfully removed his niece immediately after breakfast, not the auroral breakfast of Bertram, but the comfortable meal of ten o'clock; and except for a rehearsal of the *bolero* in the room over the library John was able to put in a morning of undisturbed diligence. Beatrice took Viola for a walk in the afternoon, and when Bertram arrived back from school about six o'clock she nearly spoilt her own dinner by the assistance she gave him with his tea. John had a couple of quiet hours with *Joan of Arc* before dinner, when he was only once interrupted by Beatrice's coming as her nephew's ambassador to ask what was the past participle of some Latin verb, which cost him five minutes' search for a dictionary. After dinner John played two sets of piquet with his sister-in-law and having won both began to feel that there was a good deal to be said for a woman's presence in the house.

But about eleven o'clock on the morning of the next day James arrived, and not only James but Beyle the bulldog, who had, if one might judge by his behavior, as profound a contempt as his master for John's library, and a much more unpleasant way of showing it.

"I wish you'd leave your dog in the hall," John protested. "Look at him now; he's upset the paper-basket. Get down off that chair! I say, do look at him!"

Beyle was coursing round the room, steering himself with the kinked blob that served him for a tail.

"He likes the soft carpet," his master explained. "He thinks it's grass."

"What an idiotic dog," John scoffed. "And I suppose he thinks my Aubusson is an herbaceous border. Drop it, you brute, will you. I say, do put him downstairs. He's going to worry it in a minute, and all agree that bulldogs can't be induced to let go of anything they've once fairly gripped. Lie down, will you!"

James roared with laughter at his brother's disgust, but finally he turned the dog out of the room, and John heard what he fancied was a panic-stricken descent of the stairs by Maud or . . .

"I say, I hope he isn't chasing Mrs. Worfolk up and down the house," he ejaculated as he hurried out on the landing. What ever Beyle had been doing, he was at rest now and smiling up at John from the front-door mat. "I hope it *wasn't* Mrs. Worfolk," he said, coming back. "She's in a very delicate state just at present."

"What?" James shouted, incredulously.

"Oh, not in that way, my dear fellow, not in that way. But she's not used to having so many visitors in the house."

"I'm going to take one of them away with me, if that'll be any consolation to her," James announced.

"Not Beatrice?" his brother stammered.

James nodded grimly.

"It's all very fine for you with a mob of servants to look after you: but I can't spare Beatrice any more easily than you could spare Mrs. Worfolk. I've been confoundedly uncomfortable for nearly two days, and my wife must come back."

"Oh, but look here," John protested. "She's been managing the children magnificently. I've hardly known they were in the house. You can't take Beatrice away."

"Sorry, Johnnie, but my existence is not so richly endowed with comforts as yours. You'd better get a wife for yourself. You can afford one."

"But can't we arrive at a compromise?" John pleaded. "Why don't you come and camp out with me, too?"

"Camp out, you hypocrite!" the critic jeered. "No, no, you can't bribe me with your luxuries. Do you think that I could work with two children careering all over the place? I dare say they don't disturb your plays. I dare say you can't hear them above the clash of swords and the rolling of thunder, but for critical work I want absolute quiet. Sorry, but I'm afraid I must carry off Beatrice."

"Well, of course, if you must. . . ." John murmured, despondently. And it was very little consolation to think, while Viola practised the *fandango* in the library preparatory to dislocating the household by removing Maud from her work to escort her to the dancing-class, that Beatrice herself would have liked to stay.

"However," John sternly resolved, "the next time that James tries to scoff at married life I shall tell him pretty plainly what I think of his affectation."

He decided ultimately to keep the children at Church Row for a week, to give them some kind of treat on Saturday, and on Saturday evening, before dinner, to take them back to their father and insist upon his being responsible for them. If by chance George proved to be really ill, which he did not suppose for a moment that he would, he should take matters firmly into his hands and export the children to Ambles until their mother came home: Viola could practise every known variety of Spanish dance over Laurence's head, or even in Laurence's room; and as for Bertram he could corrupt Harold to his heart's content.

On the whole, the week passed off well. Although Viola had fallen like Lucifer from being an angel in Maud's mind, she won back her esteem by behaving like a human little girl when they went to the dancing-class together and did not try to assume diabolic attributes in exchange for the angelic position she had forfeited. John was allowed to gather that Viola's chief claim to Maud's forgiveness was founded upon her encouragement of the advances made to her escort by a handsome young sergeant of the Line whom they had encountered in the tube.

"Miss Viola behaved herself like a little lady," Maud had informed John when they came home.

"You enjoyed taking her?"

"Yes, indeed, sir, it's a pleasure to go about with anyone so lady-like. Several very nice people turned round to admire her."

"Did they, Maud, did they?"

Later, when Viola's account of the afternoon reached him he wondered if the sergeant was one of those nice people.

Mrs. Worfolk, too, was reconciled to Bertram by the profound respect he accorded to her tales and by his appreciation of an album of family photographs she brought out for him from the bottom of her trunk.

"The boy can be as quiet as a mouse," she assured John, "as long as he isn't encouraged to make a hullabaloo."

"You think I encourage him, Mrs. Worfolk?"

"Well, sir, it's not my place to offer an opinion about managing children, but giving them a calf's head is as good as telling them to misbehave theirselves. It's asking for trouble. There he is now, doing what he calls his home work with a little plate of toffee I made for him—as good as gold. But what I do ask is where's the use in filling up a child's head with Latin and Greece. Teach a child to be a heathen goddess and a heathen goddess he'll be. Teach him the story of the Infant Samuel and he'll behave like the Infant Samuel, though I must say that one child who I told about God's voice, in the family to which I was nursemaid, had a regular fit and woke up screaming in the middle of the night that he could hear God routing about for him under the bed. But then he was a child with very old-fashioned notions and took the whole story for gospel, and his mother said after that no one wasn't to read him nothing except stories about animals."

"What happened to him when he grew up?" John asked.

"Well, sir, I lost sight of the whole family, but I dare say he became a clergyman, for he never lost this habit of thinking God was dodging him all the time. It was God here, and God there, till I fairly got the jumps myself and might have taken up with the Wesleans if I hadn't gone as third housemaid to a family where the master kept race-horses which gave me something else to think about, and I never had anything more to do with children until my poor sister's Herbert."

"That must have been a great change, Mrs. Worfolk."

"Yes, sir, so it was; but life's only one long changing about, though they do say there's nothing new under the sun. But good gracious me, fellows who make up mottoes always exaggerate a bit: they've got to, so as to keep up with one another."

When Friday evening arrived John nearly emphasized Mrs. Worfolk's agreement with Heraclitus by keeping the children at Church Row. But by the last post there came a letter from Janet Bond to beg an earlier production of *Joan of Arc* if it was by any means possible, and John looking at the infinitesimal amount he had written during the week resolved that he must stick to his intention of taking the children back to their father on the following day.

"What would you like to do to-morrow?" he inquired "I happen to have a free afternoon, and—er—I'm afraid your father wants you back in Earl's Court, so it will be your last opportunity of enjoying yourselves for some time—

I mean of our enjoying ourselves for some time, in fact, until we all meet at Ambles for Christmas."

"Oh, I say," Bertram protested. "Have we got to go back to rotten old Earl's Court? What a sell!"

"I thought we were going to live here always," Viola exclaimed.

"But don't you want to go back to your father?" John demanded in what he hoped was a voice brimming with reproaches for their lack of filial piety, but which he could not help feeling was bubbling over with something very near elation.

"Oh, no," both children affirmed, "we like being with you much best."

John's gratification was suddenly darkened by the suspicion that perhaps Eleanor had told them to flatter him like this; he turned swiftly aside to hide the chagrin that such a thought gave him, and when he spoke again it was almost roughly, because in addition to being suspicious of their sincerity he was vexed with himself for displaying a spirit of competitive affection. It occurred to him that it was jealousy rather than love which made the world go round— a dangerous reflection for a romantic playwright.

"I'm afraid it can't be helped," he said. "To-morrow is definitely our last day. So choose your own method of celebrating it without dressing up."

"Oh, we only dress up on Sundays," Viola said, loftily.

"I vote we go to the Zoo," Bertram opinionated after a weighty pause.

Had his nephew Harold suggested a visit to the Zoo, John would have shunned the proposal with horror; but with Bertram and Viola the prospect of such an expedition was positively enticing.

"I must beware of favoritism," John warned himself. "Yes, and I must beware of being blarneyed." Then aloud he added:

"Very well, we will visit the Zoo immediately after lunch to-morrow.

"Oh, but we must go in the morning," Bertram cried. "There won't be nearly time to see everything in the afternoon."

"What about our food?"

"We can eat there."

"But, my dear boy," John said. "You are confusing us with the lions. I much doubt if a human being *can* eat at the Zoo, unless he has a passion for peanuts and stale buns, which I have not."

"I swear you can," Bertram maintained. "Anyhow, I know you can get ices there in the summer."

"We'll risk it," John declared, adventurously; and the children echoed his enthusiasm with joy.

"We must see the toucans this time," Bertram announced in a grave voice, "and last time we missed the zebu."

"I shouldn't have thought that possible," John demurred, "with all those stripes."

"Not the zebra," Bertram severely corrected him. "The zebu."

"Never heard of the beast," John said.

"I say, V,' Bertram exclaimed, incredulously. "He's never heard of the zebu."

Viola was too much shocked by her uncle's ignorance to do more than smile sadly.

"We'll show it you to-morrow," Bertram promised.

"Thanks very much. I shall enjoy meeting the zebu," John admitted, humbly. "And any other friends of yours in the animal world whose names begin with Z."

"And we also missed the ichneumon," Viola reminded her brother.

"Your last visit seems to have been full of broken appointments. It's just as well you're going again to-morrow. You'll be able to explain that it wasn't your fault."

"No, it wasn't" said Bertram, bitterly. "It was Miss Coldwell's."

"Yes," said Viola. "She simply tore past everything And when Bertram gave the chimpanzee a brown marble instead of a nut and he nearly broke one of his teeth, she said it was cruel."

"Yes, fancy thinking *that* was cruel," Bertram scoffed. "He was in an awful wax, though; he bunged it back at me like anything. But I swopped the marble on Monday with Higginbotham Minor for two green commonys: at least I said it was the marble; only really I dropped it while we were waiting for the bus."

"You're a kind of juvenile Lord Elgin," John declared.

"What did he do?"

"He did the Greek nation over marbles, just as you did the chimpanzee and Higginbotham Minor."

Next morning John made arrangements to send the children's luggage to Earl's Court so that he should be able when the Zoological Gardens were closed to take them directly home and not be tempted to swerve from his determination: then under the nearest approach to a blue sky that London can produce in November they set out for Regent's Park.

John with his nephew and niece for guides spent a pleasant if exhausting day. Remembering the criticism leveled against Miss Coldwell's rapidity of transit, he loitered earnestly by every cage, although he had really had no previous conception of how many animals the Zoo included and began to dread a long list of uninvited occupants at the day's end. He had a charming triumph in the discovery of two more animals beginning with Z, to wit, the zibet and the zoril, which was the sweeter for the fact that they were both new beasts to the children. There was an argument with the keeper of the snake's house, because Bertram nearly blinded a lethargic alligator with his sister's umbrella, and another with the keeper of the giraffes, because in despite of an earnest plea not to feed them, Viola succeeded in tempting one to sniff moistly a piece of raspberry noyau. If some animals were inevitably missed, there were several welcome surprises such as seeing much more of the hippopotamus than the tips of his nostrils floating like two bits of mud on the surface of the water; others included the alleged visibility of a beaver's tail, a conjugal scene between the polar-bears, a truly demoniac exhibition of rage by the Tasmanian-devil, some wonderful gymnastics by a baby snow-leopard, a successful attempt to touch a kangaroo's nose, an indisputable wriggle of vitality from the anaconda, and the sudden scratching of its ear by a somnolent fruit-eating bat.

About ten minutes before the Gardens closed John, who was tired out and had somehow got his cigar-case full of peanuts, declared it was time to go home.

"Oh, but we must just have a squint at the Small Cats' House," Bertram cried, and Viola clasped her hands in apprehension at the bare idea of not doing so.

"All right," John agreed. "I'll wait for you three minutes, and then I'm going slowly along towards the exit."

The three minutes passed, and since the children still lingered he walked on as he had promised. When they did not catch him up as soon as he expected, he waited for a while and then with an exclamation of annoyance turned back.

"What on earth can they find to enjoy in this awful smell?" he wondered, when he entered the Small Cats' House to drag them out. The house was empty except for a bored keeper thinking of his tea.

"Have you seen two children?" John asked, anxiously.

"No, sir, this is the Small Cats' House," replied the keeper.

"Children," repeated John, irritably.

"No, sir. Or, yes, I believe there *was* a little boy and a little girl in here, but they've been gone some minutes now. It's closing time," he added, significantly.

John rushed miserably along deserted paths through the dusk, looking everywhere for Bertram and Viola without success.

"All out," was being shouted from every direction.

"Two children," he panted to a keeper by the exit.

"All out."

"But two children are lost in the Gardens."

"Closing time, sir. They must have gone out by another gate."

He herded John through the turnstile into the street as he would have herded a recalcitrant gnu into its inclosure.

"But this is terrible," John lamented. "This is appalling. I've lost George's children."

He hailed a taxi, drove to the nearest police-station, left their descriptions, and directed the driver to Halma House, Earl's Court Square.

CHAPTER VII

JOHN came to the conclusion while he was driving to Earl's Court that the distinctive anxiety in losing two children was to be sought for in an acute consciousness of their mobility. He had often enough lost such articles as sovereigns, and matchboxes, and income-tax demands; but in the disappearance of these he had always been consoled by the knowledge that they were stationary in some place or another at any given moment, and that somebody or another must find them at some time or another, with profit or disappointment to himself. But Bertram and Viola might be anywhere; if at this moment they were somewhere, before the taxi had turned the next corner they might be somewhere else. The only kind of loss comparable to this was the loss of a train, in which case also the victim was dismayed by the thought of its mobility. Moreover, was it logically possible to find two children, any more than it was possible to find a lost train? They could be caught like a train by somebody else; but except among gipsies, who were practically extinct, the sport of catching children was nowadays unknown. The classic instance of two lost children—and by the way an uncle came into that—was *The Babes in the Wood,* in which story they were neither caught nor found, though certainly their bodies were found owing to the eccentric behavior of some birds in the vicinity. It would be distressing to read in the paper to-morrow of two children's having been found under a drift of paper-bags in the bear-pit at the Zoo, hugged to death not by each other, but by the bears. Or they might have hidden themselves in the Reptile House—Bertram had displayed a dreadful curiosity about the effect of standing upon one of the alligators—and their fate might remain for ever a matter of conjecture. Yet even supposing that they were not at this moment regarding with amazed absorption—absorption was too ominous a word—with amazed interest the nocturnal gambols of the great cats, were they on that account to be considered safe? If it was a question of being crunched up, it made little difference whether one was crunched up by the wheels of an omnibus or by the jaws of a panther. To be sure, Bertram was accustomed to go to school by tube every morning, and obviously he must know by this time how to ask the way to any given spot. . . .

The driver of the taxi was taking no risks with the traffic, and John's tightly strung nerves were relaxed; he began to perceive that he was agitating himself foolishly. The wide smoothness of Cromwell Road was all that was needed to persuade him that the shock had deprived him for a short time of common sense. How absurd he had been! Of course the children would be all right; but he should take good care to administer no less sharp a shock to George than he had experienced himself. He did not approve of George's attitude, and if the temporary loss of Bertram and Viola could rouse him to a sense of his paternal responsibilities, this disturbing climax of a jolly day would not have been led up to in vain. No, George's moral, mental, and physical laziness must no longer be encouraged.

"I shall make the whole business out to be as bad as possible," he decided. "Though, now that I have had time to think the situation out, I realize that there is really not the least likelihood of anything's serious having happened to them."

For James even when he was most exasperating John always felt an involuntary deference that stood quite apart from the sentimental regard which he always tried to owe him as head of the family; for his second brother George he had nothing but contempt. James might be wrongheaded; but George was fatheaded. James kept something of their father's fallen day about him; George was a kind of gross caricature of his own self. Every feature in this brother's face reproduced the corresponding feature in his own with such compelling suggestiveness of a potentially similar degeneration that John could never escape from the reproach of George's insistent kinship. Many times he had been seized by a strong impulse to cut George ruthlessly out of his life; but as soon as he perceived that gibbous development of his own aquiline nose, that reduplication of his own rounded chin, that bull-like thickening of his own sanguine neck, and that saurian accentuation of the eloquent pouches beneath his own eyes, John surrendered to the claims of fraternity and lent George as much as he required at the moment. If Daniel Curtis's desire to marry Hilda had always puzzled him, Eleanor's willingness to be tied for life to George was even more incomprehensible. Still, it was lucky that she had been taken with such a whim, because she was all that stood between George and absolute dependence upon his family, in other words upon his younger brother. Whatever Eleanor's faults, however aggressive her personality, John recognized that she was a hard worker and that the incubus of a husband like George (to whom she seemed curiously and inexplicably devoted) entitled her to a great deal of indulgence.

It was strange to look back now to the time when he and George were both in the city, himself in dog-biscuits and George in wool, and to remember that except their father everybody in the family had foretold a prosperous commercial career for George. Beyond his skill at Solo Whist and a combination of luck with judgment in betting through July and August on weight for age selling-plates and avoiding the big autumn handicaps, John could not recall that George had ever shown a glimmer of financial intelligence. Once or twice when he had visited his brother in the wool-warehouse he had watched an interview between George and a bale of wool, and he had often chuckled at the reflection that the protagonists were well matched—there had always been something woolly about George in mind and body; and when one day he rolled stolidly forth from the warehouse for the last time in order to enter into partnership with a deluded friend to act as the British agents for a society of colonial housewives, John felt that the deluded friend would have been equally well served by a bale of wool. When George and his deluded friend had tried the patience of the colonial housewives for a year by never once succeeding in procuring for them what they required, the partnership was dissolved, and George processed from undertaking to undertaking till he became the business manager of a theatrical touring company. Although as a business manager he reached the nadir of his incompetence he emerged from the post with Eleanor for wife, which perhaps gave rise to a family legend that George had never been so successful as when he was a business manager. This legend he never dispelled by a second exhibition of himself in the part, although he often spoke regretfully of the long Sundays in the train, playing nap for penny points. After he married Eleanor he was commission-agent for a variety of gentlemanly commodities like whisky and cigars; but he drank and smoked much more than he sold, and when bridge was introduced and popularized, having decided that it was the best investment for his share of Eleanor's salary, he abandoned everything else. Moreover, John's increasing prosperity gave his play a fine stability and confidence; he used to feel that his wife's current account merely lapped the base of a solid cliff of capital. A bad week at Bridge came to be known as another financial disappointment; but he used to say cheerfully when he signed the I.O.U. that one must not expect everybody in the family to be always lucky, and that it was dear old John's turn this week. John himself sometimes became quite giddy in watching the swift revolutions of the wheel of fortune as spun by George. The effect of sitting up late at cards usually made George wake with a headache, which he called "feeling overworked"; he was at his best in the dusky hours before dinner, in fact just at the time when John was on his way to explode in his ear the news of the children's disappearance; it was then that among the attenuated spinsters of Halam House his grossness seemed nothing more than a ruddy well-being and that his utter indifference to any kind of responsibility acquired the characteristics of a ripe geniality.

Halma House, Earl's Court Square, was a very large boarding-house, so large that Miss Moxley, the most attenuated spinster who lived in it, once declared that it was more like a residential hotel than a boarding-house, a theory that was eagerly supported by all the other attenuated spinsters who clung to its overstuffed furniture or like dusty cobwebs floated about its garish saloons. Halma House was indeed two houses squeezed or knocked (or whatever other uncomfortable verb can be found to express the welding) into one. Above the front-door of number 198 were the large gilt letters that composed HALMA: above the front-door of what was once number 200 the equally large gilt letters that made up HOUSE. The division between the front-door steps had been removed so as to give an almost Medician grandeur to the entrance, at the top of which beneath a folded awning a curved garden-seat against the disused door of number 20 suggested that it was the resort for the intimate gayety of the boarders at the close of a fine summer day; as Miss Moxley used to vow, it was really quite an oasis, with the plane-trees of the square for contemplation not to mention the noising of the sparrows and the distant tinkling of milk-cans, quite an oasis in dingy old London. But then Miss Moxley had the early symptoms of exophthalmus, a malady that often accompanies the poetic temperament; Miss Moxley, fluttering out for five minutes' fresh air before dinner on a gentle eve in early June, was capable of idealizing to the semblance of a careless pastoral group the spectacle of a half-pay major, a portly widow or two up from the country, and George Touchwood, all brushing the smuts from their noses while they gossiped together on that seat: this was by no means too much for her exophthalmic vision.

John's arrival at Halma House in raw November was not greeted by such evidence of communal felicity; on the contrary, when he walked up the steps, the garden-seat looked most defiantly uninviting; nor did the entrance hall with its writhing gilt furniture symbolize anything more romantic than the competitive pretentiousness of life in a boarding-house that was almost a residential hotel. A blond waiter whose hair would have been dishevelled but for the uses of perspiration informed him that Mr. Tooshvood was in his sitting-room, and led him to a door at the end of the hall opposite another door that gave descent to the dungeons of supply, the inmates of which seemed to spend their time in throwing dishes at one another.

The possession of this sitting-room was the outstanding advantage that George always claimed for Halma House, whenever it was suggested that he should change his quarters: Adam discoursing to his youngest descendant upon the glories of Eden could hardly have outbragged George on the subject of that sitting-room. John on the other hand disliked it and took pleasure in pointing out the impossibility of knowing whether it was a conservatory half transformed into a box-room or a box-room nearly turned into a conservatory. He used to call it George's amphibious apartment, with justice indeed, for Bertram and Viola with true appreciation had once selected it as the appropriate setting in which to reproduce Jules Verne's *Twenty Thousand Leagues under the Sea*. The wallpaper of dark blue flock was smeared with the glistening pattern as of seaweed upon rocks at low tide; the window was of ground-glass tinted to the hue of water in a swimming-bath on Saturday afternoon, and was surrounded by an elaborate arrangement of cork that masked a number of flower pots filled with unexacting plants; while as if the atmosphere was not already sufficiently aqueous, a stage of disheartened aspidistras cast a deep-sea twilight upon the recesses of the room, in the middle of which was a jagged table of particolored marble, and upon the walls of which were hung cases of stuffed fish. Mrs. Easton, the proprietress of Halma House, only lent the room to George as a favor: it was not really his own, and while he lay in bed of a morning she used to quarrel there with all the servants in turn. Moreover, any of the boarders who had bicycles stabled them in this advantageous apartment, the fireplace of which smoked. Nevertheless, George liked it and used to knit there for an hour after lunch, sitting in an armchair that smelt like the cushions of a third-class smoker and looking with his knitting needles and opaque eyes like a large lobster preening his antennæ in the corner of a tank.

When John visited him now, he was reading an evening paper by the light of a rugged mantle of incandescent gas and calculating how much he would have won if he had backed the second favorite for every steeplechase of the day.

"Hullo, is that you, John?" he inquired with a yawn, and one hand swam vaguely in his brother's direction while the other kept its fingers spread out upon the second favorites like a stranded starfish.

"Yes, I'm afraid I've got very bad news for you, George."

George's opaque eyes rolled slowly away from the races and fixed his brother's in dull interrogation.

"Bertram and Viola are lost," John proclaimed.

"Oh, that's all right," George sighed with relief. "I thought you were serious for a minute. Crested Grebe at 4 to 1—yes, my theory that you ought to back second favorites works out right for the ninth time in succession. I should have been six pounds up to-day, betting with level sovereigns. Tut-tut-tut!"

John felt that his announcement had not made quite the splash it ought to have made in George's deep and stagnant pool.

"I don't think you heard what I said," he repeated. "Bertram and Viola—*your* children—are definitely lost."

"I don't expect they are really," said George, soothingly. "No, no, not really. The trouble is that not one single bookie will take on this second-favorite system. Ha-ha—they daren't, the cowards! Don't you bother about the kids; no, no, they'll be all right. They're probably hanging on behind a van—they often do that when I'm out with them, but they always turn up in the end. Yes, I should have made twenty-nine pounds this week."

"Look here," said John, severely, "I want you clearly to understand that this is not a simple question of losing them for a few minutes or so. They have been lost now since the Zoo was closed this afternoon, and I am not yet convinced that they are not shut up inside for the night."

"Ah, very likely," said George. "That's just the kind of place they might get to."

"The prospect of your children's passing the night in the Zoo leaves you unaffected?" John demanded in the tone of an examining counsel.

"Oh, they'll have been cleared out by now," said George. "You really mustn't bother yourself about them, old boy."

"You have no qualms, George, at the notion of their wandering for hours upon the outskirts of Regent's Park?"

"Now don't you worry, John. I'm not going to worry, and I don't want you to worry. Why worry? Depend upon it, you'll find them safe and sound in Church Row when you get back. By the way, is your taxi waiting?"

"No, I dismissed it."

"I was afraid it might be piling up the twopences. Though I dare say a pyramid of twopences wouldn't bother you, you old plutocrat. Yes, these second favorites . . ."

"Confound the second favorites," John exclaimed. "I want to discuss your children."

"You wouldn't, if you were their father. They involve me in far too many discussions. You see, you're not used to children. I am."

John's eyes flashed as much as the melancholy illumination permitted; this was the cue for which he had been waiting.

"Just so, my dear George. You are used to children: I am not. And that is why I have come to tell you that the police have been instructed to return them, when found, to *you* and not to me."

George blinked in a puzzled way.

"To me?" he echoed.

"Yes, to you. To their father. Hasn't their luggage arrived? I had it sent back here this morning."

"Ah, yes," George said. "Of course! I was rather late getting up this morning. I've been overworking a bit lately, and Karl did mutter something about luggage. Didn't it come in a taxi?"

John nodded.

"Yes, I remember now, in a prepaid taxi; but as I couldn't remember that I was expecting any luggage, I told Karl to send it back where it came from."

"Do you mean to say that you sent their luggage back after I'd taken the trouble to . . ."

"That's all right, old boy. I was feeling too tired to deal with any problems this morning. The morning is the only opportunity I get for a little peace. It never occurred to me whose luggage it was. It might have been a mistake; in fact I thought it was a mistake. But in any case it's very lucky I did send it back, because they'll want it to-night."

"I'm afraid I can't keep them with me any longer."

Though irony might be lost on George's cold blood, the plain fact might wake him up to the actuality of the situation and so it did.

"Oh, but look here, old boy," he expostulated, "Eleanor won't be home for another five weeks. She'll be at Cardiff next week."

"And Bertram and Viola will be at Earl's Court," said John, firmly.

"But the doctor strongly recommended me to rest. I've been very seedy while you were in America. Stomachic, old boy. Yes, that's the trouble. And then my nerves are not as strong as yours. I've had a lot of worry lately."

"I'm sorry," John insisted. "But I've been called away on urgent business, and I can't leave the children at Church Row. I'm sorry, George, but as soon as they are found, I must hand them over to you."

"I shall send them down to the country," George threatened.

"When they are once more safely in your keeping, you can do what you like with them."

"To your place, I mean."

Normally John would have given a ready assent to such a proposal; but George's attitude had by now aroused his bitter disapproval, and he was determined that Bertram and Viola should be planted upon their father without option.

"Ambles is impossible," he said, decidedly. "Besides, Eleanor is anxious that Viola shouldn't miss her series of Spanish dances. She attends the dancing-class every Tuesday and Friday. No doubt your landlady will lend you Karl to escort her."

"Children are very difficult in a boarding-house," George argued. "They're apt to disturb the other guests. In fact, there was a little trouble only last week over some game—"

"Robinson Crusoe," John put in.

"Ah, they told you?"

"No, no, go on. I'm curious to know exactly what we missed at Church Row."

"Well, they have a habit, which Eleanor most imprudently encourages, of dressing up on Sundays, and as I've had to make it an understood thing that *none* of *my* clothes are to be used, they are apt to borrow other people's. I must admit that generally people have been very kind about lending their clothes; but latterly this dressing up has taken a more ambitious form, and on Sunday week—I think it was—"

"Yes, it would have been a Sunday," John agreed.

"On Sunday week they borrowed Miss Moxley's parrot for Robinson Crusoe. You remember poor Miss Moxley, John?"

"Yes, she lent you five pounds once," said John, sternly.

"Precisely. Oh yes, she did. Yes, yes, that was why I was so vexed about her lending her parrot."

"Why shouldn't she lend her parrot?"

"No reason at all why she shouldn't lend it; but apparently parrots are very excitable birds, and this particular one went mad under the strain of the children's performance, bit Major Downman's finger, and escaped by an upper window. Poor Miss Moxley was extremely upset, and the bird has never been seen since. So you see, as I told you, children are apt to be rather a nuisance to the other guests."

"None of the guests at Halma House keeps a tame calf?"

George looked frightened.

"Oh no, I don't think so. There's certainly never been the least sign of mooing in the garden. Besides, I'm sure Mrs. Easton would object to a calf. She even objects to dogs, as I had to tell James the other day when he came to see me *very* early about signing some deed or other. But what made you ask about a calf? Do you want one?"

"No, I don't want one: I hate cows and calves. Bertram and Viola, however, are likely to want one next week."

"You've been spoiling them, old chap. They'd never dare ask me for a calf. Why, it's preposterous. Yes, you've been spoiling them. Ah, well, you can afford it; that's one thing."

"Yes, I dare say I have been spoiling them, George; but you'll be able to correct that when they're once again in your sole charge."

George looked doubtful.

"I'm very strict with them," he admitted. "I had to be after they lost the parrot and burned Mrs. Easton's rug. It was most annoying."

"Yes, luckily I hadn't got any suitable fur rugs," John chuckled. "So they actually burnt Mrs. Easton's?"

"Yes, and—er—she was so much upset," George went on. "that she's—well—the fact is, they *can't* come back, John, because she's let their room."

"How much do you owe her?" John demanded.

"Oh, very little. I think only from last September. Well, you see, Eleanor was out of an engagement all the summer and had a wretched salary at the Parthenon while she was understudying—these actress-managers are awful harpies—do you know Janet Bond?"

"Yes, I'm writing a tragedy for her now."

"Make her pay, old boy, make her pay. That's my advice. And I know the business side of the profession. But to come back to Mrs. Easton—I was really very angry with her, but you see, I've got my own room here and it's uncommonly difficult to find a private room in a boarding-house, so I thought we'd stay on here till Eleanor's tour was over. She intends to save three pounds a week, and if I have a little luck over the sticks this winter, we shall be quite straight with Mrs. Easton, and then the children will be able to come back in the New Year."

"How much do you owe her?" John demanded for the second time.

"Oh, I think it's about twenty pounds—it may be a little more."

John knew how much the little more always was in George's calculations, and rang the bell, which fetched his brother out of the armchair almost in a bound.

"Old boy, I never ring the bell here," he expostulated. "You see, I never consider that my private room is included in the attendance."

George moved nervously in the direction of the door to make his peace with whoever should answer the unwonted summons; but John firmly interposed himself and explained that he had rung for Mrs. Easton herself.

"Rung for Mrs. Easton?" George repeated in terrified amazement. "But she may come!"

"I hope she will," replied John, becoming more divinely calm every moment in the presence of his brother's agitation.

A tangled head flung itself round the door like one of the minor characters in a Punch and Judy show.

"Jew ring?" it asked, hoarsely.

"Please ask Mrs. Easton to come down to Mr. Touchwood's sitting-room," said John, seriously.

The head sniffed and vanished.

"I wish you could realize, old chap, that in a boarding-house far more tact is required than anywhere else in the world," George muttered in melancholy apprehension. "An embassy isn't in it with a boarding-house. For instance, if I hadn't got the most marvelous tact, I should never have kept this room. However," he added more cheerfully, "I don't suppose for a moment that she'll come—unless of course she thinks that the chimney is on fire. Dash it, John, I wish you could understand some of the difficulties of my life. That's why I took up knitting. My nerves are all to pieces. If I were a rich man I should go for a long sea-voyage."

George fell into a silent brooding upon his misfortunes and ill-health and frustrated ambitions; John examined the stuffed fish upon the walls, which made him think of wet days upon the river and waiting drearily in hotel smoking-rooms for the weather to clear up. Then suddenly Mrs. Easton filled the room. Positive details of this lady's past were lacking, although the gossip of a long line of attenuated spinsters had evolved a rich apocrypha. It was generally accepted, however, that Halma House was founded partly upon settlements made in her favor long ago by a generous stockbroker and partly upon an insurance-policy taken out by her late husband Dr. Easton, almost on the vigil of his death, the only successful operation he ever performed. The mixed derivation of her prosperity was significantly set forth in her personal appearance: she either wore widow's black and powdered her face with pink talcum or she wore bright satins with plumed hats and let her nose shine: so that although she never looked perfectly respectable, on the other hand she never looked really fast.

"Good evening, ma'am," John began at once, assuming an air of Grandisonian courtesy. "My brother is anxious to settle his account."

The clouds rolled away from Mrs. Easton's brow; the old Eve glimmered for a moment in her fierce eye; if he had been alone with her, John would have thought that she was about to wink at him.

"I hear my nephew and niece have been taking liberties with your rug," he went on, but feeling that he might have expressed the last sentence better, he hurriedly blotted the check and with a bow handed it to the proprietress. "No doubt," he added, "you will overlook it this time? I am having a new rug sent to you immediately. What—er—skin do you prefer? Bear? I mean to say, the rug."

He tried to think of any other animal whose personality survived in rugs, but could think of none except a rabbit, and condemning the ambiguity of the English language waited in some embarrassment for Mrs. Easton to reply. She was by this time so surely convinced of John's interest in her that she opened to him with a trilling flutter of complacency like a turkey's tail.

"It happened to be a bearskin," she murmured. "But children *will* be children. We oughtn't to forget that we were all children once, Mr. Touchwood."

"So no doubt," John nervously continued, "you will be glad to see them when they come back to-night. Their room . . ."

"I shall give orders at once, Mr. Touchwood."

He wished that she would not harp upon the Mr. Touchwood; he seemed to detect in it a kind of reproachful formality; but he thanked her and hoped nervously she would now leave him to George.

"Oh dear me, why the girl hasn't lit the fire," Mrs. Easton exclaimed, evidently searching for a gracious action.

George eying his brother with a glance between admiration and disquietude told his landlady that he thought the fire smoked a little.

"I shall have the chimney swept to-morrow," she answered as grandly as if she had conferred a dukedom upon John and an earldom upon George.

Then with a special smile that was directed not so much toward the successful author as toward the gallant male she tucked away the check in her bodice, where it looked as forlorn as a skiff upon the tumultuous billows of the Atlantic, and went off to put on her green satin for dinner.

"We shall all hope to see you at half-past seven," she paused in the doorway to assure John.

"You know, I'll tell you what it is, old chap," said George when they were alone again. "*You* ought to have taken up the commission business and *I* ought to have written plays. But thanks very much for tiding me over this difficult time."

"Yes," said John, a little sharply. "Your wife's current account wasn't flowing quite strongly enough, was it?"

"Wonderful woman, Mrs. Easton," George declared. "She has a keen eye for business."

"And for pleasure too, I should imagine," said John, austerely. "But get on your coat, George," he added, "because we must go out and inquire at all the police stations in turn for news of Bertram and Viola. We can't stop here discussing that woman."

"I tell you the kids will be all right. You mustn't get fussy, John. It's absurd to go out now," George protested. "In fact I daren't. I must think of my health. Dr. Burnham who's staying here for a congress of medical men has given me a lot of advice, and as he has refused to charge me a penny for it, the least I can do is to pay attention to what he says. Besides, what are we going to do?"

"Visit all the police stations in London."

"What shall we gain by doing that? Have you ever been to a police station? They're most uncomfortable places to hang about in before dinner."

"Get on your coat," John repeated.

George sighed.

"Well, if you insist, I suppose you have the right to insist; but in my opinion it's a waste of time. And if the kids are in a police station, I think it would teach them a dashed good lesson to keep them there for awhile. You don't want to encourage them to lose themselves every day. I wish *you* had half a dozen kids."

John, however, was inflexible; the sight of his brother sitting in that aqueous room and pondering the might-have-beens of the race course had kindled in his breast the fire of a reformer; George must be taught that he could not bring children into the world without being prepared to look after them. He must and should be taught.

"Why, you'd take more trouble," he declared, "if you'd lost a fox terrier."

"Of course I should," George agreed. "I should have to."

John reddened with indignation.

"Don't be angry, old chap. I didn't mean that I should think more of a fox terrier. But, don't you see, a dog is dependent upon its collar, whereas Bertram and Viola can explain where they come from. Is it very cold out?"

"You'd better wear your heavy coat."

"That means I shall have to go all the way upstairs," groaned George.

The two brothers walked along the hall, and John longed to prod George with a heavy, spiked pole.

"Going out, Touchwood?" inquired an elderly man of military appearance, who was practicing golf putts from one cabbage rose to another on the Brussels carpet.

"Yes, I'm going out, Major. You know my brother, don't you? You remember Major Downman, John?"

George left his brother with the major and toiled listlessly upstairs.

"I think I once saw a play of yours, Mr. Touchwood."

John smiled as mechanically as the major might have returned a salute.

"*The Fall of Nineveh,* wasn't it?"

The author bowed an affirmative: it was hardly worth while differentiating between Nineveh and Babylon when he was just going out.

"Yes," the major persisted. "Wasn't there a good deal of talk about the scantness of some of the ladies' dresses?"

"There may have been," John said. "We had to save on the dresses what we spent on the hanging gardens."

"Quite," agreed the major, wisely. "But I'm not a puritan myself.

John bowed again to show his appreciation of the admission.

"Oh, no. Rather the reverse, in fact. I play golf every Sunday, and if it's wet I play bridge."

John wished that George would be quick with his coat.

"But I don't go in much for the theater nowadays."

"Don't you?"

"No, though I used to when I was a subaltern. By gad, yes! But it was better, I think, in my young days. No offense to you, Mr. Touchwood."

"Distance does lend enchantment," John assented.

"Quite, quite. I suppose you don't remember a piece at the old Prince of Wales? What was it called? Upon my soul, I've forgotten. It was a capital piece, though. I remember there was a scene in which the uncle—or it may not have been the uncle—no, I'm wrong. It was at the Strand. Or was it? God bless my soul, I don't know which it was. You don't remember the piece? It was either at the Prince of Wales or the Strand, or, by Jove, was it Toole's?"

Was George never coming? Every moment would bring Major Downman nearer to the heart of his reminiscence, and unless he escaped soon he might have to submit to a narrative of the whole plot.

"Do you know what I'm doing?" the Major began again. "I'm confusing two pieces. That's what I'm doing. But I know an uncle arrived suddenly."

"Yes, uncles are often rather fidgety," John agreed. "Ah, excuse me, Major. I see my brother coming downstairs. Good-by, Major, good-by. I should like to have a chat with you one of these days about the mid-Victorian theater."

"Delighted," the Major said, fervently. "I shall think of that play before to-night. Don't you be afraid. Yes, it's on the tip of my tongue. On the very tip. But I'm confusing two theaters. I see where I've gone wrong."

At that moment there was the sound of a taxi's arrival at Halma House; the bell rang; when George opened the door for John and himself to pass out, they were met by Mrs. Worfolk holding Viola and Bertram tightly, one in each hand.

"I told you they'd turn up," George said, and immediately took off his overcoat with a sigh of relief. "Well, you've given us a nice hunt," he went on with an indignant scowl at the children. "Come along to my room and explain where you've been. Good evening, Mrs. Worfolk."

In their father's sitting-room Bertram and Viola stood up to take their trial.

"Yes," opened Mrs. Worfolk, on whom lay the burden of narrating the malefactors' behavior. "Yes, I've brought back the infant prodigals, and a nice job I've had to persuade them to come quiet. In fact, I never had such a job since I took my poor sister's Herbert hollering to the hospital with a penny as he'd nearly choked himself with, all through him sucking it to get at some sweet stuff which was stuck to the edge. He *didn't* choke, though, because I patted him all down the street the same as if I'd been bowling a hoop, and several people looked at me in a very inquisitive way. Not that I ever pay attention to how people looks, except in church. To begin with, the nerve they've got. Well, I mean to say, when any one packs up some luggage and sends it off in a taxi, whoever expects to see it come back again almost at once? It came bouncing back, I do declare, as if it had been India rubber. 'Well,' as I said to Maud, 'It just shows how deep they are, and Mr. Touchwood'll have trouble with them before the day's done. You mark my words.' And, sure enough, just as I'd made up my mind that you wouldn't be in to tea, rat-a-tat-tat on the front door, and up drives my lord and my lady as grand as you like in a taxi. Of course, it give me a bit of a turn, not seeing you, sir, and I was just going to ask if you'd had an accident or something, when my lord starts in to argue with the driver that he'd only got to pay half fare for himself and his sister, the same as his father does when they travel by train. Oh, yes; he was going to pay the man himself. Any one would of thought it was the Juke of Wellington, to hear him arguing with that driver. Well, anyway, in the end, of course I had to pay the difference out of my housekeeping money, which you'll find entered in the book. And then, without so much as a blink, my lord starts in to tell how they'd gone into the Small Rat's House—"

"Cats," interrupted Viola, solemnly.

"Well, rats or cats, what does it matter, you naughty girl? It wasn't of rats or cats you were thinking, but running away from your poor uncle, as you perfeckly well know. Yes, indeed, sir, they went into this small house and dodged you like two pickpockets and then went careering out of the Zoo in the opposite direction. The first taxi that came along they caught hold of and drove back to Church Row. 'But your uncle intended for you to go back to your father, Mr. George, in Earl's Court,' I remarked very severely. 'We know,' they says to me, laughing like two hyenas. 'But we don't want to go back to Earl's Court,' putting in a great deal of rudeness about Earl's Court, which, not wanting to get them into worse trouble than what they will get into as it is, I won't repeat. 'And we won't go back to Earl's Court,' they said, what's more. 'We *won't* go back.' Well, sir, when I've had my orders given me, I know where I am, and the policeman at the corner being a friend of Elsa's, he helped; for, believe me or not, they struggled like two convicks with Maud and I. Well, to cut a long story short, here they are, and just about fit to be put to bed on the instant."

John could not fancy that Eleanor had contrived such an elaborate display of preference for his company, and with every wish to support Mrs. Worfolk by an exhibition of avuncular sternness he could only smile at his nephew and niece. Indeed, it cost him a great effort not to take them back with him at once to Hampstead. He hardened himself, however, and tried to look shocked.

"We wanted to stay with you," said Bertram.

"We wanted to stay with you," echoed Viola.

"We didn't *want* to dodge you in the Small Cats' House. But we had to," said Bertram.

"Yes, we had to," echoed Viola.

"Their luggage 'as come back with them," interrupted Mrs. Worfolk, grimly.

"Oh, of course, they must stay here," John agreed. "Oh, unquestionably! I wasn't thinking of anything else."

He beckoned to Bertram and Viola to follow him out of the room.

"Look here," he whispered to them in the passage, "be good children and stay quietly at home. We shall meet at Christmas." He pressed a sovereign into each hand.

"Good lummy," Bertram gasped. "I wish I'd had this on the fifth of November. I'd have made old Major Downman much more waxy than he was when I tied a squib to his coat."

"Did you, Bertram, did you? You oughtn't to have done that. Though I can understand the temptation. But don't waste this on fireworks."

"Oh no," said Bertram. "I'm going to buy Miss Moxley a parrot, because we lost hers."

"Are you, Bertram?" John exclaimed with some emotion. "That shows a fine spirit, my boy. I'm very pleased with you."

"Yes," said Bertram, "because then with what you gave V we'll buy a monkey at the same time."

"Good heavens," cried John, turning pale. "A monkey?"

"That will be nice, won't it, Uncle John?" Viola asked, tenderly.

But perhaps it would escape from an upper window like the parrot, John thought, before Christmas.

When the children had been sent upstairs and Mrs. Worfolk had gone back to Hampstead, John told his brother that he should not stop to dinner after all.

"Oh, all right," George said. "But I had something to talk over with you. Those confounded children put it clean out of my mind. I had a strange letter from Mama this week. It seems that Hugh has got into rather a nasty fix. She doesn't say what it is, and I don't know why she wrote to me of all people. But she's evidently frightened about Hugh and asks me to approach you on his behalf."

"What on earth has he been doing now?" asked John, gloomily.

"I should think it was probably money," said George. "Well, I told you I'd had a lot of worry lately, and I *have* been very worried about this news of Hugh. Very worried. I'm afraid it may be serious this time. But if I were you, old chap, I should refuse to do anything about it. Why should he come to you to get him out of a scrape? You've done enough for him, in my opinion. You mustn't let people take advantage of your good nature, even if they are relations. I'm sorry my kids have been a bit of a nuisance, but, after all, they are still only kids, and Hugh isn't. He's old enough to know better. Mama says something about the police, but that may only be Hugh's bluff. I shouldn't worry myself if I were you. It's no good for us all to worry."

"I shall go and see Hugh at once," John decided. "You're not keeping anything from me, George? He's not actually under arrest?"

"Oh, no, you won't have to visit any more police stations to-night," George promised. "Hugh is living with his friend, Aubrey Fenton, at 22 Carlington Road, West Kensington."

"I shall go there to-night," John declared.

He had almost reached the front door when George called him back.

"I've been trying to work out a riddle," he said, earnestly. "You know there's a medicine called Easton's Syrup? Well, I thought . . . don't be in such a hurry; you'll muddle me up . . . and I shall spoil it . . ."

"Try it on Major Downman," John advised, crossly, slamming the door of Halma House behind him. "Fatuous, that's what George is, utterly fatuous," he assured himself as he hurried down the steps.

CHAPTER VIII

JOHN decided to walk from Earl's Court to West Kensington. Being still in complete ignorance of what Hugh had done, he had a presentiment that this time it was something really grave, and he was now beginning to believe that George knew how grave it was. Perhaps his decision to go on foot was not altogether wise, for he was tired out by a convulsive day, and he had never experienced before such a fathomless sinking of the stomach on the verge of being mixed up in a disagreeable family complication, which was prolonged by the opportunity that the walk afforded him for dismal meditation. While he hurried with bowed head along one ill-lighted road after another a temptation assailed him to follow George's advice and abandon Hugh, and not merely Hugh, but all the rest of his relations, a temptation that elaborated itself into going back to Church Row, packing up, and escaping to Arizona or British East Africa or Samoa. In the first place, he had already several times vowed never more to have anything to do with his youngest brother; secondly, he was justified in resenting strongly the tortuous road by which he had been approached on his behalf; thirdly, it might benefit Hugh's morals to spend a week or two in fear of the ubiquitous police, instead of a few stay-at-home tradesmen; fourthly, if anything serious did happen to Hugh, it would serve as a warning to the rest of his relations, particularly to George; finally, it was his dinner hour, and if he waited to eat his dinner before tackling Hugh, he should undoubtedly tackle him afterward in much too generous a frame of mind. Yes, it would be wiser to go home at once, have a good dinner, and start for Arizona to-morrow morning. The longer he contemplated it, the less he liked the way he had been beguiled into visiting Hugh. If the—the young bounder—no, really bounder was not too strong a word—if the young bounder was in trouble, why could he not have come forward openly and courageously to the one relation who could help him? Why had he again relied upon his mother's fondness, and why had she, as always, chosen the indirect channel by writing to George rather than to himself? The fact of the matter was that his mother and George and Hugh possessed similar loose conceptions of integrity, and now that it was become a question of facing the music they had instinctively joined hands. Yet George had advised him to have nothing more to do with Hugh, which looked as if his latest game was a bit too strong even for George to relish, for John declined to believe that George possessed enough of the spirit of competitive sponging to bother about trying to poach in Hugh's waters; Hilda or Eleanor might, but George . . . George was frightened, that was it; obviously he knew more than he had told, and he did not want to be exposed . . . it would not astonish him to learn that George was in the business with Hugh and had invented that letter from Mama to invoke his intervention before it was too late to save himself. What could it all be about? Curiosity turned the scale against Arizona, and John pressed forward to West Kensington.

The houses in Carlington Road looked like an overcrowded row of tall, thin men watching a football match on a cold day; each red-faced house had a tree in front of it like an umbrella and trim, white steps like spats; in a fantastic mood the comparison might be prolonged indefinitely, even so far as to say that, however outwardly uncomfortable they might appear, like enthusiastic spectators, they were probably all aglow within. If John had been asked whether he liked an interior of pink lampshades and brass gongs, he would have replied emphatically in the negative; but on this chill November night he found the inside of number 22 rather pleasant after the street. The maid looked doubtful over admitting him, which was not surprising, because an odor of hot soup in the hall and the chink of plates behind a closed door on the right proclaimed that the family was at dinner.

"Will you wait in the drawing-room, sir?" she inquired. "I'll inform Mr. Touchwood that you're here."

John felt a grim satisfaction in thus breaking in upon Hugh's dinner; there was nothing so well calculated to disturb even a tranquil conscience as an unexpected visit at such an hour; but the effect upon guilt would be . . .

"Just say that a gentleman wishes to speak to him for a minute. No name," he replied.

The walk through the dim streets, coupled with speculations upon the various crimes that his brother might have committed, had perhaps invested John's rosy personality with an unusual portentousness, for the maid accepted his instructions fearfully and was so much flustered by them that she forgot to turn up the gas in the drawing-room, of which John was glad; he assured himself that the heavily draped room in the subdued light gave the final touch to the atmosphere of horror which he aimed at creating; and he could not resist opening the door to enjoy the consternation in the dining-room just beyond.

"What is it?"

A murmur from the maid.

"Well, you'd better finish your soup first. I wouldn't let my soup get cold for anybody."

There followed a general buzz from the midst of which Hugh emerged, his long, sallow face seeming longer than usual in his anxiety, his long, thin neck craning forward like an apprehensive bird's, and his bony fingers clutching a napkin with which he dusted his legs nervously.

"Like a flag of truce," John thought, and almost simultaneously felt a sharp twinge of resentment at Hugh's daring to sport a dinner jacket with as much effrontery as if his life had been as white as that expanse of shirt.

"Good Lord," Hugh exclaimed when he recognized his brother. "I thought you were a detective, at least. Come in and have some grub, won't you? Mrs. Fenton will be awfully glad to see you."

John demurred at the invitation. Judging by what he had been told about Mrs. Fenton's attitude toward Hugh, he did not think that Touchwood was a welcome name in 22 Carlington Road.

"Aubrey!" Hugh was shouting. "One of my brothers has just blown in."

John felt sure that the rapid feminine voice he could faintly hear had a distinct note of expostulation in it; but, however earnest the objection, it was at once drowned in the boisterous hospitality of Aubrey, who came beaming into the hall—a well set up young man of about twenty-five with a fresh complexion, glasses, an opal solitaire in his shirt, and a waxy white flower in his buttonhole.

"Do come in," he begged, with an encouraging wave of his napkin. "We've only just begun."

Although John felt that by dining in this house he was making himself an accessory after the still undivulged fact, he was really so hungry by now that he could not bring himself to refuse. He knew that he was displaying weakness, but he compounded with his austere self by arguing that he was more likely to arrive at the truth if he avoided anything in the nature of precipitate action.

Mrs. Fenton did not receive her guest as cordially as her son; in fact, she showed plainly that she resented extremely his having been invited to dinner. She was a well-preserved woman and reminded John of a pink crystallized pear; her frosted transformation glistened like encrusted sugar round the stalk, which was represented by a tubular head ornament on the apex of the carefully tended pyramid; her greeting was sticky.

"My son's friend has spoken of you," Mrs. Fenton was saying, coldly, in reply to John's apologies for intruding upon her like this. He for his part was envying her ability to refer to Hugh without admitting his individual existence, when somebody kicked him under the table, and, looking up, he saw that Hugh was frowning at him in a cautionary manner.

"I've already met your brother, the writer," his hostess continued.

"My brother, James?" asked John in amazement. He could not envisage James in these surroundings.

"No, I have not had the pleasure of meeting him *yet*. I was referring to the dramatist, who has dined with me several times."

"But," John began, when another kick under the table silenced him.

"Pass the salt, will you, George, old boy?" Hugh said loudly.

John's soup was cold, but in the heat of his suppressed indignation he did not notice it. So George had been masquerading in this house as himself; no wonder he had not encouraged the idea of an interview with Hugh. Evidently a dishonest outrage had been perpetrated in his name, and though Hugh might kick him under the table, he should soon obtain his revenge by having Hugh kicked out of the house. John took as much pleasure in his dinner that evening as a sandbag might have taken in being stuffed with sand. He felt full when it was over, but it was a soulless affair; and when Mrs. Fenton, who had done nothing except look down her nose all through the meal, left the table, he turned furiously upon Hugh.

"What does this gross impersonation mean?" he demanded.

Aubrey threw himself figuratively between the brothers, which only seemed to increase John's irritation.

"We wanted to jolly the mater along," he explained. "No harm was intended, but Hughie was keen to prove his respectability; so, as you and he weren't on the most cordial terms, we introduced your brother, George, as yourself. It was a compliment, really, to your public character; but old George rather enjoyed dining here, and I'm bound to say he sold the mater some very decent port. In fact, you're drinking it now."

"And I suppose," said John, angrily, "that between you all you've perpetrated some discreditable fraud, what? I suppose you've been ordering shirts in my name as well as selling port, eh? I'll disown the bill. You understand me? I won't have you masquerading as a gentleman, Hugh, when you can't behave like one. It's obtaining money under false pretenses, and you can write to your mother till you're as blue in the face as the ink in your bottle—it won't help you. I can put up with laziness; I can tolerate stupidity; I can endure dissipation; but I'm damned if I'll stand being introduced as George. Port, indeed! Don't try to argue with me. You must take the consequences. Mr. Fenton, I'm sorry I allowed myself to be inveigled like this into your mother's house. I shall write to her when I get home, and I hope she will take steps to clear that impostor out. No, I won't have a cigar—though I've no doubt I shall presently receive the bill for them, unless I've also been passed off as a tobacconist's agent by George. As for him, I've done with him, too. I shall advertise in the *Times* that neither he nor Hugh has any business to order things in my name. I came here to-night in response to an urgent appeal; I find that I've been made a fool of; I find myself in a most undignified position. No, I will not have another glass of port. I don't know how much George exacted for it, but let me tell you that it isn't even good port: it's turbid and fiery."

John rose from the table and was making for the door, when Hugh took hold of his arm.

"Look here, old chap," he began.

"Don't attempt to soften me with pothouse endearments," said John, fiercely. "I will not be called 'old chap.'"

"All right, old chap, I won't," said Hugh. "But before you go jumping into the street like a lighted cracker, please listen. Nobody has been ordering anything in your name. You're absolutely off the lines there. Why, I exhausted your credit years ago. And I don't see why you should grudge poor old George a few dinners."

"You rascal," John stammered. "You impudent rascal!"

"Don't annoy him, Hughie," Aubrey advised. "I can see his point."

"Oh, you can, sir, can you?" John snapped. "You can understand, can you, how it affects me to be saddled with brothers like these and port like this?"

John was so furious that he could not bring himself to mention George or Hugh by name: they merely represented maddening abstractions of relationship, and he longed for some phrase like "my son's friend" with which he might disown them forever.

"You mustn't blame your brother George, Mr. Touchwood," urged Aubrey. "He's not involved in this latest affair. I'm sorry we told the mater that he was you, but the mater required jollying along, as I explained. She can't appreciate Hugh. He's too modern for her."

"I sympathize with Mrs. Fenton."

"You must forgive a ruse. It's just the kind of ruse I should think a playwright would appreciate. You know. Charley's Aunt and all that."

John clenched his fist: "Don't you mutter to me about a sense of humor," he said to Hugh, wrathfully.

"I wasn't muttering," replied Hugh. "I merely observed that a little sense of humor wouldn't be a bad thing. I'm sorry that George has been dragged like a red herring across the business, because it's a much more serious matter than simply introducing George to Mrs. Fenton as you and selling her some port which personally I think is not at all bad, eh, Aubrey?"

He poured himself out another glass to prove his conviction.

"You may think all this a joke," John retorted. "But I don't. I consider it a gross exhibition of bad taste."

"All right. Granted. Let's leave it at that," sighed Hugh, wearily. "But you don't give a fellow much encouragement to own up when he really is in a tight corner. However, personally I've got past minding. If I'm sentenced to penal servitude, it'll be your fault for not listening. Only don't say I disgraced the family name."

"Hugh's right," Aubrey put in. "We really are in a deuce of a hole."

"Disgrace the family name?" John repeated. "Allow me to tell you that when you hawk George round London as your brother, the playwright, I consider *that* is disgracing the family name."

"So that if I'm arrested for forgery," Hugh asked, "you won't mind?"

"Forgery?" John gasped.

Hugh nodded.

"Yes, we had bad luck in the straight," he murmured, tossing off two more glasses of port. "Cleared every hurdle like a bird and . . . however, it's no good grumbling. We just didn't pull it off."

"No," sighed Aubrey. "We were beaten by a short head."

John sat down unsteadily, filled up half a glass of Burgundy with sherry, and drank it straight off without realizing that George's port was even worse than he had supposed.

"Whose name have you forged?" he brought himself to ask at last.

"Stephen Crutchley's."

"Good heavens!" he groaned. "But this is horrible. And has he found out? Does he know who did it?"

It was characteristic of John that he did not ask for how much his friend's name had been forged.

"He has his suspicions," Hugh admitted. "And he's bound to know pretty soon. In fact, I think the only thing to do is for you to explain matters. After all, in a way it was a joke."

"Yes, a kind of experimental joke," Aubrey agreed.

"But it has proved to me how easy it is to cash a forged check," Hugh continued, hopefully. "And, of course, if you talk to Crutchley he'll be all right. He's not likely to be very severe on the brother of an old friend. That was one of the reasons we experimented on him—that, and also partly because I found an old check book of his. He's awfully careless, you know, is Stephen—very much the high-brow architect and all that, though he doesn't forget to charge. In fact, so many people have had to pay for his name that it serves him right to find himself doing the same for once."

"Does Mrs. Fenton know anything of this?" John asked.

"Why, no," Aubrey answered, quickly. "Well, women don't understand about money, do they? And the mater has less idea of the wicked world than most. My father was always a bit of a recluse, don't you see?"

"Was he?" John said, sarcastically. "I should think his son will be a bit of a recluse, too, before he's done. But forgery! No, it's incredible—incredible!"

"Don't worry, Johnnie," Hugh insisted. "Don't worry. I'm not worrying at all, now that you've come along. Nobody knows anything for certain yet. George doesn't know. Mama doesn't know. Mrs. Fenton doesn't know. And Stevie only guesses."

"How do you know that he guesses?" John demanded.

"Well, that's part of the story, eh, Aubrey?" said Hugh, turning to his accomplice, who nodded sagely.

"Which I suppose one ought to tell in full, eh, Aubrey?" he went on.

"I think it would interest your brother—I mean—quite apart from his being your brother, it would interest him as a playwright," Aubrey agreed.

"Glasses round, then," called Hugh, cheerfully.

"There's a vacant armchair by the fireplace," Aubrey pointed out to John.

"Thanks," said John, stiffly. "I don't suppose that the comfort of an armchair will alleviate my feelings. Begin, sir," he commanded Hugh. "Begin, and get it finished quickly, for heaven's sake, so that I can leave this house and think out my course of action in solitude."

"Do you know what it is, Johnnie?" Hugh said, craning his neck and examining his brother with an air of suddenly aroused curiosity. "You're beginning to dramatize yourself.

I suppose it's inevitable, but I wish you wouldn't. It gives me the same kind of embarrassed feeling that I get when a woman starts reciting. You're not subjective. That's the curse of all romantic writers. You want to get an objective viewpoint. You're not the only person on in this scene. I'm on. Aubrey's on. Mrs. Fenton and Stevie Crutchley are waiting in the wings, as it were. And, for all I know, the police may be waiting there, too, by this time. Get an objective viewpoint, Johnnie. Subjectivity went out with Rousseau."

"Confound your impudence," John spluttered.

"Yes, that's much better than talking about thinking out a course of action in solitude," Hugh approved. "But don't run away with the idea that I'm trying to annoy you. I'm not. I've every reason to encourage the romantic side of you, because finally it will be the romantic side of you that will shudder to behold your youngest brother in the dock. In fact, I'm going the limit on your romance. At the same time I don't like to see you laying it on too thick. I'll give you your fine feelings and all that. I'll grant you your natural mortification, etcetera, etcetera. But try to see my point of view as well as your own. When you're thinking out a course of action in solitude, you'll light a cigar with a good old paunch on it, and you'll put your legs up on the mantelpiece, unless you've grown old-maidish and afraid of scratching the furniture, and you'll pat your passbook, which is probably suffering from fatty degeneration. That's a good phrase, Aubrey?"

"Devilish good," the accomplice allowed. "But, look here, Hugh, steady—the mater gets rather bored if we keep the servants out of the dining-room too long, and I think your brother is anxious to have the story. So fire ahead, there's a good fellow."

Hugh looked hurt at the lack of appreciation which greeted the subtler shades of his discourse, but, observing that John looked still more hurt at being kept waiting, he made haste to begin without further reference to style.

"Well, you see, Johnnie, I've always been unlucky."

John made a gesture of impatience; but Hugh raised a sedative hand.

"I know there's nothing that riles lucky people so much as when unlucky people claim the prerogatives of their bad luck. I'm perfectly willing to admit that I'm lazier than you. But remember that energy is a gift, not an attainment. And I was born tired. The first stunning blow I had was when the old man died. You remember he always regarded me as a bit of an infant prodigy? So I was from his point of view, for he was over sixty when he begot me, and he used to look at me just as some people look at the silver cups they've won for races. But when he died, all the advantages of being the youngest son died with him, and I realized that I was an encumbrance. I'm willing to grant that I was a nuisance, too, but . . . however, it's no use raking up old scores . . . I'm equally willing to admit that you've always treated me very decently and that I've always behaved very rottenly. I'll admit also that my taste in clothes was beyond my powers of gratification; that I liked wine and women—or to put a nicer point upon it—whisky and waitresses. I did. And what of it? You'll observe that I'm not going to try to justify myself. Have another glass of port? No? Right-o; well, I will. I repeat I'm not going to attempt to justify myself, even if I couldn't, which I can, but in vino veritas, which I think you'll admit is Latin. Latin, I said. Precisely. Where was I?"

"Hugh, old boy, buck up," his friend prompted, anxiously.

"Come, sir," John said, trembling visibly with indignation. "Get on with your story while you can. I don't want to waste my time listening to the meanderings of a drunkard."

Hugh's eyes were glazing over like a puddle in frost, but he knitted his brows and regarded his brother with intense concentration.

"Don't try to take any literary advantage of me, Johnnie. You can dig out the longest word in the dictionary, but I've got a longer. Metempsychosis! Hear that? I'm willing to admit that I don't like having to say it, but you find me another man who can say it at all after George's port. Metempsychosis! And it's not a disease. No, no, no, no, don't you run away with the idea that it's a disease. Not at all. It's a religion. And for three years I've been wasting valuable knowledge like that on an architect's office. Do you thing Stevie wants to hear about metempsychosis—that's the third time I've cleared it—of course he doesn't. Stephen Crutchley is a Goth. What am I? I'm a Palladian. There you have it. Am I right, Aubrey?"

"Quite right, old boy, only come to the point."

"That's all right, Aubrey, don't you be afraid. I'm nursing her along by the rails. You can lay a hundred pounds to a box of George's cigars bar one. And that one's me. Where was I? Ah, yes. Well, I'm not going to say a word against Stephen, Johnnie. He's a friend of yours. He's my boss. He's one of England's leading ecclesiastical architects. But that doesn't help me when I find myself in a Somersetshire village seven miles from the nearest station arguing with a deaf parson about the restoration of his moldy church. Does it? Of course not. It doesn't help me when I find myself sleeping in damp sheets and woken up at seven o'clock by a cross between a gardener and a charwoman for early service. Does it? Of course not. Architecture like everything else is a good job when you're waving the flag on top of the tower; but when you're digging the foundations it's rotten. Stevie and I have had our little differences, but when he's sober—I mean when I'm sober—he'll tell you that there's not one of his juniors he thinks better of than me. I'm against Gothic. I consider Gothic the muddle-headed expression of a muddle-headed period. But I've been loyal to Stevie, only. . . ."

Hugh paused solemnly, while his friend regarded him with nervous solicitude.

"Only," Hugh repeated in a loud voice. "Metempsychosis," he murmured, and drinking two more glasses of wine, he sat back in his chair and shook his head in mute despair of human speech.

Aubrey took John aside.

"I'm afraid Hugh's too far gone to explain all the details to-night," he whispered. "But it's really very serious. You see he found an old check book of Mr. Crutchley's, and more from a joke than anything else he tried to see if it was difficult to cash a check. It wasn't. He succeeded. But he's suspected. I helped him indirectly, but of course I don't come into the business except as an accessory. Only, if you take my advice, you'll call on Mr. Crutchley as soon as you can, and I'm sure you'll be able to square things up. You'll know how to manage him; but Hugh has a way of exasperating him."

All the bland, the almost infantine simplicity of Aubrey Fenton's demeanor did not avail to propitiate John's rage; and when the maid came in with a message from his hostess to ask if it would soon be convenient to allow the table to be cleared, he announced that he should not remain another minute in the house.

"But can Hugh count on your support?" Aubrey persisted. He spoke like an election agent who is growing rapidly doubtful of his candidate's prospects.

"He can count on nothing," said John, violently. "He can count on nothing at all. On absolutely nothing at all."

Anybody who had seen Hugh's condition at this moment would have agreed with John. His eyes had already lost even as much life as might have been discerned in the slow freezing of a puddle, and had now assumed the glassy fixity and perfect roundness of two bottle-stoppers.

"He can count on nothing," John asseverated.

"I see," said Aubrey, tactfully. "I'll try and get that across to him. Must you really be going?"

"Immediately."

"You'll trot in and say ta-ta to the mater?"

John had no wish ever again to meet this crystallized lady, but his politeness rose superior to his indignation, and he followed the son of the house into the drawing-room. His last glimpse of Hugh was of a mechanical figure, the only gesture of which was awkwardly to rescue every glass in turn that the maid endeavored to include in her clearance of the table.

"It's scandalous," muttered John. "It's—it's abominable! Mrs. Fenton," he said with a courtly bow for her hospitality, "I regret that your son has encouraged my brother to impose himself upon your good-nature. I shall take steps to insure that he shall do so no longer. I beg your pardon, Mrs. Fenton, I apologize. Good-night."

"I've always spoilt Aubrey," she said. "And he always had a mania for dangerous toys which he never could learn to work properly. Never!" she repeated, passionately.

For an instant the musty sugar in which she was inclosed cracked and allowed John a glimpse of the feminine humanity underneath; but in the same instant the crystallization was more complete than ever, and when John released her hand he nearly took out his handkerchief to wipe away the stickiness.

"I say, what steps *are* you going to take to-morrow?" Aubrey asked.

"Never mind," John growled. Inasmuch as he himself had no more idea of what he intended to do than Aubrey, the reply was a good one.

Where Carlington Road flows into Hammersmith Road John waited for a passing taxi, apostrophizing meanwhile the befogged stars in the London sky.

"I shall not forget to-night. No, I certainly sha'n't. I doubt if any dramatist ever spent such another. A glimpse at all the animals of the globe, a lunch that would have made a jackal vomit, a search for two lost children, an interview with a fatuous brother, a loan of over thirty pounds, a winking landlady, a narrow escape from being bored to death by a Major, a dinner that gave me the sensation of being slowly buried alive, a glass of George's port, and for climax the news that my brother has committed a forgery.

How can I think about Joan of Arc? A few more days like this and I shall never be able to think or write again—however, please God, there'll always be the cinema."

Whirring home to Hampstead John fell asleep, and when he had supplemented that amount of repose in the taxi by eight hours in his own bed, he woke next morning with his mind made up to square matters with Stephen Crutchley, to withdraw Hugh from architecture, to intern him until Christmas at Ambles, and in the New Year to transport him to British Honduras as a mahogany-planter. He had met on board the *Murmania* a mahogany-planter who was visiting England for the first time in thirteen years: the profession must be an enthralling one.

It was only when John reached the offices of Stephen Crutchley in Staple Inn that he discovered it was Sunday, which meant another whole day's idleness and suspense, and he almost fell to wishing that he was in church again with Bertram and Viola. But there was a sweet sadness in this old paved court, where a few sparrows chirped their plaintive monotone from an overarching tree, the branches of which fretted a sky of pearly blue, and where several dreary men were sitting upon the benches regarding their frayed boots. John could not remain unsusceptible to the antique charm of the scene, and finding an unoccupied bench he rested there in the timid sunlight.

"What a place to choose for a forgery," he murmured, reproachfully, and tried to change the direction of his thoughts by remembering that Dr. Johnson had lived here for a time. He had no sooner concentrated upon fancies of that great man than he began to wonder if he was not mistaken in supposing that he had lived here, and he looked round for some one who could inform him. The dreary men with frayed boots were only counting the slow minutes of divine service before the public-houses could open: they knew nothing of the lexicographer. But the subject of forgery was not to be driven away by memories of Dr. Johnson, because his friend, Dr. Dodd, suddenly jumped into the train of thought, and it was impossible not to conjure up that poor and learned gentleman's last journey to Tyburn nor to reflect how the latticed dormers on the Holborn side of the Inn were the same now as then and had actually seen Dr. Dodd go jolting past. John had often thought how incomprehensible it was that scarcely a century ago people should have been hanged for such crimes as forgery; but not it seemed rather more comprehensible. Of course, he should not like to know that his brother was going to be hanged; but for the sake of his future it would be an excellent thing to revive capital punishment for minor crimes. He should like when all this dreadful business was settled to say to his brother, "Oh, by the way, Hugh, I hear they've just passed a bill making forgery a capital offense once more. I think you'll like mahogany-planting."

But would the fear of death act as a deterrent upon such an one as Hugh, who after committing so dishonorable a crime had lacked even the grace to make his confession of it soberly? It was doubtful: Hugh was without shame. From boyhood his career had been undistinguished by a single decent action; but on the contrary it had been steadily marred by vice and folly from the time when he had stolen an unused set of British North Borneo stamps from the locker of his best friend at school to this monstrous climax. Forgery! Great heavens, had he ever yet envisaged Hugh listening abjectly (or worse impudently) to the strictures of a scornful judge? Had he yet imagined the headlines in the press? *Brother of distinguished dramatist sent to penal servitude. Judge's scathing comments.* Mr. Touchwood breaks down in court. *Miss Janet Bond's production indefinitely postponed.* Surely Stephen would not proceed to extreme measures, but for the sake of their lifelong sympathy spare his old friend this humiliation; yet even as John reached this conclusion the chink-chink of the sparrows in the plane-tree sounded upon the air like the chink-chink of the picks on Dartmoor. Hugh a convict! It might well befall thus, if his jaunty demeanor hardened Stephen's heart.

Suppose that Stephen should be seized with one of those moral crises that can only be relieved by making an example of somebody? Would it not be as well to go down at once to his place in the country and try to square matters, unembarrassed by Hugh's brazen impenitence? Or was it already too late? John could not bring himself to believe that his old friend would call in the police without warning him. Stephen had always had a generous disposition, and it might well be that rather than wound John's pride by the revelation of his brother's disgrace he had made up his mind to say nothing and to give Hugh another chance: that would be like Stephen. No, he should not intrude upon his week-end; though how he was going to pass the long Sunday unless he occupied himself with something more cheerful than his own thoughts he did not know. Should he visit James and Beatrice, and take them out to lunch with a Symphony Concert to follow? No, he should never be able to keep the secret of Hugh's crime, and James would inevitably wind up the discussion by making it seem as if it were entirely his own fault. Should he visit George and warn him that the less intercourse he had with Hugh the better, yes, and incidentally observe to George that he resented his impersonation of himself at Mrs. Fenton's? No, George's company would be as intolerable as his port. And the children? No, no, let them dress up with minds still untainted by their Uncle Hugh's shame; let them enact Robinson Crusoe and if they liked burn Halma House to the ground. What was unpremeditated arson compared with deliberate forgery? But if there was a genuine criminal streak in the Touchwoods, how was he ever again to feel secure of his relations' honor? To-morrow he might learn that James had murdered Beatrice because she had slept through the opening chapters of *Lord Ormont and his Aminta*. To-morrow he might learn that George was a defaulting bookmaker, that Hilda had embezzled the whole of Laurence's board, and that Harold was about to be prosecuted by the Society for Prevention of Cruelty to Animals. Why, even his mother might have taken to gin-drinking in the small hours of the morning!

"God forgive me," said John. "I am losing my faith in humanity and my respect for my mother. Yet some imbeciles prate about the romance of crime."

John felt that if he continued to sit here brooding upon his relations he should be in danger of taking some violent step such as joining the Salvation Army: he remembered how an actor in *The Fall of Babylon* had brooded upon his inability to say his lines with just the emphasis he as author had required, until on the night before the opening he had left the theater and become a Salvationist. One of the loafers in the court shuffled up to John and begged him for a match; when John complied he asked for something to use it on, and John was so much distressed by the faint likeness he bore to his eldest brother that he gave him a cigar.

"Without me that is what they would all be by now, every one of them, James, George, and Hugh," he thought. "But if I hadn't been lucky, so might I," he added, reprovingly, to himself, "though at any rate I should have tried to join a workhouse and not wasted my time cadging for matches in Staple Inn."

John was not quite clear about workhouses; he had abandoned realistic writing before he dealt with workhouse life as it really is.

"However, I can't sit here depressing myself all day; besides, this bench is damp. What fools those sparrows are to stay chirping in that tree when they might be hopping about in Hampshire—out of reach of Harold's airgun of course—and what a fool I am! But it's no use for me to go home and work at Joan of Arc. The English archers will only be shooting broad arrows all the time. I'll walk slowly to the Garrick, I think, and have an early lunch."

Perversely enough the club did not seem to contain one sympathetic acquaintance, let alone a friend, that Sunday; and after lunch John was reduced to looking at the portraits of famous dead players, who bored him nearly as much as one or two of the live ones who were lounging in the smoking-room.

"This is getting unendurable," he moaned, and there seemed nothing for it but to sally forth and walk the hollow-sounding city. From Long Acre he turned into St. Martin's Lane, shook off the temptation to bore himself still more hopelessly by a visit to the National Gallery, and reached Cockspur Street. Three or four Sabbath loiterers were staring at a window, and John saw that it was the office of the Cunard Line and that the attraction was a model of the *S.S. Murmania.*

"What a fool I am!" John murmured much more emphatically than in Staple Inn. He was just going to call a taxi to drive him to Chelsea, when he experienced from yesterday a revulsion against taxis. Yesterday had been a nightmare of taxis, between driving to the Zoo and driving to the police station and driving home after that interview with the forger—by this time John had discarded Hugh as a relation—not to mention Mrs. Worfolk in a taxi, and the children in a taxi, and their luggage buzzing backward and forward between Earl's Court and Hampstead in a taxi. No, he should walk to Chealsea: a brisk walk with an objective would do him good. 83 Camera Square. It was indeed rather a tribute to his memory, he flattered himself, that he could remember her address without referring to her card. He should walk along the Embankment; it was only half-past two now.

It was pleasant walking by the river on that fine afternoon, and John felt as he strode along Grosvenor Road, his spirit rising with the eager tide, that after all there was nothing like the sea, nothing!

"As soon as I've finished Joan of Arc, I shall take a sea-voyage. It's all very well for George to talk about sea-voyages, but let him do some work first. Even if I do send him for a sea-voyage, how will he spend his time? I know perfectly well. He'll feel seasick for the first week and play poker for the rest of the passage. No, no, after the Christmas holidays at Ambles he'll be as right as a trivet without a sea-voyage. What is a trivet by the way? Now if I had a secretary, I should make a note of a query like that. As it is, I shall probably never know what a trivet is; but if I had a secretary, I should ask her to look it up in the dictionary when we got home. I dare say I've lost thousands of ideas by not having a secretary at hand. I shall have to advertise—or find out in some way about a secretary. Thank heaven, neither Hilda nor Beatrice nor Eleanor nor Edith knows shorthand. But even if Edith did know shorthand, she'd be eternally occupied with the dactylography—as I suppose *he'd* call it—of Laurence's apostolic successes—there's another note I might make. Of course, it's nothing wonderful as a piece of wit, but I might get an epigram worth keeping, say three times a week, if I had a secretary at my elbow. I don't believe that Stephen will make any difficulties about Hugh. Oh no, I don't think so. I was tired this morning after yesterday. This walk is making me see events in their right proportion. Rosification indeed! James brings out these things as if he were a second Sydney Smith; but in my opinion wit without humor is like marmalade without butter. And even if I do rosify things, well, what is it that Lady Teazle says? *I wish it were spring all the year round and that roses grew under our feet.* And it takes something to rosify such moral anemia as Hugh's. By the way I wonder just exactly whereabouts in Chelsea Camera Square is."

Now if there was one thing that John hated, if there was one thing that dragged even his buoyant spirits into the dust, if there was one thing worse than having a forger for a blood-relation, it was to be compelled to ask his way anywhere in London within the four miles radius. He would not even now admit to himself more than that he did not know the *exact* whereabouts of Camera Square. Although he really had not the remotest idea beyond its location in the extensive borough of Chelsea where Camera Square was, he wasted half-an-hour in dancing a kind of Ladies' Chain with all the side-streets off King's Road and never catching a glimpse of his destination. It was at last borne in upon him that if he wanted to call on Mrs. Hamilton at a respectable hour for afternoon tea he should simply have to ask his way.

Now arose for John the problem of choosing the oracle. He walked on and on, half making up his mind every moment to accost somebody and when he was on the point of doing so perceiving in his expression a latent haughtiness that held him back until it was too late. Had it not been Sunday, he would have entered a shop and bought sufficiently expensive to bribe the shopman from looking astonished at his ignorance. Presently, however, he passed a tobacconist's, and having bought three of the best cigars he had, which were not very good, he asked casually as he was going out the direction of Camera Square. The shopman did not know. He came to another tobacconist's, bought three more cigars, and that shopman did not know either. Gradually with a sharp sense of impending disgrace John realized that he must ask a policeman. He turned aside from the many inviting policemen in the main road, where the contemptuous glances of wayfarers might presume his rusticity, and tried to find a policeman in a secluded by-street. This took another half-an-hour, and when John did accost this ponderous hermit of the force he accosted him in broken English.

"Ees thees ze vay to Cahmehra Squah?" he asked, shrugging his shoulders in what he conceived to be the gesture of a Frenchman who had landed that morning from Calais.

"Eh?"

"Cahmehra Squah?" John repeated.

The policeman put his hand in his pocket, and John thought he was going to whistle for help; but it was really to get out a handkerchief to blow his nose and give him time to guess what John wanted to know.

"Say it again, will yer?" the policeman requested.

John repeated his Gallic rendering of Camera.

"I ain't seen it round here. Where do you say you dropped it?"

"Eet ees a place I vants."

What slow-witted oafs the English were, thought John with a compassionate sigh for the poor foreigners who must be lost in London every day. However, this policeman was so loutish that he felt he could risk an almost perfect pronunciation.

"Oh, Kemmerer Squer," said the policeman with a huge smile of comprehension. "Why, you're looking at it." He pointed along the road.

"Damn," thought John. "I needn't have asked at all. Sank you. Good-evening," he said aloud.

"The same to you and many of them, Napoleon," the policeman nodded.

John hurried away, and soon he was walking along a narrow garden, very unlike a London garden, for it was full of frost-bitten herbaceous flowers and smelt of the country. Not a house on this side of the square resembled its neighbor; but Number 83 was the most charmingly odd of all, two stories high with a little Chinese balcony and jasmine over a queer pointed porch of wrought iron.

"Yes, sir, Mrs. Hamilton is at home," said the maid.

The last bars of something by Schumann or Chopin died away; in the comparative stillness that succeeded John could hear a canary singing, and the tinkle of tea-cups; there was also a smell of muffins and—mimosa, was it? Anyway it was very delicious, he thought, while he made his overcoat as small as possible, so as not to fill the tiny hall entirely.

"Mr. Touchwood was the name?" the maid asked.

"What an intelligent young woman," he thought. "How much more intelligent than that policeman. But women are more intelligent in small things."

John felt very large as he bowed his head to enter the drawing-room.

CHAPTER IX

A SUDDEN apprehension of his bulk (though he was only comparatively massive) overcame John when he stood inside the tiny drawing-room of 83 Camera Square; and it was not until the steam from the tea-pot had materialized into Miss Hamilton, who in a dress of filmy gray floated round him as a cloud swathes a mountain, that he felt at ease.

"Why, how charming of you to keep your word," her well-remembered voice, so soft and deep, was murmuring. "You don't know my mother, do you? Mother, this is Mr. Touchwood, who was so kind to Ida and me on the voyage back from America."

Mrs. Hamilton was one of those mothers that never destroy the prospects of their children by testifying outwardly to what their beauty may one day come: neither in face nor in expression nor in gesture nor in voice did she bear the least resemblance to her daughter. At first John was inclined to compare her to a diminutive clown; but presently he caught sight of some golden mandarins marching across a lacquer cupboard and decided that she resembled a mandarin; after which wherever he looked in the room he seemed to catch sight of her miniature—on the willow-pattern plates, on the mantelpiece in porcelain, and even on the red lacquer bridge that spanned the tea-caddy.

"We've all heard of Mr. Touchwood," she said, picking up a small silver weapon in the shape of a pea-shooter and puffing out her already plump cheeks in a vain effort to extinguish the flame of the spirit-lamp. "And I'm devoted to the drama. Pouf! I think this is a very dull instrument, dear. What would England be without Shakespeare? Pouf! Pouf! One blows and blows and blows and blows till really

—well, it has taught me never to regret that I did not learn the flute when there was a question of my having lessons. Pouf! Pouf!"

John offered his services as extinguisher.

"You have to blow very hard," she warned him; and he being determined at all costs to impress Miss Hamilton blew like a knight-errant at the gate of an enchanted castle. It was almost too vigorous a blast: besides extinguishing the flame, it blew several currants from the cake into Mrs. Hamilton's lap, which John in an access of good-will tried to blow off again less successfully.

"Bravo," the old lady exclaimed, clapping her hands. "I'm glad to see that it can be done. But didn't you write *The Walls of Jericho?* Ah no, I'm thinking of Joshua and his trumpet."

"*The Fall of Babylon,* mother," Miss Hamilton put in with a smile, in the curves of which quivered a hint of scornfulness.

"Then I was not so far out. *The Fall of Babylon* to be sure. Oh, what a fall was there, my countrymen."

She beamed at the author encouragingly, who beamed responsively back at her; presently she began to chuckle to herself, and John, hoping that in his wish to be pleasant to Miss Hamilton's mother he was not appearing to be imitating a hen, chuckled back.

"I'm glad you have a sense of humor," she exclaimed, suddenly assuming an intensely serious expression and throwing up her eyebrows like two skipping-ropes.

John, who felt as if he was playing a game, copied her expression as well as he was able.

"I live on it," she pursued. "And thrive moreover. A small income and an ample sense of humor. Yes, for thus one avoids extravagance oneself, but enjoys it in other people."

"And how is Miss Merritt?" John inquired of Miss Hamilton, when he had bowed his appreciation of the witticism. But before she could reply, her mother rattled on:

"Miss Merritt will not take Doris to America again. Miss Merritt has written a book called *The Aphorisms of Aphrodite.*"

The old lady's remarkable eyebrows were darting about her forehead like forked lightning while she spoke. .

"The Aphorisms of Aphrodite!" she repeated. "A collection of some of the most declassical observations that I have ever encountered." Like a diver's arms the eyebrows drew themselves together for a plunge into unfathomable moral depths.

"My dear mother, lots of people found it very amusing," her daughter protested.

"Miss Merritt," the old lady asserted, "was meant for bookkeeping by double-entry, instead of which she had taken to book-writing by double-entente. The profits may be treble, but the method is base. How did she affect you, Mr. Touchwood?"

"She frightened me," John confessed. "I thought her manner somewhat severe."

"You hear that, Doris? Her ethical exterior frightened him."

"You're both very unfair to Ida. I only wish I had half her talents."

"Wrapped in a napkin," said the old lady, "you have your shorthand."

John's heart leapt.

"Ah, you know shorthand," he could not help ejaculating with manifest pleasure.

"I studied for a time. I think I had vague ideas once of a commercial career," she replied, indifferently.

"The suggestion being," Mrs. Hamilton put in, "that I discouraged her. But how is one to encourage shorthand? If she had learnt the deaf and dumb alphabet I might have put aside half-an-hour every day for conversation. But it is as hard to encourage shorthand as to encourage a person who is talking in his sleep."

John fancied that beneath the indifference of the daughter

and the self-conscious humor of the mother he could detect cross-currents of mutual disapproval; he could have sworn that the daughter was beginning to be perpetually aware of her mother's presence.

"Or is it due to my obsession that relations should never see too much of each other?" he asked himself. "Yet she knows shorthand—an extraordinary coincidence. What a delightful house you have," he said aloud with as much fervor as would excuse the momentary abstraction into which he had been cast.

"My husband was a sinologue," Mrs. Hamilton announced.

"Was he indeed?" said John, trying to focus the word.

"And the study of Chinese is nearly as exclusive as shorthand," the old lady went on. "But we traveled a great deal in China when I was first married and being upon our honeymoon had but slight need of general conversation."

No wonder she looked like a mandarin.

"And to me their furniture was always more expressive than their language. Hence this house." Her black eyebrows soared like a condor to disappear in the clouds of her snowy hair. "But do not let us talk of China," she continued. "Let us rather talk of the drama. Or will you have another muffin?"

"I think I should prefer the muffin," John admitted.

Presently he noticed that Miss Hamilton was looking surreptitiously at her watch and glancing anxiously at the deepening twilight; she evidently had an appointment elsewhere, and he rose to make his farewells.

"For I'm sure you're wanting to go out," he ventured.

"Doris never cares to stay at home for very long," said her mother; and John was aware once again, this time unmistakably, of the cross-currents of mutual discontent.

"I had promised to meet Ida in Sloane Square."

"On the holy mount of Ida," the old lady quoted; John laughed out of politeness, though he was unable to see the point of the allusion; he might have concluded that after all Mrs. Hamilton was really rather stupid, perhaps even vain and tiresome, had she not immediately afterward proposed that he should give Doris time to get ready and have the benefit of her company along King's Road.

"For I assume you are both going in the same direction," she said, evoking with her eyebrows the suggestion of a signpost.

"My dear mother, Mr. Touchwood doesn't want to be bored with escorting me," her daughter was protesting.

John laughed at the idea of being bored; then he fancied that in such a small room his laughter might have sounded hysterical, and he raised the pitch of his voice to give the impression that he always laughed like that. In the end, after a short argument, Miss Hamilton agreed somewhat ungraciously to let John wait for her. When she was gone to get ready, her mother leaned over and tapped John's arm with a fan.

"I'm getting extremely anxious about Doris," she confided; the eyebrows hovering in her forehead like a hawk about to strike gave her listener the impression that she was really going to say something this time.

"Her health?" he began, anxiously.

"Her health is perfect. It is her independence which worries me. Hence this house! Her father's brother is only too willing to do anything for her, but she declines to be a poor relation. Now such an attitude is ridiculous, because she *is* a poor relation. To each overture from her uncle she replies with defiance. At one moment she drowns his remarks in a typewriter; at another she flourishes her shorthand in his face; and this summer she fled to America before he had finished what he was saying. Mr. Touchwood, I rely on you!" she exclaimed, thumping him on the shoulder with the fan.

John felt himself to be a very infirm prop for the old lady's ambition, and wobbled in silence while she heaped upon him her aspirations.

"You are a man of the world. All the world's a stage!

Prompt her, my dear Mr. Touchwood, prompt her. You must have had a great experience in prompting. I rely on you. Her uncle *must* be allowed to help her. For pray appreciate that Doris's independence merely benefits charitable institutions, and in my opinion there is a limit to anonymous benevolence. Perhaps you've heard of the Home for Epileptic Gentlewomen? They can have their fits in peace and comfort entirely because my daughter refuses to accept one penny from her uncle. To a mother, of course, such behavior is unaccountable. And what is so unjust is that she won't allow me to accept a penny either, but has even gone so far as to threaten to live with Miss Merritt if I do. Aphorisms of Aphrodite! I can assure you that there are times when I do not regret that I possess an ample sense of humor. If you were a mother, Mr. Touchwood . . ."

"I *am* an uncle," said John, quickly. He was not going to let Mrs. Hamilton monopolize all the privileges of kinship.

"Then who more able to advise a niece? She will listen to you. Friends, Romans, countrymen, lend me your ears. You must remember that she already admires you as a playwright. Insist that in future she must admire you from the stalls instead of from the pit—as now. At present she is pinched. Do not misunderstand me. I speak in metaphors. She is pinched by straitened circumstances just as the women of China are pinched by their shoes. She declines to wear a hobble-skirt; but decline or not, she hobbles through life. She cannot do otherwise, which is why we live here in Camera Square like two spoonfuls of tea in an old caddy!"

"But you know, personally," John protested while the old lady was fanning back her lost breath, "personally, and I am now speaking as an uncle, personally I must confess that independence charms me."

"Music hath charms," said Mrs. Hamilton. "Who will deny it? And independence with the indefinite article before it also hath charms; but independence with no article at all, independence, the abstract noun, though it may be a public virtue, is a private vice. Vesuvius lends variety to the Bay of Naples; but a tufted mole on a woman's cheek affects the observer with abhorrence, like a woolly caterpillar lurking in the heart of a rose. Let us distinguish between the state and the individual. Do, my dear Mr. Touchwood, let us always preserve a distinction between wild nature and human nature."

John was determined not to give way, and he once more firmly asserted his admiration for independence.

"All the world's a stage," said Mrs. Hamilton. "Yes, and all the men and women merely players; yet life, Mr. Touchwood, is not a play. I have realized that since my husband died. The widow of a sinologue has much to realize. At first I hoped that Doris would marry. But she has never wanted to marry. Men proposed in shoals. But as I always said to them, 'What is the use of proposing to my daughter? She will never marry.'"

For the first time John began to pay a deep and respectful attention to the conversation.

"Really I should have thought," he began; but he stopped himself abruptly, for he felt that it was not quite chivalrous for him to appraise Miss Hamilton's matrimonial chances. "No doubt Miss Hamilton is very critical," he substituted.

"She would criticize anybody," the old lady exclaimed. "From the Creator of us all in general to her own mother in particular she would criticize anybody. Anybody that is, except Miss Merritt. Do not suppose, for instance, that she will not criticize you."

"Oh, I have no hope of escaping," John said.

"But pay no attention and continue to advise her. Really, when I think that on account of her obstinacy a number of epileptic females are enjoying luxurious convulsions while I am compelled to alternate between muffins and scones every day of the week, though I never know which I like better, really I resent our unnecessary poverty. As I say to her, whether we accept her uncle's offer or not, we are always poor relations; so we may as well be comfortably off poor relations."

"Don't you suppose that perhaps her uncle is all the fonder of her because of this independence?" John suggested. "I think I should be."

"But what is the use of that?" Mrs. Hamilton demanded. "Nothing is so bad for people as stunted affection. My husband spent all his patrimony—he was a younger son—everything he had in fact upon his passion for Chinese—well, not quite everything, for he was able to leave me a small income, which I share with Doris. Pray remember that I have never denied her anything that I could afford. Although she has many times plotted with her friend Ida Merritt to earn her own living, I have never once encouraged her in such a step. The idea to me has always been painful. A sense of humor has carried *me* through life; but Doris, alas, is infected with gloom. Whether it is living in London or whether it is reading Nietzsche I don't know, but she is infested with gloom. Therefore when I heard of her meeting you I was glad; I was almost reconciled to the notion of that vulgar descent upon America. Pray do not imagine that I am trying to flatter: you should be used to public approbation by now. John Hamilton is her uncle's name, and he has a delightful estate near the Mull of Kintyre—Glencockic House—some of the rents of which provide carpets for the fits of epileptic gentlewomen and some the children of indigent tradesmen in Ayr with colonial opportunities. Yet his sister-in-law must choose every morning between muffins and scones."

John tried unsuccessfully to change the conversation; he even went so far as to ask the old lady questions about her adventures in China, although it was one of the rules of his conduct never to expose himself unnecessarily to the reminiscences of travelers.

"Yes, yes," she would reply, impatiently, "the bells in the temple gardens are delicious. Ding-dong! ding-dong! But, as I was saying, unless Doris sees her way to be at any rate outwardly gracious . . ." and so it went on until Doris herself, dressed in that misty green Harris tweed of the *Murmania*, came in to say that she was ready.

"My dear child," her mother protested. "The streets of London are empty on Sunday evening, but they are not a Highland moor. What queer notions of dress you do have, to be sure."

"Ida and I are going out to supper with some friends of hers in Norwood, and I want to keep warm in the train."

"One of the aphorisms of Aphrodite, I suppose, to wear a Norfolk-jacket—or should I say a Norwood jacket?—on Sunday evening. You must excuse her, Mr. Touchwood."

John was by this time thoroughly bored by the old lady's witticisms and delighted to leave her to fan herself in the firelight, while he and her daughter walked along toward King's Road.

"No sign of a taxi," said John, whose mind was running on shorthand, though he was much too shy to raise the topic for a second time. "You don't mind going as far as Sloane Square by motor-bus?"

A moment later they were climbing to the outside of a motor-bus; when John pulled the waterproof rug over their knees and felt the wind in his face while they swayed together and apart in the rapid motion, he could easily have fancied that they were once again upon the Atlantic.

"I often think of our crossing," he said in what he hoped was an harmonious mixture of small talk and sentiment.

"So do I."

He tried to turn eagerly round, but was unable to do so on account of having fastened the strap of the rug.

"Well, in Camera Square, wouldn't you?" she murmured.

"You're not happy there?" In order to cover his embarrassment at finding he had asked what she might consider an impertinent question John turned away to fasten the rug more tightly, which nearly kept him from turning around again at all.

"Don't let's talk about me," she begged, dismissing the

subject with a curt little laugh. "How fast they do drive on Sunday."

"Yes, the streets are empty," he agreed. Good heavens, at this rate they would be at Sloane Square in five minutes, and he might just as well never have called on her. What did it matter if the streets were empty? They were not half as empty as this conversation.

"I'm working hard," he began.

"Lucky you!"

"At least when I say I'm working hard," he corrected himself, "I mean that I have been working hard. Just at present I'm rather worried by family matters."

"Poor man, I sympathize with you."

She might sympathize with him; but on this motor-bus her manner was so detached that nobody could have guessed it, John thought, and he had looked at her every time a street-lamp illuminated her expression.

"I often think of our crossing," he repeated. "I'm sure it would be a great pity to let our friendship fade out into nothing. Won't you lunch with me one day?"

"With pleasure."

"Wednesday at Princes? Or no, better say the Carlton Grill."

"Thanks so much."

"It's not easy to talk on a motor-bus, is it?" John suggested.

"No, it's like trying to talk to somebody whom you're seeing off in a train."

"I hope you'll enjoy your evening. You'll remember me to Miss Merritt?"

"Of course."

Sloane Square opened ahead of them; but at any rate, John congratulated himself, he had managed to arrange a lunch for Wednesday and need no longer reproach himself for a complete deadlock.

"I must hurry," she warned him when they had descended to the pavement.

"Wednesday at one o'clock then."

He would have liked to detain her with elaborate instructions about the exact spot on the carpet where she would find him waiting for her on Wednesday; but she had shaken him lightly by the hand and crossed the road before he could decide between the entrance in Regent Street and the entrance in Pall Mall.

"It is bcoming every day more evident, Mrs. Worfolk," John told his housekeeper after supper that evening, " that I must begin to look about for a secretary."

"Yes, sir," she agreed, cheerfully. "There's lots of deserving young fellows would be glad of the job, I'm shaw."

John left it at that, acknowledged Mrs. Worfolk's wishes for his night's repose, poured himself out a whisky and soda, and settled himself down to read a gilded work at fifteen shillings net entitled *Fifteen Famous Forgers*. When he had read three shillings' worth, he decided that the only crime which possessed a literary interest for anybody outside the principals was murder, and went to bed early in order to prepare for the painful interview at Staple Inn next morning.

Stephen Crutchley, the celebrated architect, was some years older than John, old enough in fact to have been severely affected by the esthetic movement in his early twenties; he had a secret belief that was nourished both by his preeminence in Gothic design and by his wife's lilies and languors that he formed a link with the Pre-Raphaelites. His legs were excessively short, but short though they were one of them had managed to remain an inch shorter than the other, which in conjunction with a ponderous body made his gait something between a limp and a shamble. He had a long ragged beard which looked as if he had dropped egg or cigarette-ash on it according to whether the person who was deciding its color thought it was more gray or more yellow. His appearance was usually referred to by paragraph writers as leonine, and he much regretted that his beard was turning gray so soon, when what the same writers called his "tawny mane of hair" was still unwithered. He affected the Bohemian costume of the 'eighties, that is to say the velvet jacket, the flowered silk waistcoat, and the unknotted tie of deep crimson or old gold kept in place by a prelate's ring; he lunched every day at the Arts Club, and since he was making at least £6000 a year, he did not bother to go back to his office in the afternoon. John had met him first soon after his father's death in 1890 somewhere in Northamptonshire where Crutchley was restoring a church—his first big job—and where John was editing temporarily a local paper. In those days John reacting from dog-biscuits was every bit as romantic as he was now; he and the young architect had often talked the sun up and spoken ecstatically of another medieval renaissance, of the nobility of handicrafts and of the glory of the guilds. Later on, when John in the reaction from journalism embarked upon realistic novels, Crutchley was inclined to quarrel with him as a renegade, and even went so far as to send him a volume of Browning's poems with *The Lost Leader* heavily marked in red pencil. Considering that Crutchley was making more money with his gargoyles than himself with his novels John resented the accusation of having deserted his friend for a handful of silver; and as for the ribbon which he was accused of putting in his coat, John thought that the architect was the last person to underline such an accusation, when himself for the advancement of his work had joined every ecclesiastical society from the English Church Union to the Alcuin Club. There was not a ritualistic parson in the land who wanted with or without a faculty to erect a rood or reredos but turned to Crutchley for his design, principally because his watch-chain jingled with religious labels; although to do him justice, even when he was making £6000 a year he continued to attend Choral Eucharists as regularly as ever. When John abandoned realistic novels and made a success as a romantic playwright his friend welcomed him back to the Gothic fold with emotion and enthusiasm.

"You and I, John, are almost the only ones left," the architect had said, feelingly.

"Come, come, Stephen, you mustn't talk as if I was William de Morgan. I'm not yet forty, and you're not yet forty-five," John had replied, slightly nettled by this ascription of them to a bygone period.

Yet with all his absurdities and affectations Stephen was a fine fellow and a fine architect, and when soon after this he had agreed to take Hugh into his office John would have forgiven him if he had chosen to perambulate Chelsea in doublet and hose.

Thinking of Stephen as he had known him for twenty years John had no qualms when on Monday morning he ascended the winding stone steps that led up to his office in the oldest portion of Staple Inn; nor apparently had Hugh, who came in as jauntily as ever and greeted his brother with genial self-possession.

"I thought you'd blow in this morning. I betted Aubrey half-a-dollar that you'd blow in. He tells me you went off in rather a bad temper on Saturday night. But you were quite right, Johnnie; that port of George's is not good. You were quite right. I shall always respect your verdict on wine in future."

"This is not the moment to talk about wine," said John, angrily.

"I'm afraid that owing to George and his confounded elderberry ink I didn't put my case quite as clearly as I ought to have done," Hugh went on, serenely. "But don't worry. As soon as you've settled with Stevie, I shall tell you all about it. I think you'll be thrilled. It's a pity you've moved into Wardour Street, or you might have made a good story out of it."

One of the clerks came back with an invitation for John to follow him into Mr. Crutchley's own room, and he was glad to escape from his brother's airy impenitence.

"Wonderful how Stevie acts up to the part, isn't it?" commented Hugh, when he saw John looking round him at the timbered rooms with their ancient furniture and medieval blazonries through which they were passing.

"I prefer to see Crutchley alone," said John, coldly. "No doubt he will send for you when your presence is required."

Hugh nodded amiably and went over to his desk in one of the latticed oriel windows, the noise of the Holborn traffic surging in through which reminded the listener that these perfectly medieval rooms were in the heart of modern London.

"I should rather like to live in chambers here myself," thought John. "I believe they would give me the very atmosphere I require for Joan of Arc; and I should be close to the theaters."

This project appealed to him more than ever when he entered the architect's inmost sanctum, which containing nothing that did not belong to the best period of whatever it was, wrought iron or carved wood or embroidered stuff, impressed John's eye for a scenic effect. Nor was there too much of it: the room was austere, not even so full as a Carpaccio interior. Modernity here wore a figleaf; wax candles were burned instead of gas or electric light; and even the telephone was enshrined in a Florentine casket. When the oaken door covered with huge nails and floriated hinges was closed, John sat down upon what is called a Glastonbury chair and gazed at his friend who was seated upon a gilt throne under a canopy of faded azure that was embroidered with golden unicorns, wyverns, and other fabulous monsters in a pasture of silver fleurs-de-lys.

"Have a cigar," said the Master, as he liked to be called, pushing across the refectory table that had come out of an old Flemish monastery a primitive box painted with scenes of saintly temptations, but lined with cedar wood and packed full of fat Corona Coronas.

"It seems hardly appropriate to smoke cigars in this room," John observed. "Even a churchwarden-pipe would be an anachronism here."

"Yes, yes," Stephen assented, tossing back his hair with the authentic Vikingly gesture. "But cigars are the chief consolation we have for being compelled to exist in this modern world. I haven't seen you, John, since you returned from America. How's work?"

"*Lucretia* went splendidly in New York. And I'm in the middle of *Joan of Arc* now."

"I'm glad, I'm glad," the architect growled as fiercely as one of the great Victorians. "But for Heaven's sake get the coats right. Theatrical heraldry is shocking. And get the ecclesiastical details right. Theatrical ritual is worse. But I'm glad you're giving 'em Joan of Arc. Keep it up, keep it up. The modern drama wants disinfecting."

"I suppose you wouldn't care to advise me about the costumes and processions and all that," John suggested, offering his friend a pinch of his romantic Sanitas.

"Yes, I will. Of course, I will. But I must have a free hand. An absolutely free hand, John. I won't have any confounded play-actor trying to tell me that it doesn't matter if a bishop in the fifteenth century does wear a sixteenth century miter, because it's more effective from the gallery. Eh? I know them. You know them. A free hand or you can burn Joan on an asbestos gasfire, and I won't help you."

"Your help would be so much appreciated," John assured him, "that I can promise you an absolutely short hand."

The architect stared at the dramatist.

"What did I say? I mean free hand—extraordinary slip," John laughed a little awkwardly. "Yes, your name, Stephen, is just what we shall require to persuade the skeptical that it *is* worth while making another attempt with Joan of Arc. I can promise you some fine opportunities. I've got a particularly effective tableau to show the miserable condition of France before the play begins. The curtain will rise upon the rearguard of an army marching out of a city, heavy snow will fall, and above the silence you will hear the howling of the wolves following in the track of the troops. This is an historical fact. I may even introduce several wolves upon the stage. But I rather doubt if trained wolves are procurable, although at a pinch we could use large dogs —but don't let me run away with my own work like this.

I did not come here this morning to talk about Joan of Arc, but about my brother Hugh."

John rose from his chair and walked nervously up and down the room, while Stephen Crutchley managed to exaggerate a slight roughness at the back of his throat into a violent fit of coughing.

"I see you feel it as much as I do," John murmured, while the architect continued to express his overwrought feelings in bronchial spasms.

"I would have spared you this," the architect managed to gasp at last.

"I'm sure you would," said John, warmly. "But since in what I hope was a genuine impulse of contrition not entirely dictated by motives of self-interest Hugh has confessed his crime to me, I am come here this morning confident that you will allow me to—in other words—what was the exact sum? I shall of course remove him from your tutelage this morning."

John's eloquence was not spontaneous; he had rehearsed this speech on the way from Hampstead that morning, and he was agreeably surprised to find that he had been able owing to his friend's coughing-fit to reproduce nearly all of it. He had so often been robbed of a prepared oration by some unexpected turn of the conversation that he felt now much happier than he ought under the weight of a family scandal.

"Your generosity . . ." he continued.

"No, no," interrupted the architect, "it is you who are generous."

The two romantics gazed at one another with an expression of nobility that required no words to enhance it.

"We can afford to be generous," said John, which was perfectly true, though the reference was to worth of character rather than to worth of capital.

"Eighty-one pounds six and eightpence," Crutchley murmured. "But I blame myself. I should not have left an old check book lying about. It was careless—it was, I do not hesitate to say so, criminally careless. But you know my attitude towards money. I am radically incapable of dealing with money."

"Of course you are," John assented with conviction. "So am I. Money with me is merely a means to an end."

"Exactly what it is with me," the architect declared. "Money in itself conveys nothing to me. What I always say to my clients is that if they want the best work they must pay for it. It's the work that counts, not the money."

"Precisely my own attitude," John agreed. "What people will not understand is that an artist charges a high price when he does not want to do the work. If people insist on his doing it, they must expect to pay."

"And of course," the architect added, "we owe it to our fellows to sustain the dignity of our professions. Art in England has already been too much cheapened."

"You've kept all your old enthusiasms," John told his friend. "It's splendid to find a man who is not spoilt by success. Eighty-one pounds you said? I've brought my check book."

"Eighty-one pounds six and eightpence, yes. It was like you, John, to come forward in this way. But I wish you could have been spared. You understand, don't you, that I intended to say nothing about it and to blame myself in silence for my carelessness? On the other hand, I could not treat your brother with my former confidence. This terrible business disturbed our whole relationship."

"I am not going to enlarge on my feelings," said John as he handed the architect the stolen sum. "But you will understand them. I believe the shock has aged me. I seem to have lost some of my self-reliance. Only this morning I was thinking to myself that I must really get a private secretary."

"You certainly should have one," the architect agreed.

"Yes, I must. The only thing is that since this dreadful escapade of Hugh's I feel that an unbusinesslike creature such as I am ought not to put himself in the hands of a young man. What is your experience of women? From a business point of view, I mean."

"I think that a woman would do your work much better than a man," said the architect, decidedly.

"So do I. I'm very glad to have your advice though."

After this John felt no more reluctant at parting with eighty-one pounds six and eightpence than he would have felt in paying a specialist two guineas for advising him to take a long rest when he wanted to take a long rest. His friend's aloofness from money had raised to a higher level what might easily have been a most unpleasant transaction: not even one of his heroes could have extricated himself from an involved situation more poetically and more sympathetically. It now only remained to dispose of the villain.

"Shall we have Hugh in?" John asked.

"I wish I could keep him with me," the architect sighed. "But I don't think I have a right to consult my personal feelings. We must consider his behavior in itself."

"In any case," said John, quickly, "I have made arrangements about his future; he is going to be a mahogany-planter in British Honduras."

"Of course I don't use mahogany much in my work, but if ever .. . ." the architect was beginning, when John waved aside his kindly intentions.

"The impulse is generous, Stephen, but I should prefer that so far as you are concerned Hugh should always be as if he had never been. In fact, I'm bound to say frankly that I'm glad you do not use mahogany in your work. I'm glad that I've chosen a career for Hugh which will cut him completely off from what to me will always be the painful associations of architecture."

While they were waiting for the sinner to come in, John tried to remember the name of the mahogany-planter whom he had met in the *Murmania;* but he could get no nearer to it than a vague notion that it might have been Raikes, and he decided to leave out for the present any allusion to British Honduras.

Hugh entered his chief's room without a blush: he could not have bowed his head, however sincere his repentance, because his collars would not permit the least abasement; though at least, his brother thought, he might have had the decency not to sit down until he was invited, and when he did sit down not to pull up his trousers in that aggressive way and expose those very defiant socks.

Stephen Crutchley rose from his throne and shambled over to the fireplace, leaning against the stone hood of which he took up an attitude that would have abashed anybody but Hugh.

"Touchwood," he began, "no doubt you have already guessed why I have asked you to speak to me."

Hugh nodded encouragingly.

"I do not wish to enlarge upon the circumstances of your behavior, because your brother, my old friend, has come forward to shield you from the consequences. Nor do I propose to animadvert upon the forgery itself. However lightly you embarked upon it, I don't doubt that by now you have sufficiently realized its gravity. What tempted you to commit this crime I do not hope to guess; but I fear that such a device for obtaining money must have been inspired by debts, whether for cards or for horse-racing, or perhaps even for women I do not pretend to know."

"Add waistcoats and whisky and you've got the motive," Hugh chirped. "I say, I think your trousers are scorching," he added on a note of anxious consideration.

"I do not propose to enlarge on any of these topics," said the architect, moving away from the fire and sniffing irritably the faint odor of overheated homespun. "What I do wish to enlarge upon is your brother's generosity in coming forward like this. Naturally I who have known him for twenty years expected nothing else, because he is a man of ideals, a writer of whom we are all proud, from whom we all expect great things and—however I am not going to enlarge upon his obvious qualities. What I do wish to say is that he and I have decided that after this business you must leave me. I don't suppose that you expected to remain; nor, even if you could, do I suppose that you would wish to remain. Perhaps you are not enough in sympathy with my aspirations for the future of English architecture to regret our parting; but I hope that this lesson you have had will be the means of bringing you to an appreciation of what your brother has done for you and that in British Honduras you will behave in such a way as to justify his generosity. Touchwood, good-by! I did not expect when you came to me three years ago that our last farewell would be fraught— would be so unpleasant."

John was probably much more profoundly moved by Crutchley's sermon than Hugh; indeed he was so much moved that he rose to supplement it with one of his own in which he said the same things about the architect that the architect had said about him, after which the two romantics looked at each other admiringly, while they waited for Hugh to reply.

"I suppose I ought to say I'm very sorry and all that," Hugh managed to mutter at last. "Good-by, Mr. Crutchley, and jolly good luck. I'll just toddle through the office and say good-by to all the boys, John, and then I dare say you'll be ready for lunch."

He swaggered out of the room; when the two friends were left together they turned aside with mutual sympathy from the topic of Hugh to discuss Joan of Arc and a new transept that Crutchley was designing. When the culprit put his head round the door and called out to John that he was ready, the two old friends shook hands affectionately and parted with an increased regard for each other and themselves.

"Look here, what's all this about British Honduras?" Hugh asked indignantly when he and his brother had passed under the arched entry of Staple Inn and were walking along Holborn. "I see you're bent on gratifying your appetite for romance even in the choice of a colony. British Honduras! British humbug!"

"I prefer not do discuss anything except your immediate future," said John.

"It's such an extraordinary place to hit on," Hugh grunted in a tone of irritated perplexity.

"The immediate future," John repeated, sharply. "To-night you will go down to Hampshire and if you wish for any more help from me, you will remain there in the strictest seclusion until I have time to settle your ultimate future."

"Oh, I sha'n't at all mind a few weeks in Hampshire. What I'm grumbling at is British Honduras. I shall rather enjoy Hampshire in fact. Who's there at present?"

John told him, and Hugh made a grimace.

"I shall have to jolly them up a bit. However it's a good job that Laurence has lost his faith. I shall be spared his Chloral Eucharists, anyway. Where are we going to lunch?"

"Hugh!" exclaimed his outraged brother stopping short in the middle of the crowded pavement. "Have you no sense of shame at all? Are you utterly callous?"

"Look here, Johnnie, don't start in again on that. I know you had to take that line with Stevie, and you'll do me the justice of admitting that I backed you up; but when we're alone, do chuck all that. I'm very grateful to you for forking out—by the way, I hope you noticed the nice little touch in the sum? Eighty-one pounds six and eightpence. The six and eightpence was for my lawyer."

"Do you adopt this sickeningly cynical attitude," John besought. "Forgery is not a joke."

"Well, this forgery was," Hugh contradicted. "You see, I got hold of Stevie's old check book and found he had quite a decent little account in Croydon. So I faked his signature—you know how to do that?"

"I don't want to know."

"You copy the signature upside down. Yes, that's the way. Then old Aubrey disguised himself with blue glasses and presented the check at the bank, just allowing himself five minutes to catch the train back to town. I was waiting at the station in no end of a funk. But it was all right. The clerk blinked for a minute, but old Aubrey blinked back at him as cool as you please, and he shoveled out the gold. Aubrey came jingling on to the platform like a milk-can just as the train was starting."

"I wish to hear no more."

"And then I found that Stevie was cocking his eye at this check book and scratching his head and looking at me and—well, he suspected me. The fact of the matter is that Stevie's as keen on his cash as anybody. I suppose this is a side account for the benefit of some little lady or other."

"Silence," John commanded.

"And then I lost my nerve, so that when Stevie started questioning me about his check book I must have looked embarrassed."

"I'm surprised to hear that," John put in, bitterly.

"Yes, I dare say I could have bluffed it out, because I'd taken the precaution to cash the check through Aubrey whom Stevie knows nothing about. But I don't know. I lost my nerve. Well, thanks very much for stumping up, Johnnie; I'm only glad you got so much pleasure out of it yourself."

"What do you mean—pleasure?"

"Shut up—don't pretend you didn't enjoy yourself, you old Pharisee. Look here where *are* we going to lunch? I'm carrying a bag full of instruments, you know."

John told Hugh that he declined to lunch with him in his present mood of bravado, and at the corner of Chancery Lane they parted.

"Mind," John warned him, "if you wish for any help from me you are to remain for the present at Ambles."

"My dear chap, I don't want to remain anywhere else; but I wish you could appreciate the way in which the dark and bloody deed was done, as one of your characters would say. You haven't uttered a word of congratulation. After all, it took some pluck, you know, and the signature was an absolutely perfect fake—perfect. The only thing that failed was my nerve afterwards. But I suppose I should be steadier another time."

John hurried away in a rage and walked up the Strand muttering:

"What *was* the name of that mahogany-planter? *Was* it Raikes or wasn't it? I must find his card."

It was not until he had posted the following letter that he recovered some of his wonted serenity.

>36 Church Row,
>>Hampstead, N.W.,
>>>*Nov. 28, 1910.*

My dear Miss Hamilton,—In case I am too shy to broach the subject at lunch on Wednesday I am writing to ask you beforehand if in your wildest dreams you have ever dreamt that you could be a private secretary. I have for a long time been wanting a secretary, and as you often spoke with interest of my work I am in hopes that the idea will not be distasteful to you. I should not have dared to ask you if you had not mentioned shorthand yesterday and if Mrs. Hamilton had not said something about your typewriting. This seems to indicate that at any rate you have considered the question of secretarial work. The fact of the matter is that in addition to my plays I am much worried by family affairs, so much so that I am kept from my own work and really require not merely mechanical assistance, but also advice on many subjects on which a woman is competent to advise.

I gathered also from your mother's conversation that you yourself were sometimes harassed by family problems and I thought that perhaps you might welcome an excuse to get away from them for awhile.

My notions of the salary that one ought to offer a private secretary are extremely vague. Possibly our friend Miss Merritt would negotiate the business side, which to me as an author is always very unpleasant. I should of course accept whatever Miss Merritt proposed without hesitation. My idea was that you would work with me every morning at Hampstead. I have never yet attempted dictation myself, but I feel that I could do it after a little practice. Then I thought you could lunch with me, and that after lunch we could work on the materials—that is to say that I should give you a list of things I wanted to know, which you would search for either in my own library or at the British Museum. Does this strike you as too heavy a task? Perhaps Miss Merritt will advise you on this matter too.

If Mrs. Hamilton is opposed to the idea, possibly I might call upon her and explain personally my point of view. In the meantime I am looking forward to our lunch and hoping very much that you will set my mind at rest by accepting the post. I think I told you I was working on a play with Joan of Arc as the central figure. It is interesting, because I am determined not to fall into the temptation of introducing a factitious love-interest, which in my opinion spoilt Schiller's version.

Yours sincerely,
JOHN TOUCHWOOD.

CHAPTER X

WHEN after lunch on Wednesday afternoon John relinquished Miss Hamilton to the company of her friend Miss Merritt at Charing Cross Station, he was relinquishing a secretary from whom he had received an assurance that the very next morning she would be at his elbow, if he might so express himself. In his rosiest moments he had never expected so swift a fulfilment of his plan, and he felt duly grateful to Miss Merritt, to whose powers of persuasion he ascribed the acceptance in spite of Mrs. Hamilton's usually only too effective method of counteracting any kind of independent action on her daughter's part. On the promenade deck of the *Murmania* Miss Merritt had impressed John with her resolute character; now she seemed to him positively Napoleonic, and he was more in awe of her than ever, so much so indeed that he completely failed to convey his sense of obligation to her good offices and could only beam at her like a benevolent character in a Dickens novel. Finally he did manage to stammer out his desire that she would charge herself with the financial side of the agreement and was lost in silent wonder when she had no hesitation in suggesting terms based on the fact that Miss Hamilton had no previous experience as a secretary.

"Later on, if you're satisfied with her," she said, "you must increase her salary; but I will be no party to overpayment simply because she is personally sympathetic to you."

How well that was put, John thought. Personally sympathetic! How accurately it described his attitude toward Miss Hamilton. He took leave of the young women and walked up Villiers Street, cheered by the pleasant conviction that the flood of domestic worries which had threatened to destroy his peace of mind and overwhelm his productiveness was at last definitely stayed.

"She's exactly what I require," he kept saying to himself, exultantly. "And I think I may claim without unduly flattering myself that the post I have offered her is exactly what she requires. From what that very nice girl Miss Merritt said, it is evidently a question of asserting herself now or never. With what a charming lack of self-consciousness she agreed to the salary and even suggested the hours of work herself. Oh, she's undoubtedly practical—very practical; but at the same time she has not got that almost painfully practical exterior of Miss Merritt, who must have broken in a large number of difficult employers to acquire that tight set of her mouth. Probably I shall be easy to manage, so working for me won't spoil her unbusinesslike appearance. To-morrow we are to discuss the choice of a typewriter; and by the way, I must arrange which room she is to use for typing. The noise of a machine at high speed would be as prejudicial to composition as Viola's stepdancing. Yes, I must arrange with Mrs. Worfolk about a room."

John's faith in his good luck was confirmed by the amazing discovery that Mrs. Worfolk had known his intended secretary as a child.

"Her old nurse in fact!" he exclaimed joyfully, for such a melodramatic coincidence did not offend John's romantic palate.

"No, sir, not her nurse. I never was not what you might call a nurse proper. Well, I mean to say, though I was always fond of children I seemed to take more somehow to the house itself, and so I never got beyond being a nursemaid. After that I gave myself up to rising as high as a housemaid *can* rise until I married Mr. Worfolk. Perhaps you may remember me once passing the remark that I'd been in service with a racing family? Well, after I left them I took a situation as upper housemaid with a very nice family in the county of Unts, and who came up to London for the season to Grosvenor Gardens. Then I met Mr. Worfolk who was a carpenter and he made packing-cases for Mr. Hamilton who was your young lady's pa. Oh, I remember him well. There was a slight argument between Mr. Worfolk and I—well, not argument, because ours was a very happy marriage, but a slight conversation as to whether he was to make cases for Chi-ner or Chi-nese knick-knacks, and Mr. Worfolk was wrong."

"But were you in service with Mr. Hamilton? Did he live in Huntingdonshire?"

"No, no, sir. You're getting very confused, if you'll pardon the obsivation. Very confused, you're getting. This Mr. Hamilton was a customer of Mr. Worfolk and through him coming to superintend his Chi-nese valuables being packed I got to know his little girl—your secretary as is to be. Oh, I remember her perfickly. Why, I mended a hole in her stocking once. Right above the garter it was, and she was so fond of our Tom. Oh, but he *was* a beautiful mouser. I've heard many people say they never saw a finer cat nowhere."

"You have a splendid memory, Mrs. Worfolk."

"Yes, sir. I have got a good memory. Why, when I was a tiny tot I can remember my poor grandpa being took sudden with the colic and rolling about on the kitchen hearthrug, groaning, as you might say, in a agony of pain. Well, he died the same year as the Juke of Wellington, but though I was taken to the Juke's funeral by my poor mother, I've forgotten that. Well, one can't remember everything, and that's a fact; one little thing will stick and another little thing won't. Well, I mean to say, it's a good job anybody can't remember everything. I'm shaw there's enough trouble in the world as it is."

Mrs. Worfolk startled the new secretary when she presented herself at 36 Church Row next day by embracing her affectionately in the hall before she had explained the reason for such a demonstration. It soon transpired, however, that Miss Hamilton's memory was as good as Mrs. Worfolk's and that she had not forgotten those jolly visits to the carpenter long ago, nor even the big yellow Tomcat. As for the master of the house, he raised his housekeeper's salary to show what importance he attached to a good memory.

For a day or two John felt shy of assigning much work to his secretary; but she soon protested that, if she was only going to type thirty to fifty lines of blank verse every other morning, she should resign her post on the ground that it was an undignified sinecure.

"What about dictating your letters? You made such a point of my knowing shorthand."

"Yes, I did, didn't I?" John agreed.

Dictation made him very nervous at first; but with a little practice he began to enjoy it, and ultimately it became something in the nature of a vice. He dictated immensely long letters to friends whose very existence he had forgotten for years, the result of which abrupt revivals of intercourse was a shower of appeals to lend money to these companions of his youth. Yet this result did not discourage him from the habit of dictating for dictation's sake, and every night before he turned over to go to sleep he used to poke about in the rubbish-heap of the past for more forgotten friends. As a set off to incommoding himself with a host of unnecessary correspondents he became meticulously businesslike, and after having neglected Miss Janet Bond for several weeks he began to write to her daily about the progress of the play, which notwithstanding his passion for dictation really was progressing at last. Indeed he worked up the manageress of the Parthenon to such a pitch of excitement that one morning she appeared suddenly at Church Row and made a dramatic entrance into the library when John, who had for the moment exhausted his list of friends, was dictating a letter to *The Times* about the condition of some trees on Hampstead Heath.

"I've broken in upon your inspiration," boomed Miss Bond in tones that she usually reserved for her most intensely tragic moments.

In vain did the author asseverate that he was delighted to

see her; she rushed away without another word; but that evening she wrote him an ecstatic letter from her dressing-room about what it had meant to her and what it always would mean to her to think of his working like that for her."

"But we mustn't deride Janet Bond," said the author to his secretary, who was looking contemptuously at the actress's heavy caligraphy. "We must remember that she will create Joan of Arc."

"Yes, it's a pity, isn't it?" Miss Hamilton commented, dryly.

"Oh, but won't you allow that she's a great actress?"

"I will indeed," she murmured with an emphatic nod.

Carried along upon his flood of correspondence John nevertheless managed to steer clear of his relations, and in his present frame of mind he was inclined to attribute his successful course like everything else that was prospering just now to the advent of Miss Hamilton. However, it was too much to expect that with his newly discovered talent he should resist dictating at any rate one epistolary sermon to his youngest brother, of whose arrival at Ambles he had been sharply notified by Hilda. This weighty address took up nearly a whole morning, and when it was finished John was disconcerted by Miss Hamilton's saying:

"You don't really want me to type all this out?"

"Why not?"

"Oh, I don't know. But it seems to me that whatever he's done this won't make him repent. You don't mind my criticizing you?"

"I asked you to," he reminded her.

"Well, it seems to me a little false—a little, if I may say so, complacently wrathful. It's the sort of thing I seem to remember reading and laughing at in old-fashioned books. Of course, I'll type it out at once if you insist, but it's already after twelve o'clock, and we have to go over the material for the third act. I can't somehow fit in what you've just been dictating with what you were telling me yesterday about the scene between Gilles de Rais and Joan. I'm so afraid that you'll make Joan preach, and of course she mustn't preach, must she?"

"All right," conceded John, trying not to appear mortified. "If you think it isn't worth sending, I won't send it."

He fancied that she would be moved by his sensitiveness to her judgment; but, without a tremor, she tore the pages out of her shorthand book and threw them into the wastepaper basket. John stared at the ruthless young woman in dismay.

"Didn't you mean me to take you at your word?" she asked, severely.

He was not altogether sure that he had, but he lacked the courage to tell her so and checked an impulse to rescue his stillborn sermon from the grave.

"Though I don't quite like the idea of leaving my brother at Ambles with nothing to occupy his energies," John went on, meditatively, "I'm doubtful of the prudence of exposing him to the temptations of idleness."

"If you want to give him something to do, why don't you intrust him with getting ready the house for your Christmas party? You are always worrying about its emptiness."

"But isn't that putting in his way temptations of a more positive kind?" he suggested.

"Not if you set a limit to your expenditure. Can you trust his taste? He ought to be an adept at furnishings."

"Oh, I think he'd do the actual furnishing very well. But won't it seem as if I am overlooking his abominable behavior too easily?"

With a great effort John kept his eyes averted from the waste-paper basket.

"You must either do that or refuse to have anything more to do with him," Miss Hamilton declared. "You can't expect him to be the mirror of your moral superiority for the rest of his life."

"You seem to take quite an interest in him," said John, a little resentfully.

Miss Hamilton shrugged her shoulders.

"All right," he added, hurriedly. "I'll authorize him to prepare the house for Christmas. He must fight his own battles with my sister, Hilda. At any rate, it will annoy her."

Miss Hamilton shook her head in mock reproof.

"Act Three. Scene One," the dramatist announced in the voice of a mystic who has at last shaken himself free from earthly clogs and is about to achieve levitation. It was consoling to perceive that his secretary's expression changed in accord with his own, and John decided that she really was a most attractive young woman and not so unsympathetic as he had been upon the verge of thinking. Moreover, she was right. The important thing at present, the only thing, in fact, was the progress of the play, and it was for this very purpose that he had secured her collaboration—well, perhaps collaboration was too strong a word—but, indeed, so completely had she identified herself with his work that really he could almost call it collaboration. He ought not to tax his invention at this critical point with such a minor problem as the preparation of Ambles for a family reunion. Relations must go to the deuce in their own way, at any rate until the rough draft of the third act was finished, which, under present favorable conditions, might easily happen before Christmas. His secretary was always careful not to worry him with her own domestic bothers, though he knew by the way she had once or twice referred to her mother that she was having her own hard fight at home. He had once proposed calling upon the old lady; but Doris had quickly squashed the suggestion. John liked to think about Mrs. Hamilton, because through some obscure process of logic it gave him an excuse to think about her daughter as Doris. In other connections he thought of her formally as Miss Hamilton, and often told himself how lucky it was that so charming and accomplished a young woman should be so obviously indifferent to—well, not exactly to himself, but surely he might allege to anything except himself as a romantic playwright.

Meanwhile, the play itself marched on with apparent smoothness, until one morning John dictated the following letter to his star:

My Dear Miss Bond,—Much against my will, I have come to the conclusion that without a human love interest a play about Joan of Arc is impossible. You will be surprised by my abrupt change of front, and you will smile to yourself when you remember how earnestly I argued against your suggestion that I might ultimately be compelled to introduce a human love interest. The fact of the matter is that now I have arrived at the third act I find patriotism too abstract an emotion for the stage. As you know, my idea was to make Joan so much positively enamoured of her country that the ordinary love interest would be superseded. I shall continue to keep Joan herself heart free; but I do think that it would be effective to have at any rate two people in love with her. My notion is to introduce a devoted young peasant who will follow her from her native village, first to the court at Chinon, and so on right through the play until the last fatal scene in the market place at Rouen. I'm sure such a simple lover could be made very moving, and the contrast would be valuable; moreover, it strikes me as a perfectly natural situation. Further, I propose that Gilles de Rais should not only be in love with her, but that he should actually declare his love, and that she should for a brief moment be tempted to return it, finally spurning him as a temptation of the Devil, and thereby reducing him to such a state of despair that he is led into the horrible practices for which he was finally condemned to death. Let me know your opinion soon, because I am at this moment working on the third act.

Yours very sincerely,
John Touchwood.

To which Miss Bond replied by telegram:

Complete confidence in you, and think suggestion magnificent, there should be exit speech of renunciation for Joan to bring down curtain of third act.

JANET BOND.

"You agree with these suggestions?" John asked his secretary.

"Like Miss Bond, I have complete confidence in you," she replied.

He looked at her earnestly to see if she was laughing at him, and put down his pen.

"Do you know that in some ways you yourself remind me of Joan?"

It was a habit of John's, who had a brain like a fly's eye, to perceive historical resemblances that were denied to an ordinary vision. Generally he discovered these reincarnations of the past in his own personality. While he was writing *The Fall of Babylon* he actually fretted himself for a time over a fancied similarity between his character and Nebuchadnezzar's, and sometimes used to wonder if he was putting too much of himself into his portrayal of that dim potentate; and during his composition of *Lucretia* he was so profoundly convinced that Cæsar Borgia was simply John Touchwood over again in a more passionate period and a more picturesque costume that, as the critics pointed out, he presented the world with an aspect of him that would never have been recognized by Machiavelli. Yet, even when Harold was being most unpleasant, or when Viola and Bertram were deafening his household, John could not bring himself to believe that he and Gilles de Rais, who was proved to have tortured over three hundred children to death, had many similar traits; nor was he willing to admit more than a most superficial likeness to the feeble Dauphin Charles. In fact, at one time he was so much discouraged by his inability to adumbrate himself in any of his personages that he began to regret his choice of Joan of Arc and to wish that he had persevered in his intention to write a play about Sir Walter Raleigh, with whom, allowing for the sundering years, he felt he had more in common than with any other historical figure. Therefore he was relieved to discover this resemblance between his heroine and his secretary, in whom he was beginning to take nearly as much interest as in himself.

"Do you mean outwardly?" asked Miss Hamilton, looking at an engraving of the bust from the church of St. Maurice, Orleans. "If so, I hope her complexion wasn't really as scaly as that."

"No, I mean in character."

"I suppose a private secretary ought not to say 'what nonsense' to her employer, but really what else can I say? You might as well compare Ida Merritt to Joan of Arc; in fact, she really is rather like my conception of her."

"I'm sorry you find the comparison so far-fetched," John said, huffily. "It wasn't intended to be uncomplimentary."

"Have you decided to introduce those wolves in the first act, because I think I ought to begin making inquiries about suitable dogs?"

When Miss Hamilton rushed away from the personal like this, John used to regret that he had changed their relationship from one of friendship to one of business. Although he admired practicalness, he realized that it was possible to be too practical, and he sighed sometimes for the tone that his unknown admirers took when they wrote to him about his work. Only that morning he had received a letter from one of these, which he had tossed across the table for his secretary's perusal before he dictated a graceful reply.

> HILLCREST,
>   Highfield Road,
>   Hornsey, N.,
>   *Dec. 14, 1910.*

DEAR SIR:—I have never written to an author before, but I cannot help writing to ask you *when* you are going to give us another play. I cannot tell you how much I enjoy your plays—they take me into another world. Please do not imagine that I am an enthusiastic schoolgirl. I am the mother of four dear little children, and my husband and I both act in a dramatic club at Hornsey. We are very anxious to perform one of your plays, but the committee is afraid of the expense. I suppose it would be asking too much of you to lend us some of the costumes of *The Fall of Babylon*. I think it is your greatest work up till now, and I simply live in all those wonderful old cities now and read everything I can find about them. I was brought up very strictly when I was young and grew to hate the Bible—please do not be shocked at this—but since I saw *The Fall of Babylon* I have taken to reading it again. I went nine times—twice in the gallery, three times in the pit, twice in the upper circle and twice in the dress circle, once in the fifth row at the side and once right in the middle of the front row! I cut out the enclosed photo of you from *The Tatler,* and, would it be asking too much to sign your name? Hoping for the pleasure of a reply, I remain,

Your sincere admirer,

(Mrs.) Enid Foster.

"What extraordinary lunatics there are in this world," Miss Hamilton had commented. "Have you noticed the one constant factor in these letters? All the women begin by saying that it is the first time they have ever written to an author; of course, they would say the same thing to a man who kissed them. The men, however, try to convey that they're in the habit of writing to authors. I think there's a moral to be extracted from that observation."

Now, John had not yet attained—and perhaps it was improbable that he ever would attain—those cold summits of art out of reach alike of the still, sad music and the hurdy-gurdies of humanity, so that these letters from unknown men and women, were they never so foolish, titillated his vanity, which he called "appealing to his imagination."

"One must try to put oneself in the writer's place," he had urged, reproachfully.

"Um—yes, but I can't help thinking of Mrs. Enid Foster living in those wonderful old cities. Her household will crash like Babylon if she isn't careful, and her family will be reduced to eating grass like Nebuchadnezzar, if the greengrocer's book is neglected any longer."

"You won't allow the suburbs to be touched by poetry?"

John had tried to convey in his tone that Miss Hamilton in criticizing the enthusiasm of Mrs. Foster was depreciating his own work. But she had seemed quite unconscious of having rather offended him and had taken down his answer without excusing herself. Now when in a spirit that was truly forgiving he had actually compared her to his beloved heroine, she had scoffed at him as if he was a kind of Mrs. Foster himself.

"You're very matter-of-fact," he muttered.

"Isn't that a rather desirable quality in a secretary?"

"Yes, but I think you might have waited to hear why you reminded me of Joan of Arc before you began talking about those confounded wolves, which, by the way, I have decided to cut out."

"Don't cut out a good effect just because you're annoyed with me," she advised.

"Oh no, there are other reasons," said John, loftily. "It is possible that in an opening tableau the audience may not appreciate that they are wolves, and if they think they're only a lot of stray dogs, the effect will go for nothing. It was merely a passing idea, and I have discarded it."

Miss Hamilton left him to go and type out the morning's correspondence, and John settled down to a speech by the Maid on the subject of perpetual celibacy: he wrote a very good one.

"She may laugh at me," said the author to himself, "but she *is* like Joan—extraordinarily like. Why, I can hear her making this very speech."

Miss Hamilton might sometimes profane John's poetic

sanctuaries and sometimes pull his leg when he was on tiptoe for a flight like Mr. Keats' sweetpeas, but she made existence much more pleasant for him, and he had already reached the stage of wondering how he had ever managed to get along without her. He even went so far in his passion for historical parallels as to compare his situation before she came to the realm of France before Joan of Arc took it in hand. He knew in his heart that these weeks before Christmas were unnaturally calm; he had no hope of prolonging this halcyon time much further; but while it lasted he would enjoy it to the full. Any one who had overheard John announcing to his reflection in the glass an unbridled hedonism for the immediate future might have been pardoned for supposing that he was about to amuse himself in a very desperate fashion. As a matter of fact, the averred intention was due to nothing more exciting than the prospect of a long walk over the Heath with Miss Hamilton to discuss an outline of the fourth act, which John knew would gradually be filled in with his plans for writing other plays and finally be colored by a conversation, or, anyhow, a monologue about himself as a human being without reference to himself as an author.

"What is so delightful about Miss Hamilton," he assured that credulous and complaisant reflection, "is the way one can talk to her without there being the least danger of her supposing that one has any ulterior object in view. Notwithstanding all the rich externals of the past, I'm bound to confess that the relations between men and women are far more natural nowadays. I suppose it was the bicycle that began female emancipation; had bicycles been invented in the time of Joan of Arc she would scarcely have had to face so much ecclesiastical criticism of her behavior."

The walk was a success; amongst other things, John discovered that if he had had a sister like Miss Hamilton, most of his family troubles would never have arisen. He shook his head sadly at the thought that once upon a time he had tried to imagine a Miss Hamilton in Edith, and in a burst of self-revelation, like the brief appearance of two or three acres of definitely blue sky overhead, he assured his secretary that her coming had made a difference to his whole life.

"Well, of course you get through much more in the day now," she agreed.

John would have liked a less practical response, but he made the best of it.

"I've got so much wrapped up in the play," he said, "that I'm wondering now if I shall be able to tear myself away from London for Christmas. I dread the idea of a complete break—especially with the most interesting portion just coming along. I think I must ask you to take your holiday later in the year, if you don't mind."

He had got it out, and if he could have patted himself on the back without appearing ridiculous in a public thoroughfare he would have done so. His manner might have sounded brusque, but John was sure that the least suggestion of any other attitude except that of an employer compelled against his will to seem inconsiderate would have been fatal.

"That would mean leaving my mother alone," said Miss Hamilton, doubtfully.

John looked sympathetic, but firm, when he agreed with her.

"She would understand that literary work takes no account of the church calendar," he pointed out. "After all, what is Christmas?"

"Unfortunately, my mother is already very much offended with me for working with you at all. Oh, well, bother relations!" she exclaimed, vehemently. "I'm going to be selfish in future. All right, if you insist, I must obey—or lose my job, eh?"

"I might have to engage a locum tenens. You see, now that I've got into the habit of dictating my letters and relying upon somebody else to keep my references in order and—"

"Yes, yes," she interrupted. "I quite see that it would put you to great inconvenience if I cried off. All the same, I can't help being worried by the notion of leaving mother alone on Christmas Day itself. Why shouldn't I join you on the day after?"

"The very thing," John decided. "I will leave London on Christmas Eve, and you shall come down on Boxing Day. But I should travel in the morning, if I were you. It's apt to be unpleasant, traveling in the evening on a Bank Holiday. Hullo, here we are! This walk has given me a tremendous appetite, and I do feel that we've made a splendid start with the fourth act, don't you?"

"The fourth act?" repeated his secretary. "It seems to me that most of the time you were talking about the position of women in modern life."

John laughed gayly.

"Ah, I see you haven't even yet absolutely grasped my method of work. I was thinking all the while of Joan's speech to her accusers. I can assure you that all my remarks were entirely relevant to what I had in my head. That's the way I get my atmosphere. I told you that you reminded me of her, but you wouldn't believe me. In doublet and hose you would *be* Joan."

"Should I? I think I should look more like Dick Whittington in a touring pantomime. My legs are too thin for tights."

"By the way, I wonder if Janet Bond has good legs?" said John, pensively.

It was charming to be able to talk about women's legs like this without there being the slightest suggestion that they had any; yet, somehow the least promising topics were rehabilitated by the company of Miss Hamilton, and most of them, even the oldest, acquired a new and absorbing interest. John had registered a vow on the first day his secretary came that he would watch carefully for the least signs of rosifying her and he had renewed this vow every morning before his glass; but it was sometimes difficult not to attribute to her all sorts of mysterious fascinations, as on those occasions when he would have kept her working later than usual in the afternoon and when she would have been persuaded to stay for tea, for which she made a point of getting home to please her mother, who gave it a grand importance. John was convinced that even James would forgive him for thinking that in all England there was not a more competent, a more charming, a more—he used to pull himself up guiltily at about the third comparative and stifle his fancies in the particularly delicious cake that Mrs. Worfolk always seemed to provide on the days when his secretary stayed to tea.

It was on one of these rosified afternoons, full of candle-light and firelight and the warmed scent of hyacinths that Miss Hamilton rallied John about his exaggerated dread of his relations.

"For I've been working with you now for nearly three weeks, and you've not been bothered by them once," she declared.

"My name! My name!" he cried. "Touchwood?"

"I begin to think it's nothing but an affectation," she persisted. "*You're* not pestered by charitable uncles who want to boast of what they've done for their poor brother's only daughter. *You're* not made to feel that you've wrecked your mother's old age by earning your own living."

"Yes, they have been quiet recently," he admitted. "But there was such a terrible outbreak of Family Influenza just before you came that some sort of prostration for a time was inevitable. I hope you don't expect my brother, Hugh, to commit a forgery every week. Besides, that excellent suggestion of yours about preparing Ambles for Christmas has kept him busy, and probably all the rest of them down there too. But it's odd you should raise the subject, because I was going to propose your having supper here some Sunday soon and inviting my eldest brother and his wife to meet you."

"To-morrow is the last Sunday before Christmas. The Sunday after is Christmas Day."

"Is it really? Then I must dictate an invitation for to-morrow, and I must begin to see about presents on Monday. By Jove, how time has flown!"

"After all, what is Christmas?" she laughed.

"Oh, you must expect children to be excited about it," John murmured. "I don't like to disappoint *them*. But I'd no idea Christmas was on top of us like this. You'll help me with my shopping next week? I hope to goodness Eleanor won't come and bother me. She'll be getting back to town to-morrow. It's really extraordinary, the way the time has passed."

John dictated an urgent invitation to James and Beatrice to sup with them the following evening, and since it was too late to let them know by post, he decided to see Miss Hamilton as far as the tube and leave the note in person at Hill Road.

James arrived for supper in a most truculent mood, and this being aggravated by his brother's burgundy, of which he drank a good deal, referring to it all the while as poison, much to John's annoyance, embroiled him half way through supper in an argument with Miss Hamilton on the subject of feminine intelligence.

"Women are not intelligent," he shouted. "The glimmering intelligence they sometimes appear to exhibit is only one of their numerous sexual allurements. A woman thinks with her nerves, reasons with her emotions, and speculates with her sensations."

"Rubbish," said Miss Hamilton, emphatically.

"Now, Jimmie dear," his wife put in, "you'll only have indigestion if you get excited while you're eatin'."

"I shall have indigestion anyway," growled her husband. "My liver will be like dough to-morrow after this burgundy. I ought to drink a light moselle."

"Well, you can have moselle," John began.

"I loathe moselle. I'd as soon drink syrup of squills," James bellowed.

"All right, you shall have syrup of squills next time."

"Oh, Johnnie," Beatrice interposed with a wide reproachful smile. "Jimmie's only joking. He doesn't really like syrup of squills."

"For heaven's sake, don't try to analyze my tastes," said James to his wife.

John threw a glance at Miss Hamilton, which was meant to express "What did I tell you?" But she was blind to his signal and only intent upon attacking James on behalf of her sex.

"Women have not the same kind of intelligence as men," she began, "because it is denied to them by their physical constitution. But they have. I insist, a supplementary intelligence without which the great masculine minds would be as ineffective as convulsions of nature. Women work like the coral polyps. . . ."

"Bravo!" John cried. "A capital comparison!"

"An absurd comparison!" James contradicted. "A ludicrous comparison! Woman is purely individualistic. The moment she begins to take up with communal effort, she tends to become sterile."

"Do get on with your supper, dear," urged Beatrice, who had only understood the last word and was anxious not "to be made to feel small," as she would have put it, in front of an unmarried woman.

John perceived her mortification and jumped through the argument as a clown through a paper hoop.

"Remember I'm expecting you both at Ambles on Christmas Eve," he said, boisterously. "We're going to have a real old-fashioned Christmas party."

James forgot all about women in his indignation; but before he could express his opinion Beatrice held up another paper hoop for the distraction of the audience.

"I'm simply longin' for the country," she declared. "Christmas with a lot of children is the nicest thing I know."

John went through the hoop with aplomb and refused to be unseated by his brother.

"James will enjoy it more than any of us," he chuckled.

"What!" shouted the critic. "I'd sooner be wrecked on

a desert island with nothing to read but a sixpenny edition of the Christmas Carol. Ugh!"

John looked at Miss Hamilton again, and this time his appeal was not unheeded; she said no more about women and let James rail on at sentimental festivities, which, by the time he had finished with them, looked as irreparable as the remains of the tipsy-cake. There seemed no reason amid the universal collapse of tradition to conserve the habit of letting the ladies retire after dinner. As there was no drawing-room in his bachelor household, it would have been more comfortable to smoke upstairs in the library; but James returned to Fielding after demolishing Dickens and protested against being made to hurry over his port; so his host had to watch Beatrice escort Miss Hamilton from the dining-room with considerable resentment at what he thought was her unjustifiably protective manner.

"As my secretary," he felt, "Miss Hamilton is more at home in my house than Beatrice is. I suppose, though, that like everything else I have my relations are going to take possession of her now."

"Where did you pick up your lady-help?" James asked, when he and his brother were left alone with the wine.

"If you're alluding to Miss Hamilton," John said, sharply, "I met her on board the *Murmania,* crossing the Atlantic."

"I never heard any good come of traveling acquaintances. She has a good complexion; I suppose she took your eye by not being seasick. Beware of women with good complexions who aren't seasick, Johnnie. They always flirt."

"Are you supposed to be warning me against my secretary?"

"Any woman who finds herself at a man's elbow is dangerous. Nurses, of course, are the most notoriously dangerous—but a secretary who isn't seasick is nearly as bad."

"Thanks very much for your brotherly concern," said John, sarcastically. "You will be relieved to hear that the relationship between Miss Hamilton and myself is a purely practical one, and likely to remain so."

"Platonism was never practical," James answered with a snort. "It was the most impractical system ever imagined."

"Fortunately Miss Hamilton is sufficiently interested in her work and in mine not to bother her head about the philosophy of the affections."

James was irritating when he was criticizing contemporary literature; but his views of modern life were infuriating.

"I'm not accusing your young woman—how old is she, by the way? About twenty-nine, I should guess. A damned dangerous age, Johnnie. However, as I say, I'm not accusing her of designs upon you. But a man who writes the kind of plays that you do is capable of any extravagance, and you're much too old by now to be thinking about marriage."

"I don't happen to be thinking about marriage," John retorted. "But I refuse to accept your dictum about my age. I consider that the effects of age have been very much exaggerated by the young. You cannot call a man of forty-two old."

"You look much more than forty-two. However, one can't write plays like yours without exposing oneself to a good deal of emotional wear and tear. No, no, you're making a great mistake in introducing a woman into the house. Believe me, Johnnie, I'm speaking for your good. If I hadn't married, I might have preserved my illusions about women and compounded just as profitable a dose of dramatic nux vomica as yourself."

"What do you mean by a dose of dramatic nux vomica?"

"That's my name for the sort of plays you write, which unduly accelerate the action of the heart and make a sane person retch. However, don't take my remarks in ill part. I was simply commenting on the danger of letting a good-looking young woman make herself indispensable."

"I'm glad you allow her good looks," John said, witheringly. "Any one who was listening to our conversation would get the impression that she was as ugly and voracious as a harpy."

"Yes, yes. She's quite good-looking. Very nice ankles."

"I haven't noticed her ankles," John said, austerely.

"You will, though," his brother replied with an encouraging laugh. "By the way, what's that rascal, Hugh, been doing? I hear you've replanted him in the bosom of the family. Isn't Hugh rather too real for one of your Christmas parties?"

John, after some hesitation, had decided not to tell any of the others the details of Hugh's misdemeanor; he had even denied himself the pleasure of holding him up to George as a warning; hence the renewal of his interest in Hugh had struck the family as a mere piece of sentimentality.

"Crutchley didn't seem to believe he'd ever make much of architecture," he explained to James. "And I'm thinking of helping him to establish himself in British Honduras."

"Bah! For less than he'll cost you in British Honduras you could establish me as the editor of a new critical weekly," James grunted.

"There is still time for Hugh to make something of his life," John replied. He had not had the slightest intention of trying to score off his eldest brother by this remark, and he was shocked to see what a spasm of ill will twisted up his face.

"I suppose your young woman is responsible for this sudden solicitude for Hugh's career? I suppose it's she who has persuaded you that he has possibilities? You take care, Johnnie. You can't manipulate the villain in life as you can on the stage."

Now, Miss Hamilton, though she had not met him, had shown just enough interest in Hugh to give these remarks a sting; and John must have been obviously taken aback, for the critic at once recovered his good humor and proposed joining the ladies upstairs. Beatrice was sitting by the fire; her husband's absence had allowed her to begin the digestion of an unusually good dinner in peace, and the smoothness of her countenance made her look more than ever like a cabinet photograph of the early 'nineties. Miss Hamilton, on the other hand, seemed bored, and very soon she declared that she must go home lest her mother should be anxious.

"Oh, you have a mother?" James observed in such a tone that John thought it was the most offensive remark of the many he had heard him make that evening. He hoped that Miss Hamilton would not abandon him after this first encounter with his relations, and he tried to ascertain her impressions while she was putting on her things in the hall.

"I'm afraid you've had a very dull evening," he murmured, apologetically. "I hope my sister-in-law wasn't more tiresome than usual. What did she talk about?"

"She was warning me—no, I won't be malicious—she was explaining to me the difficulties of an author's wife."

"Yes, poor thing; I'm afraid my brother must be very trying to live with. I hope you were sympathetic?"

"So sympathetic," Miss Hamilton replied, with a mocking glance, "that I told her I was never likely to make the experiment. Good night, Mr. Touchwood. To-morrow as usual."

She hurried down the steps and was gone before he could utter a word.

"I don't think she need have said that," he murmured to himself on his way back to the library. "I've no doubt Beatrice was very trying; but I really don't think she need have said that to me. It wasn't worth repeating such a stupid remark. That's the way things acquire an undue importance."

With John's entrance the conversation returned to Miss Hamilton; but, though it was nearly all implied criticism of his new secretary, he had no desire to change the topic. She was much more interesting than the weekly bills at Hill Road, and he listened without contradiction to his brother's qualms about her experience and his sister-in-law's regrets for her lack of it.

"However," said John to his reflection when he was undressing, "they've got to make the best of her, even if they all think the worse. And the beauty of it is that they can't occupy her as they can occupy a house. I must see about getting Hugh off to the Colonies soon. If I don't find out about British Honduras, he can always go to Canada or Australia. It isn't good for him to hang about in England."

CHAPTER XI

WHETHER it was due to the Christmas card look of his new house or merely to a desire to flaunt a romantic hospitality in the face of his eldest brother, it is certain that John had never before in his life gone so benevolently mad as during the week that preceded Christmas in the year 1910. Mindful of that afternoon in the town of Galton when he had tried to procure for Harold and Frida gifts of such American appearance as would excuse his negligence, he was determined not to expose himself for a second time to juvenile criticism, and in the selection of toys he pandered to every idiosyncrasy he had so far observed in his nephews and nieces. Thus, for Bertram he bought a large stamp album, several sheets of tropical stamps, a toy theater, representatives of every species in the great genus marbles, a set of expensive and realistic masks, and a model fireman's outfit. For Viola he filled a trunk with remnants of embroideries and all kinds of stuffs, placing on top two pairs of ebony castanets and the most professional tambourine he could find; and, in order that nature might not be utterly subordinated to art, he bought her a very large doll, rather older in appearance than Viola herself; in fact, almost marriageable. In the hope of obliterating the disappointment of those china animals, he chose for Frida a completely furnished dolls' house with garage and stables attached, so grand a house, indeed, that by knocking all the rooms into one, she could with slight inconvenience have lived in it herself; this residence he populated with gentleman-dolls, lady-dolls, servant-dolls, nurse-dolls, baby-dolls, horses, carriages, and motors; nor did he omit to provide a fishmonger's shop for the vicinity. For Harold he bought a butterfly collector's equipment, a vacuum pistol, a set of climbing-irons, a microscope, and at the last moment a juvenile diver's equipment with air pumps and all accessories, which was warranted perfectly safe, though the wicked uncle wondered if it really was.

"I don't want a mere toy for the bathroom," he explained.

"Quite so, sir," the shopman assented, with a bow. "This is guaranteed for any ordinary village pond or small stream."

For his grown-up relations John bought the kind of presents that one always does buy for grown-up relations, the kind of presents that look very ornamental on the counter, seem very useful when the shopman explains what they are for, puzzle the recipient and the donor when the shopman is no longer there, and lie about the house on small tables for the rest of the year. In the general odor of Russia leather that clung to his benefactions John hoped that Miss Hamilton would not consider too remarkable the attaché case that he intended to give her, nor amid the universal dazzle of silver object to the few little luxuries of the writing-desk with which he had enhanced it. Then there were the presents for the servants to choose, and he counted much on Miss Hamilton's enabling him to introduce into these an utilitarian note that for two or three seasons had been missing from his donations, which to an outsider might have seemed more like lures of the flesh than sober testimonials to service. He also counted upon her to persuade Mrs. Worfolk to accompany Maud down to Ambles: Elsa was to be left in Church Row with permission to invite to dinner the policeman to whom she was betrothed and various friends and relations of the two families.

When the presents were settled John proceeded to lay in a store of eatables and drinkables, in the course of which enterprise he was continually saying:

"I've forgotten for the moment what I want next, but meanwhile you'd better give me another box of Elvas plums."

"Another drum? Yes, sir," the shopman would reply, licking his pencil in a way that was at once obsequious and pedantic, though it was not intended to suggest more than perfect efficiency.

When the hall and the adjacent rooms at 36 Church Row had been turned into rolling dunes of brown paper, John rushed about London in a last frenzy of unbridled acquisitiveness to secure plenty of amusement for the children To this end he obtained a few well-known and well-tried favorites like the kinetoscope and the magic lantern, and a number of experimental diversions which would have required a trained engineer or renowned scientist to demonstrate successfully. Finally he bargained for the wardrobe of a Santa Claus whose dignified perambulations round the Christmas Bazaar of a noted emporium had attracted his fancy on account of the number of children who followed him everywhere, laughing and screaming with delight. It was not until he had completed the purchase that he discovered it was not the exterior of the Santa Claus which had charmed his little satellites, but the free distribution of bags of coagulated jujubes.

"I expect I'd better get the Christmas tree in the country," said John, waist-deep in the still rising drift of parcels. "I dare say the Galton shops keep those silver and magenta globes you hang on Christmas trees, and I ought to patronize the local tradesmen."

"If you have any local shopping to do, I'm sure you would be wise to go down to-day," Miss Hamilton suggested, firmly. "Besides, Mrs. Worfolk won't want to arrive at the last minute."

"No, indeed, I shan't, Miss," said the housekeeper. "Well, I mean to say, I don't think we ever shall arrive, not if we wait much longer. We shall require a performing elephant to carry all these parcels, as it is."

"My idea was to go down in the last train on Christmas Eve," John argued. "I like the old-fashioned style, don't you know?"

"Yes, old-fashioned's the word," Mrs. Worfolk exclaimed. "Why, who's to get the house ready if we all go trooping down on Christmas Eve? And if I go, sir, you must come with me. You know how quick Mrs. Curtis always is to snap any one up. If I had my own way, I wouldn't go within a thousand miles of the country; that's a sure thing."

John began to be afraid that his housekeeper was going back on her word, and he surrendered to the notion of leaving town that afternoon.

"I say, what is this parcel like a long drain-pipe?" he asked in a final effort to detain Miss Hamilton, who was preparing to make her farewells and leave him to his packing.

"Ah, it would take some finding out," Mrs. Worfolk interposed. "I've never seen so many shapes and sizes of parcels in all my life."

"They must have made a mistake," said John. "I don't remember buying anything so tubular as this."

He pulled away some of the paper wrapping to see what was inside.

"Ah, of course! They're two or three boxes of Elvas plums I ordered. But please don't go, Miss Hamilton," he protested. "I am relying upon you to get the tickets to Waterloo."

In spite of a strenuous scene at the station, in the course of which John's attempts to propitiate Mrs. Worfolk led to one of the porters referring to her as his mother, they managed to catch the five o'clock train to Wrottesford. After earnestly assuring his secretary that he should be perfectly ready to begin work again on Joan of Arc the day after her arrival and begging her on no account to let herself be deterred from traveling on the morning of Boxing Day, John sank back into the pleasant dreams that haunt a warm first-class smoking compartment when it's raining hard outside in the darkness of a December night.

"We shall have a green Christmas this year," observed one of his fellow travelers.

"Very green," John assented with enthusiasm, only realizing as he spoke that the superlative must sound absurd to any one who was unaware of his thoughts and hiding his embarrassment in the *Westminster Gazette,* which in the circumstances was the best newspaper he could have chosen.

John was surprised and depressed when the train arrived at Wrottesford to find that the member of the Ambles party who had elected to meet him was Hilda; and there was a long argument on the platform who should drive in the dogcart and who should drive in the fly. John did not want to ride on the back seat of the dogcart, which he would have to do unless he drove himself, a prospect that did not attract him when he saw how impatiently the mare was dancing about through the extreme lateness of the train. Hilda objected to driving with his housekeeper in the fly, and in the end John was compelled to let Maud and Mrs. Worfolk occupy the dogcart, while he and Hilda toiled along the wet lanes in the fly. It was decided to leave the greater portion of the luggage to be fetched in the morning, but even so it was after eight o'clock before they got away from the station, and John, when he found himself immured with Hilda in the musty interior of the hired vehicle was inclined to prophesy a blue Christmas this year. To begin with, Hilda would try to explain the system she had pursued in allotting the various bedrooms to accommodate the large party that was expected at Ambles. It was bad enough so long as she confined herself to a verbal exposition, but when she produced a map of the house, evidently made by Hugh on an idle evening, and to illuminate her dispositions struck away most of John's matches, it became exasperating. His brain was already fatigued by the puzzle of fitting into two vehicles four pieces, one of which might not move to the square next two of the remaining pieces, and another of which could not move backward.

"I leave it entirely to you," he declared, introducing at last into the intellectual torment of chess some of the happy irresponsibleness of bridge. "You mustn't set me these chess problems in a jolting fly before dinner."

"Chess!" Hilda sniffed with a shiver. "Draughts would be a better name."

She did not often make jokes, and before John had recovered sufficiently from his surprise to congratulate her with a hearty laugh, she was off again upon her querulous and rambling narration of the family news.

"If everything *had* been left to me, I might have managed, but Hugh's interference, apparently authorized by you, upset all my poor little arrangements. I need hardly say that Mama was so delighted to have her favorite at home with her that she has done everything since his arrival to encourage his self-importance. It's Hughie this and Hughie that, until I get quite sick of the sound of his name. And he's very unkind to poor little Harold. Apart from being very coarse and sarcastic in front of him, he is sometimes quite brutal. Only this morning he shot him in the upper part of the leg with a pellet from the poor little man's own air-gun."

John did laugh this time, and shouted "Merry Christmas!" to a passing wagon.

"I dare say it sounds very funny to you. But it made Harold cry."

"Come, come, Hilda, it's just as well he should learn the potentialities of his own instrument. He'll sympathize with the birds now."

"Birds," she scoffed. "Fancy comparing Harold with a bird!"

"It is rather unfair," John agreed.

"However, you won't be so ready to take Hugh's part when you see what he's been doing at Ambles."

"Why, what has he been doing?"

"Oh, never mind. I'd rather you judged for yourself," said Hilda, darkly. "Of course, I don't know what Hugh has been up to in London that you've had to send him down to Hampshire. I always used to hear you vow that you would have nothing more to do with him. But I know that successful people are allowed to change their minds more often than the rest of us. I know success justifies everything. And it isn't as if Hugh was grateful for your kindness. I can assure you that he criticizes everything you do. Any stranger who heard him talking about your plays would think that they were a kind of disgrace to the family. As for Laurence, he encourages him, not because he likes him, but because Hugh fills him up with stories about the stage. Though I think that a clergyman who has got into such a muddle with his bishops would do better not to make himself so conspicuous. The whole neighborhood is talking about him."

"What is Laurence's latest?"

"Why, stalking about in a black cloak, with his hair hanging down over his collar, stopping people in quiet lanes and reciting Shakespeare to them. It's not surprising that half the county is talking about his behavior and saying that he was turned out of Newton Candover for being drunk when the bishop took a confirmation, and *some* even say that he kept a ballet girl at the vicarage. But do you think that Edith objects? Oh, no! All that Laurence does must be right, because it's Laurence. She prays for him to get back his belief in the Church of England, though who's going to offer him another living I'm sure I don't know, so she might just as well spare her knees. And when she's not praying for him, she's spoiling him. She actually came out of her room the other morning with her finger up to her lips, because Laurence wasn't to be disturbed at that moment. I need hardly tell you I paid no attention and went on saying what I had to say to Huggins about the disgraceful way he's let the pears get so sleepy."

"It's a pity you didn't succeed in waking them up instead of Laurence," John chuckled.

"It's all very well for you to laugh, John, but if you could see the way that Edith is bringing up Frida! She's turning her into a regular little molly-coddle. I'm sure poor Harold does his best to put some life into the child, but she shrinks and twitches whenever he comes near her. I told Edith that it wasn't to be wondered at if Harold did tease her sometimes. She encourages him to tease her by her affectations. I used to think that Frida was quite a nice little girl when I only saw her occasionally, but she doesn't improve on acquaintance. However, I blame her mother more than I do her. Why, Edith doesn't even make the child take her cod-liver oil regularly, whereas Harold drinks his up like a little Trojan."

"Never mind," said John, soothingly. "I'm sure we shall all feel more cheerful after Christmas. And now, if you don't mind, I'm afraid I must keep quiet for the rest of the drive. I've got a scene to think about."

The author turned up the collar of his coat and retired into the further corner while Hilda chewed her veil in ruminative indignation until the mellow voice of Laurence, who had taken up a statuesque pose of welcome by the gate, broke the dank silence of the fly.

"Ah, John, my dear fellow, we are delighted to see you. The rain has stopped."

If Laurence had still been on good terms with his Creator, John might have thought from his manner that he had personally arranged this break in the weather.

"Is Harold there?" asked Hilda, sharply.

"Here I am, mother; I've just caught a Buff-tip, and it won't go into my poison-bottle."

"And what is a Buff-tip?" inquired Laurence in a tone of patronizing ignorance.

"Oh, it's a pretty common moth."

"Harold, darling, don't bother about moths or butterflies to-night. Come and say how d'ye do to dear Uncle John."

"I've dropped the cork of my poison-bottle. Look out, Frida, bother you, I say, you'll tread on it."

The combined scents of cyanide of potassium and hot metal from Harold's bull's-eye lantern were heavy upon the moist air; when the cork was found, Harold lost control over the lantern which he flashed into everybody's face in turn, so that John, rendered as helpless as a Buff-tip, walked head foremost into a sopping bush by the side of the path. However, the various accidents of arrival all escaped being serious, and the thought of dinner shortened the affectionate greetings. Remembering how Hugh had paid out Harold with his own air-gun, John greeted his youngest brother more cordially than he could ever have supposed it was possible to greet him again.

By general consent, the owner of the house was allowed to be tired that evening, and all discussion of the Christmas preparations was postponed until the next day. Harold made a surreptitious attempt to break into the most promising parcel he could find, but he was ill rewarded by the inside, which happened to be a patent carpet sweeper.

Before old Mrs. Touchwood went to bed, she took John aside and whispered:

"They're all against Hughie. But I've tried to make the poor boy feel that he's at home, and dear Georgie will be coming very soon, which will make it pleasanter for Hugh, and I've thought of a nice way to manage Jimmie."

"I think you worry yourself needlessly over Hugh, Mama; I can assure you he's perfectly capable of looking after himself."

"I hope so," the old lady sighed. "All my patience came out beautifully this evening. So I hope Hughie will be all right. He seemed to think you were a little annoyed with him."

"Did he tell you why?"

"Not exactly, but I understand it was something to do with money. You mustn't be too strict with Hugh about money, John. You must always remember that he hasn't got all the money he wants, and you must make allowances accordingly. Ah, dear, peace on earth, good-will towards men! But I don't complain. I'm very happy here with my patience, and I dare say something can be done to get rid of the bees that have made a nest in the wall just under my bedroom window. They're asleep now, but when they begin to buzz with the warm weather Huggins must try and induce them to move somewhere else. Good-night, my dear boy."

Next morning when John leaned out of his window to inhale the Hampshire air and contemplate his domain he was shocked to perceive upon the lawn below a large quadrangular excavation in which two workmen were actually digging.

"Hi! What are you doing?" he shouted.

The workmen stared at John, stared at one another, stared at their spades, and went on with their digging.

"Hi! What the devil are you doing?"

The workmen paid no attention; but the voice of Harold came trickling round the corner of the house with a gurgle of self-satisfaction.

"*I* didn't do it, Uncle John. I began geology last week, but I haven't dug up *anything*. Mother wouldn't let me. It was Uncle Hugh and Uncle Laurence. Mother knew you'd be angry when you saw what a mess the garden was in. It does look untidy, doesn't it? Huggins said he should complain to you, first thing. He says he'd just as soon put brown sugar on the paths as *that* gravel. Did you know that Ambles is built on a gravel subsoil, Uncle John? Aren't you glad, because my geology book says that a gravel subsoil is the healthiest . . ."

John removed himself abruptly out of earshot.

"What is that pernicious mess on the front lawn?" he demanded of Hugh half-an-hour later at breakfast.

"Ah, you noticed it, did you?"

"Noticed it? I should think I did notice it. I understand that you're responsible."

"Not entirely," Laurence interposed, gently. "Hugh and I must accept a joint responsibility. The truth is that for some time now I've felt that my work has been terribly at the mercy of little household noises, and Hugh recommended me to build myself an outside study. He has made a very clever design, and has kindly undertaken to supervise its erection. As you have seen, they are already well on with the foundations. The design which I shall show you after breakfast is in keeping with the house, and of course you will have the advantage of what I call my little Gazebo when I leave Ambles. Have I told you that I'm considering a brief experience of the realities of the stage? After all, why not? Shakespeare was an actor."

If John had been eating anything more solid than a lightly boiled egg at the moment he must have choked.

"You can call it your little Gazebo as much as you like, but it's nothing but a confounded summerhouse," he shouted.

"Look here, Johnnie," said Hugh, soothingly. "You'll like it when it's finished. This isn't one of Stevie's Gothic contortions. I admit that to get the full architectural effect there should be a couple of them. You see, I've followed the design of the famous dovecotes at . . ."

"Dovecoats be damned," John exploded. "I instructed you to prepare the house for Christmas; I didn't ask you to build me a new one."

"Laurence felt that he was in the way indoors," Edith explained, timidly.

"The impression was rather forced upon me," said Laurence with a glance at Hilda, who throughout the dispute had been sitting virtuously silent; nor did she open her thin lips now.

"He was going to pay for his hermitage out of the money he ought to have made from writing *Lamp-posts*," Edith went on in a muddled exposition of her husband's motives. "He wasn't thinking of himself at all. But of course if you object to his building this Gas—oh, I am so bad at proper names—he'll understand. Won't you, dear?"

"Oh, I shall understand," Laurence admitted with an expression of painfully achieved comprehension. "Though I may fail to see the necessity for such strong language."

Frida wiggled in the coils of an endless whisper from which her mother extricated her at last by murmuring:

"Hush, darling, Uncle John is a little vexed about something."

Hilda and her son still sat in mute self-righteousness; and Grandmama, who always had her breakfast in bed, was not present to defend Hugh.

"If it had been anywhere except on the lawn right in front of my room," John began more mildly.

"We tried to combine suitability of site with facility of access," Laurence condescended to explain. "But pray do not say another word," he added, waving his fingers like magic wands to induce John's silence. "The idea of my little Gazebo does not appeal to you. That is enough. I do not grudge the money already spent upon the foundations. Further discussion will irritate us all, and I for one have no wish to disturb the harmony of the season." Then exchanging his tone of polite martyrdom for the suave jocularity of a vicar, he continued: "And when are we to expect our Yuletide guests? I hear that the greater portion of your luggage is still in the care of the station-master at Wrottesford. If I can do anything to aid in the transport of what rumor says is our Christmas commissariat, do not hesitate to call upon my services. I am giving the Muse a holiday and am ready for anything. Harold, pass the marmalade, please."

John felt incapable of further argument with Laurence and Hugh in combination, and having gained his point, he let the subject of the Gazebo drop. He was glad that Miss Hamilton was not here; he felt that she might have been rather contemptuous of what he tried to believe was "good-nature," but recognized in his heart as "meekness," even "feebleness."

"When are Cousin Bertram and Cousin Viola coming?" Harold asked.

"Wow-wow-wow!" Hugh imitated, and he was probably expressing the general opinion of Harold's re-entry into the breakfast-table conversation.

"For goodness' sake, boy, don't talk about them as if they were elderly colonial connections," John commanded with the resurgent valor that Harold always inspired. "Bertram and Viola are coming to-morrow. By the way, Hilda, is there any accommodation for a monkey? I don't know for certain, but Bertram talked vaguely of bringing a monkey down. Possibly a small annex could be attached to the chickenhouse."

"A monkey?" Edith exclaimed in alarm. "Oh, I hope it won't attack dear Frida."

"I shall shoot him, if he does," Harold boasted. "I shot a mole last week."

"No, you didn't, you young liar," Hugh contradicted. "It was killed by the trap."

"Harold is always a very truthful little boy," said his mother, glaring.

"Is he? I hadn't noticed it," Hugh retorted.

"Far be it from me to indulge in odious comparisons," Laurence interposed, grandly. "But I cannot help being a trifle—ah—tickled by so much consideration's being exhibited on account of the temporary lodging of a monkey and so much animus—however, don't let us rake up a disagreeable topic."

John thought it was a pity that his brother-in-law had not felt the same about raking up the lawn when after breakfast he was telling Huggins to fill in the hole and hearing that it was unlikely to lose the scar for a long time.

"You could have knocked me down with a feather, sir, when they started in hacking away at a lovely piece of turf like that."

"I'm sure I could," John agreed, warmly.

"But what's done can't be undone, and the best way to mend a bad job would be to make a bed for ornamental annuals. Yes, sir, a nice bed in the shape of a star—or a shell."

"No thanks, Huggins, I should prefer grass again, even if for a year or two the lawn does look as if it had been recently vaccinated."

John's Christmas enthusiasm had been thoroughly damped by the atmosphere of Ambles and he regretted that he had let himself be persuaded into coming down two days earlier than he had intended. It had been Mrs. Worfolk's fault, and when his housekeeper approached him with a complaint about the way things were being managed in the kitchen John told her rather sharply that she must make the best of the present arrangements, exercise as much tact as possible, and remember that Christmas was a season when discontent was out of fashion. Then he retreated to the twenty-acre field to lose a few golf-balls. Alas, he had forgotten that Laurence had proclaimed himself to be in a holiday humor and was bored to find that this was so expansive as to include an ambition to see if golf was as difficult as people said.

"You can try a stroke if you really want to," John offered, grudgingly.

"I understand that the theory of striking involves the correct application of the hands to the club," said the novice. "I set much store by the old adage that well begun is half done."

"The main thing is to hit the ball."

"I've no doubt whatever about being able to hit the ball; but if I decide to adopt golf as a recreation from my dramatic work I wish to acquire a good style at the outset," Laurence intoned, picking up the club as solemnly as if he was going to baptize it. "What is your advice about the forefinger of my left hand? It feels to me somewhat ubiquitous. I assume that there is some inhibition upon excessive fidgeting."

"Keep your eye on the ball," John gruffly advised him. "And don't shift your position."

"One, two, three," murmured Laurence, raising the club above his shoulder.

"Fore!" John shouted to a rash member of the household who was crossing the line of fire.

A lump of turf was propelled a few feet in the direction of the admonished figure, and the ball was hammered down into the soft earth.

"You distracted me by counting four," Laurence protested. "My intention was to strike at three. However, if at first you don't succeed . . ."

But John could stand no more of it and escaped to Galton,

where he bought a bushel of lustrous ornaments for the Christmas tree that was even now being felled by Huggins in a coppice remote from Harold's myopic explorations. Then for two days the household worked feverishly and unitedly in a prevalent odor of allspice; the children were decoyed from the house while the presents were mysteriously conveyed to the drawing-room, which had been consecrated to the forthcoming revelry; Harold, after nearly involving himself in a scandal by hiding himself under the kitchen-table during one of the servant's meals in order to verify the cubic contents of their several stockings, was finally successful in contracting with Mrs. Worfolk for the loan of one of hers; Frida whispered as ceaselessly as a grove of poplars; everybody's fingers were tattooed by holly-pricks; and the introduction of so much decorative vegetation into the house brought with it a train of somnambulant insects.

On Saturday afternoon the remaining guests arrived, and when John heard Bertram and Viola shouting merrily up and down the corridors he recognized the authentic note of Christmas gayety at last. James was much less disagreeable than he had expected, and did not even freeze Beatrice when she gushed about the loveliness of the holly and reminded everybody that she was countrified herself; Hilda and Eleanor were brought together by their common dread of Hugh's apparent return to favor; George exuded a gross reproduction of the host's good-will and wandered about the room reading jokes from the Christmas numbers to those who would listen to him; Laurence kissed all the ladies under the mistletoe, bending down to them from his majesty as patronizingly as in the days of his faith he used to communicate the poor of the parish; Edith clapped her hands every time that Laurence brought off a kiss and talked in a heartfelt tremolo about the Christmas-tides of her girlhood; Frida conceived an adoration for Viola; Hugh egged on Bertram to tease, threaten, and contradict Harold on every occasion; Grandmama in a new butter-colored gown glowed in the lamplight, and purred over her fertility, as if on the day she had accepted Robert Touchwood's hand nearly half a century ago she had foreseen this gathering and had never grumbled when she found she was going to have another baby.

"Snapdragon will be ready at ten," John proclaimed, "and then to bed, so that we're all fit for Christmas Day."

He was anxious to get the household out of the way, because he had formed a project to dress himself up that night as Santa Claus and, as he put it to himself, stimulate the children's fancy in case they should be awake when their stockings were being filled.

The clock struck ten; Mrs. Worfolk gave portentous utterance to the information that the snapdragon was burning beautiful; there was a rush for the pantry where the ceremony was to take place. Laurence picked out his raisins as triumphantly as if he were snatching souls from a discredited Romish purgatory. Harold notwithstanding his bad sight seemed to be doing well until Bertram temporarily disabled him by snatching a glowing raisin from the fiercest flame and ramming it down his neck. But the one who ate most of all, more even than Harold, was George, whose fat fingers would scoop up half-a-dozen raisins at a go, were they never so hot, until gradually the blue flames flickered less alertly and finally went out altogether in a pungency of burnt brandy.

"Half-past ten," John, who was longing to dress himself up, cried impatiently.

His efforts to urge the family up to bed were rather interfered with by Laurence, who detained Eleanor with numerous questions about going on the stage with a view to correcting a few technical deficiencies in his dramatic craftsmanship.

"I'm anxious to establish by personal experience the exact length of the interval required to change one's costume, and also the distance from one's green-room to the—ah—wings. I do not aim high. I should be perfectly satisfied with such minor parts as Rosencrantz or Metellus Cimber. Perhaps,

Eleanor, you will introduce me to some of your theatrical friends after the holidays? There is a reduced day return up to town every Thursday. We might lunch together at one of those little Bohemian restaurants where rumor says that an excellent lunch is to be had for one and sixpence."

Eleanor promised she would do all she could, because John evidently wanted her to go to bed, and he was the uncle of her children.

"Thank you, Eleanor. I hope that as a catechumen I shall do honor to you. By the way, you will be interested in the part of Pontius Pilate's wife in my play. In fact I'm hoping that you will—ah—interpret it ultimately."

"Did you ever think of writing a play about Polonius's wife?" James growled on his way upstairs. "Goodnight."

When the grown-ups were safely in their rooms, John could not understand why the children were allowed to linger in the passage, gossiping and bragging; they would never go to sleep at this rate.

"I've got two cocoons of a Crimson-underwing," Harold was saying.

"Poof!" Viola scoffed. "What are they. Bertram touched the nose of a kangaroo last time we went to the Zoo."

"Yes, and I prodded a crocodile with V's umbrella," added Bertram, acknowledging her testimonial by awarding his sister a kind of share in the exploit.

"Well, I was bitten by a squirrel once," related Harold in an attempt to keep his end up. "And that was in its nest, not in a cage."

"A squirrel!" Viola sneered. "Why, the tallest giraffe licked Bertram's fingers with his tongue, and they stayed wet for hours afterwards."

"Well, so could I, if I went to the Zoo," Harold maintained with a sob at the back of his throat.

"No, you couldn't," Bertram contradicted. "Because your fingers are too smelly."

"Much too smelly!" Viola corroborated.

Various mothers emerged at this point and put a stop to the contest; the hallowed and gracious silence of Christmas night descended upon Ambles, and John went on tiptoe up to his bedroom.

"The beard, I suppose, is the most important item," he said to himself, when he had unpacked his costume.

It was a noble beard, and when John had fixed it to his cheeks with a profusion of spirit-gum, he made up his mind that it became him so well that he would grow one of his own, which whitening with the flight of time would in another thirty years make him look what he hoped to be— the doyen of romantic playwrights. The scarlet robe of Santa Claus with its trimming of bells, icicles, and holly and its ruching of snow had been made in a single piece without buttons, so that when John put it over his head the beard caught in the folds and part of it was thinned out by an icicle. In trying to disentangle himself John managed to get one sleeve stuck to his cheek much more firmly than the beard had ever been. Nor were his struggles to free himself made easier by the bells, which tinkled with every movement and made him afraid that somebody would knock at the door soon and ask if he had rung. Finally he got the robe in place, plucked several bits of sleeve from his cheek, renovated the beard, gathered together the apples, oranges, sweets, and small toys he had collected for the stockings, looked at his watch, decided that it was at least an hour too early to begin, and lay down upon his bed, where notwithstanding the ticking of his beard he fell asleep. When he woke, it was after one o'clock; the house was absolutely still. He walked cautiously to the little room occupied by Frida, turned the handle, and felt his way breathlessly along the bed to where the stocking should be hung. Unfortunately, the bed had somehow got twisted round or else his beard had destroyed his sense of direction, for while he was groping for the stocking he dropped an orange on Frida's face, who woke with a loud scream.

"Hush, my little dear," John growled in what he supposed to be the correct depth for the character. "It's only Santa Claus."

"Go away, go away," shrieked the horrified child.

John tried to strike a match to reassure her, and at the cost of a shower of apples on the floor, which sounded like bombs in the tense darkness, he managed to illuminate his appearance for an instant. The effect on Frida was appalling; she screamed a thousand times louder than before and fled from the room. John ran after her to stop her before she woke up everybody else and spoilt his fantasy; but he was hampered by the costume and Frida gained the sanctuary of her parents' bedroom.

"I only hope the little idiot will frighten them more than I frightened her," muttered John, hurrying as fast as he could back to his own room.

Suddenly from the hall below he heard a sound of sleigh-bells that put to shame the miserable little tinkle that attended his own progress; above the bells rose peals of hearty laughter, and above the laughter Hugh's voice could be heard shouting:

"Wake up! Wake up! Good people all! Here's Santa Claus! Santa Claus! Wake up!"

Just as John reached his own room, Hugh appeared at the head of the stairs brandishing a lighted torch, while close behind him dragging Harold's toboggan loaded with toys was a really superb Santa Claus.

John locked his door and undressed himself savagely, tearing off his beard in handfuls and flinging all the properties into a corner.

"Anyway, whoever it is," he said, "he'll get the credit of driving Frida mad. That's one thing. But who is it? I suppose it's Laurence showing us how well he can act."

But it was Aubrey Fenton whom Hugh had invited down to Ambles for Christmas and smuggled into the house like this to sweeten the unpleasant surprise. What annoyed John most was that he himself had never thought of using the toboggan; but the new Santa Claus was an undoubted success with the children, and Frida's sanity was soon restored by chocolates. The mystery of the apples and oranges strewn about her bedroom remained a mystery, though Hilda tried to hint that her niece had abstracted them from the sideboard.

John was able to obtain as much sympathy as he wanted from the rest of the family over Hugh's importation of his friend. In fact they were so eager to express their disapproval of such calm self-assurance, not to mention the objectionable way in which he had woken everybody up in the middle of the night, that John's own indignation gradually melted away in the heat of their malice. As for Grandmama, she shut herself up in her bedroom on Christmas morning and threatened not to appear all day, so deep was her hatred of that young Fenton who was the author of all Hugh's little weaknesses—not even when she could shift the blame could she bring herself to call her son's vices and crimes by any stronger name. Aubrey, who lacked Hugh's serene insolence, wanted to go back to London and was so much abashed in his host's presence and so appreciative of what he had done in the affair of the check that John's compassion was aroused and he made the intruder welcome. His hospitality was rewarded, because it turned out that Aubrey's lifelong passion for mechanical toys saved the situation for many of John's purchases, nearly all of which he managed to set in motion; nor could it be laid to his account that one of the drawing-room fireworks behaved like an out-of-door firework, because while Aubrey was lighting it at the right end Harold was lighting it simultaneously at the other.

On the whole, the presentation of the Christmas gifts passed off satisfactorily. The only definite display of jealousy occurred over the diver's equipment given to Harold, which was more than Bertram notwithstanding his own fireman's outfit could suppress.

"I'll swop with you, if you like," he began mildly enough.

But Harold clutched the diver's mask to his breast and shrank from the proposal.

"I think you'd rather be a fireman," Bertram persisted. "Anybody can be a diver, can't they, V?"

Viola left her doll in a state of semi-nudity and advanced to her brother's support.

"You'd look much nicer as a fireman, Harold," she said, coaxingly. "I wish I could be a fireman."

"Well, you can if you like," he answered, sullenly, looking round with a hunted expression for his mother, who unluckily for her son was in another part of the house arguing with Mrs. Worfolk about the sauce for the plum-pudding.

"But wouldn't you rather wear a pretty brass helmet?" Viola went on.

"No, I wouldn't," said Harold, desperately wrapping himself in the rubber tubes that was so temptingly conspicuous a portion of his equipment.

"Oh, you little idiot," Viola burst out, impatiently. "What's the good of your dressing up as a diver? In those goggles you always look like a diver."

"I don't, do I, Frida?" Harold implored.

Now Frida was happy with her dolls'-house; she had no reason to be loyal to Harold, who had always treated her shamefully; but the spirit of the squaw rose in her breast and she felt bound to defend the wigwam against outside criticism. Therefore she assured Harold that in ordinary life he did not look in the least like a diver.

"Well," Bertram announced, throwing aside the last pretense of respecting property, "V and I want that diver's dress, because we often act *Twenty Thousand Leagues Under the Sea.*"

"Well, I can act *Twenty Thousand Leagues Under the Sea* too."

"No you can't because you haven't read it."

"Yes, I have."

"What a bung!" exclaimed Bertram. "You've only read

A Journey to the Center of the Earth and *Round the World in Eighty Days*."

Then he remembered Frida's attitude. "Look here, if you take the fireman's uniform you can set fire to Frida's house."

Frida yelled her refusal.

"And put it out, you little idiot," Bertram added.

"And put it out," Viola echoed.

Frida rushed to her mother.

"Mother, mother, don't let them burn my dolls'-house! Mother, you won't, will you? Bertram wants to burn it."

"Naughty Bertram!" said Edith. "But he's only teasing you, darling."

"Good lummy, what a sneak," Bertram commented, bitterly, to his sister.

Viola eyed her cousin with the scorn of an Antigon.

"Beastly," she murmured. "Come on, Bertram, you don't want the diver's dress!"

"Rather not. And anyway it won't work."

"It will. It will," cried Harold, passionately. "I'm going to practice in a water-butt the first fine day we have."

It happened that John was unable to feel himself happily above these childish jealousies, because at that moment he was himself smarting with resentment at his mother's handing over to James all that she still retained of family heirlooms. His eldest brother already had the portraits, and now he was to have what was left of the silver, which would look utterly out of place in Hill Road. If John had been as young as Bertram, he would have spoken his mind pretty freely on the subject of giving James the silver and himself a checkered woolen kettle-holder. It was really too disproportionate, and he did mildly protest to the old lady that she might have left a few things at Ambles.

"But Jimmie is the eldest, and I expect him to take poor Hugh's part. The poor boy will want somebody when I'm gone, and Jimmie is the eldest."

"He may be the eldest, but I'm the one who has to look after Hugh—and very often James for that matter."

"Ah well, you're the lucky one, but Jimmie is the eldest and Hugh is the baby."

"But James hasn't any children."

"Nor have you, my dear boy."

"But I might have," said John.

If this sort of thing went on much longer, he would, too—dozens of children.

"Bertram," John called out. "Come here, my boy, and listen to me. When I go back to London, you shall have a diving-suit too if I can find another."

Eleanor tossed her head back like a victorious gamecock; she would have crowed, if she could.

"Dinner is ready," announced Hilda fresh from a triumph over Mrs. Worfolk about the sauce and happily ignorant of the dreadful relegation of her son. After an unusually large meal even for Christmas the company lay about the drawing-room like exhausted Roman debauchees, while the pink and green paper caps out of the crackers one by one fluttered from their brows to the carpet. Snores and the occasional violent whizz of an overwound toy were all that broke the stillness. At tea-time everybody woke up, and Bertram was allowed to put on his fireman's uniform in order to extinguish a bonfire that Huggins had hoped would burn slowly over the holidays. After a comparatively light supper games were played; drawing-room fireworks were let off; Laurence blacked his nose in the magic lantern; and George walking ponderously across the room to fetch himself a cigar was struck on the ear by a projectile from the vacuum pistol, the red mark of which was visible for some time even on his florid countenance. Then, when the children became too quarrelsome to be any longer tolerated out of bed, a bowl of punch was brought in and Auld Lang Syne was sung. After which everybody agreed that it had been a very merry Christmas, and Grandmama was led weeping up to bed.

The next morning about midday John announced that he was driving to Wrottesford for the purpose of meeting Miss Hamilton.

"For though it is holiday time, I must do a certain amount of work," he explained.

"Miss Hamilton?" said Grandmama. "And who may Miss Hamilton be?"

Hilda, Edith, Eleanor, and Beatrice all looked very solemn and mysterious; James chuckled; Hugh brightened visibly.

"Well, I suppose we mustn't mind a stranger's coming to spoil our happy party," Hilda sighed.

"Ah, this will be your new secretary of whom rumor has already spoken," said Laurence. "Possibly she will give me some advice on the subject of the typing of manuscripts."

"Miss Hamilton will be very busy while she is staying here," said John, curtly.

Everybody looked at everybody else, and there was an awkward pause, which was relieved by Harold's saying that he would show her where he thought a goldfinch would make a nest in spring.

"Dear little man," murmured his mother with a sigh for his childish confidence.

"Shall *I* drive in to meet her?" Hugh suggested.

"No, thank you," said John, quickly.

"That's right, Johnnie," James guffawed. "You stick to the reins yourself."

CHAPTER XII

JOHN did not consider himself a first-class whip: if he had been offered the choice between swimming to meet his love like Leander, climbing into her father's orchard like Romeo, and driving to meet her with a dog-cart, he would certainly, had the engagement shown signs of being a long one, have chosen any mode of trysting except the last. This morning, however, he was not as usual oppressed by a sense of imperfect sympathy between himself and the mare; he did not think she was going to have hysterics when she blew her nose, nor fancy that she was on the verge of bolting when she tossed her chestnut mane; the absence of William the groom seemed a matter for congratulation rather than for regret; he felt as reckless as Phaeton, as urgent as Jehu, and the mare knew it. Generally, when her master held the reins, she would try to walk up steep banks or emulate in her capricious greed the lofty browsings of the giraffe; this morning at a steady swinging trot she kept to the middle of the road, passed two motor-cars without trying to box the landscape, and did not even shy at the new hat of the vicar's wife.

Later on, however, when John was safe in the station-yard and saw the familiar way in which Miss Hamilton patted the mare he decided not to take any risk on the return journey and in spite of his brother's parting gibe to hand over the reins to his secretary; nor was the symbolism of the action distasteful. How charming she looked in that mauve frieze! How well the color was harmonizing with the purple hedgerows! How naturally she seemed to haunt the woodland scene!

"Oh, this exquisite country," she sighed. "Fancy staying in London when you can write here!"

"It does seem absurd," the lucky author agreed. "But the house is very full at present. We shall be rather exposed to interruptions until the party breaks up."

He gave her an account of the Christmas festival, to which she seemed able to listen comfortably and appreciatively in spite of the fact that she was driving This impressed John very much.

"I hope your mother wasn't angry at your leaving town," he said, tentatively. "I thought of telegraphing an invitation to her; but there really isn't room for another person."

"I'm afraid I can't say that she was gracious about my desertion of her. Indeed, she's beginning to put pressure on me to give up my post. Quite indirectly, of course, but one feels the effect just the same. Who knows? I may succumb."

John nearly fell out of the dog-cart.

"Give up your post?" he gasped. "But, my dear Miss Hamilton, the dog-roses won't be in bloom for some months."

"What have dog-roses got to do with my post?"

He laughed a little foolishly.

"I mean the play won't be finished for some months. Did I say dog-roses? I must have been thinking of the dog-cart. You drive with such admirable unconcern. Still, you ought to see these hedgerows in summer. Now the time I like for a walk is about eight o'clock on a June evening. The honeysuckle smells so delicious about eight o'clock. There's no doubt it is ridiculous to live in London. I hope you made it quite clear to your mother you had no intention of leaving me?"

"Ida Merritt did most of the arguing."

"Did she? What a very intelligent girl she is, by the way. I confess I took a great fancy to her."

"You told mother once that she frightened you."

"Ah, but I'm always frightened by people when I meet them first. Though curiously enough I was never frightened of you. Some people have told me that *I* am frightening at first. You didn't find that did you?"

"No, I certainly did not. And I can't imagine anybody else's doing so either."

Although John rather plumed himself upon the alarm he was credited with inspiring at first sight, he did not argue the point, because he really never had had the least desire to frighten his secretary.

"And your relations don't seem to find you very frightening," she murmured. "Good gracious, what an assemblage!"

The dog-cart had just drawn clear of the beechwood, and the whole of the Ambles party could be seen vigilantly grouped by the gate to receive them, which John thought was a lapse of taste on the part of his guests. Nor was he mollified by the way in which after the introductions were made Hugh took it upon himself to conduct Miss Hamilton indoors, while he was left shouting for William the groom. If it was anybody's business except his own to escort her into the house, it was Hilda's.

"What a very extraordinary thing," said John, fretfully, "that the *only* person who's wanted is not here. Where is that confounded boy?"

"I'm here," cried Bertram, responding to the epithet instinctively.

"Not you. Not you. I wanted William to take the mare.'

When lunch was over John found that notwithstanding his secretary's arrival he was less eager to begin work again upon his play than he had supposed.

"I think I must be feeling rather worn out by Christmas," he told her. "I wonder if a walk wouldn't do you good after the journey."

"Now that's a capital notion," exclaimed Hugh, who was standing close by and overheard the suggestion. "We might tramp up to the top of Shalstead Down."

"Oh yes," Harold chimed in. "I've never been there yet. Mother said it was too far for me; but it isn't, is it, Uncle John?"

"Your mother was right. It's at least three miles too far," said John, firmly. "Oh, by the way, Hugh, I've been thinking over your scheme for that summerhouse or whatever you call it, and I'm not sure that I don't rather like the idea after all. You might put it in hand this afternoon. You'd better keep Laurence with you. I want him to have it in the way he likes it, although of course I shall undertake the expense. Where's Bertram? Ah, there you are. Bertram, why don't you and Viola take Harold down to the river and practice diving? I dare say Mr. Fenton will superintend the necessary supply of air and reduce the chances of a fatal accident."

"But the water's much too cold," Hilda protested in dismay.

"Oh well, there's always something to amuse one by a river without actually going into the water," John said. "You like rivers, don't you, Fenton? I'm afraid we can't offer you a very large one, but it wiggles most picturesquely."

Aubrey Fenton, who was still feeling twinges of embarrassment on account of his uninvited stay at Ambles, was prepared to like anything his host put forward for his appreciation, and he spoke with as much enthusiasm of a promenade along the banks of the small Hampshire stream as if he were going to view the Ganges for the first time. John, having disposed of him, looked around for other possible candidates for a walk.

"You look like hard work, James," he said, approvingly.

"I've a bundle of trash here for review," the critic growled.

"I'm sorry. I was going to propose a stroll up Shalstead Down. Never mind. You'll have to walk into your victims instead." And, by gad, he would walk into them too, John thought, after that dinner yesterday.

Beatrice and Eleanor were not about; old Mrs. Touchwood was unlikely at her age to venture up the third highest elevation in Hampshire; Hilda was occupied with household duties; Edith had a headache. Only George now remained unoccupied, and John was sure he might safely risk an invitation to him; he looked incapable of walking two yards.

"I suppose you wouldn't care for a constitutional, George?" he inquired, heartily.

"A constitutional?" George repeated, gaping like a chub at a large cherry. "No, no, no, no. I always knit after lunch. Besides I never walk in the country. It ruins one's boots."

George always used to polish his own boots with as much passionate care as he would have devoted to the coloring of a meerschaum pipe.

"Well, if nobody wants to climb Shalstead Down," said John beaming happily, "what do you say, Miss Hamilton?"

A few minutes later they had crossed the twenty-acre field and were among the chalk-flecked billows of the rising downs.

"You're a terrible fraud," she laughed. "You've always led me to believe that you were completely at the mercy of your relations. Instead of which, you order them about and arrange their afternoon and really bully them into doing all sorts of things they never had any intention of doing, or any wish to do, what's more."

"Yes, I seemed to be rather successful with my strategy to-day," John admitted. "But they were stupefied by their Christmas dinner. None of them was really anxious for a walk, and I didn't want to drag them out unwillingly."

"Ah, it's all very well to explain it away like that, but don't ever ask me to sympathize with you again. I believe you're a replica of my poor mother. Her tyranny is deeply rooted in consideration for others. Why do you suppose she is always trying to make me give up working for you? For her sake? Oh, dear no! For mine."

"But *you* don't forge my name and expect her to pay me back. *You* don't arrive suddenly and deposit children upon her doorstep."

"I dare say I don't, but for my mother Ida Merritt represents all the excesses of your relations combined in one person. I'm convinced that if you and she were to compare notes you would find that you were both suffering from acute ingratitude and thoroughly enjoying it. But come, come, this is not a serious conversation. What about the fourth act?"

"The fourth act of what?" he asked, vaguely.

"The fourth act of Joan of Arc."

"Oh, Joan of Arc. I think I must give her a rest. I don't seem at all in the mood for writing at present. The truth is that I find Joan rather lacking in humanity and I'm beginning to think I made a mistake in choosing such an abnormal creature for the central figure of a play."

"Then what have I come down to Hampshire for?" she demanded.

"Well, it's very jolly down here, isn't it?" John retorted in an offended voice. "And anyway you can't expect me to burst into blank verse the moment you arrive, like a canary that's been uncovered by the housemaid. It would be an affectation to pretend I feel poetical this afternoon. I feel like a jolly good tramp before tea. I can't stand writers who always want to be literary. I have the temperament of a country squire, and if I had more money and fewer relations I should hardly write at all."

"Which would be a great pity," said his secretary.

"Would it?" John replied in the voice of one who has found an unexpected grievance and is determined to make the most of it. "I doubt if it would. What is my work, after all? I don't deceive myself. There was more in my six novels than in anything I've written since. I'm a failure to myself. In the eyes of the public I may be a success, but in the depths of my own heart—" he finished the sentence in a long sigh, all the longer because he was a little out of breath with climbing.

"But you were so cheerful a few minutes ago. I'm sure that country squires are not the prey to such swift changes of mood. I think you must be a poet really."

"A poet!" he exclaimed, bitterly, with what he fancied was the kind of laugh that is called hollow. "Do I look like a poet?"

"If you're going to talk in that childish way I sha'n't say any more," she warned him, severely. "Oh, there goes a hare!"

"Two hares," said John, trying to create an impression that in spite of the weight of his despondency he would for her sake affect a light-hearted interest in the common incidents of a country walk.

"And look at the peewits," she said. "What a fuss they make about nothing, don't they?"

"I suppose you are comparing me to a peewit now?" John reproachfully suggested.

"Well, a moment ago you compared yourself to an uncovered canary; so if I've exceeded the bounds of free speech marked out for a secretary, you must forgive me."

"My dear Miss Hamilton," he assured her, "I beg you to believe that you are at liberty to compare me to anything you like."

Having surrendered his personality for the exercise of her wit John felt more cheerful. The rest of the walk seemed to offer with its wide prospects of country asleep in the winter sunlight a wider prospect of life itself; even Joan of Arc became once again a human figure.

It was to be feared that John's manipulation of his guests after lunch might have had the effect of uniting them against the new favorite; and so it had. When he and Miss Hamilton got back to the house for tea the family was obviously upon the defensive, so obviously indeed that it gave the impression of a sculptor's group in which each figure was contributing his posture to the whole. There was not as yet the least hint of attack, but John would almost have preferred an offensive action to this martyred withdrawal from the world in which it was suggested that he and Miss Hamilton were living by themselves. It happened that a neighbor, a colorless man with a disobedient and bushy dog, called upon the Touchwoods that afternoon, and John could not help being aware that to the eyes of his relations he and his secretary appeared equally intrusive and disturbing; the manner in which Hilda offered Miss Hamilton tea scarcely differed from the manner in which she propitiated the dog with a bun; and it would have been rash to assert that she was more afraid of the dog's biting Harold than of the secretary's doing so.

"Don't worry Miss Hamilton, darling. She's tired after her long walk. Besides, she isn't used to little boys. And don't make Mr. Wenlow's dog eat sugar if it doesn't want to."

Eleanor would ordinarily have urged Bertram to prove that he could achieve what was denied to his cousin. Yet now in the face of a common enemy she made overtures to Hilda by simultaneously calling off her children from the intruders.

"If I'd known that animals were so welcomed down here," James grumbled, "I should have brought Beyle with us."

It was not a polite remark; but the disobedient dog in an effusion of cordiality had just licked the back of James' neck, and he was not nearly so rude as he would have been about a human being who had surprised him, speaking figuratively, in the same way.

"Lie down, Rover," whispered the colorless neighbor with so rich a blush that until it subsided the epithet ceased to be appropriate.

Rover unexpectedly paid attention to the command, but chose Grandmama's lap for his resting place, which made Viola laugh so ecstatically that Frida felt bound to imitate her, with the result that a geyser of tea spurted from her mouth and descended upon her father's leg. Laurence rose and led his daughter from the room, saying:

"Little girls who choke in drawing-rooms must learn to choke outside."

"I'm afraid she has adenoids, poor child," said Eleanor, kindly.

"I know what that word means," Harold bragged with gloating knowledge.

"Shut up!" cried Bertram. "You know everything, glass-eyes. But you don't know there are two worms in your tea-cup."

"There aren't," Harold contradicted.

"All right, drink it up and see. I put them there myself."

"Eleanor!" expostulated the horrified mother. "*Do* you allow Bertram to behave like this?"

She hurriedly poured away the contents of Harold's cup, which proved that the worms were only an invention of his cousin. Yet the joke was successful in its way, because there was no more tea, and therefore Harold had to go without a third cup. Edith, whose agitation had been intense while her husband was brooding in the passage over Frida's chokes, could stay still no longer, but went out to assist with tugs and taps of consolation. The colorless visitor departed with his disobedient dog, and soon a thin pipe was heard in vain whistles upon the twilight like the lisp of reeds along the dreary margin of a December stream.

John welcomed this recrudescence of maternal competition, which seemed likely to imperil the alliance, and he was grateful to Bertram and Viola for their provocation of it. But he had scarcely congratulated himself, when Hugh came in and at once laid himself out to be agreeable to Miss Hamilton.

"You've put the summerhouse in hand?" John asked, fussily, in order to make it perfectly clear to his brother that he was not the owner of Ambles.

Hugh shook his head.

"My dear man, it's Boxing Day. Besides, I know you only wanted to get rid of me this afternoon. By the way, Aubrey's going back to town to-night. Can he have the dog-cart?"

John looked round at the unbidden guest with a protest on his lips; he had planned to keep Aubrey as a diversion for Hugh, and had taken quite a fancy to him. Aubrey however, had to be at the office next day, and John was distressed to lose the cheerful young man's company, although it had been embarrassing when Grandmama had shuddered every time he opened his mouth. Another disadvantage of his departure was the direction of the old lady's imagination toward an imminent marriage between Hugh and Miss Hamilton, which was extremely galling to John, especially as the rest of the family was united in suggesting a similar conjunction between her and himself.

"I don't want to say a word against her, Johnnie," Grandmama began to mutter one evening about a week later when every game of patience had failed in turn through congestion of the hearts. "I'm not going to say she isn't a lady, and perhaps she doesn't mean to make eyes at Hughie."

John would have liked to tell his mother that she was on the verge of senile decay; but the dim old fetish of parental respect blinked at him from the jungle of the past, and in a vain search for a way of stopping her without being rude he let her ramble on.

"Of course, she has very nice eyes, and I can quite understand Hughie's taking an interest in her. I don't grudge the dear boy his youth. We all get old in time, and its natural that with us old fogies round him he *should* be a little interested in Miss Hamilton. All the same, it wouldn't be a prudent match. I dare say she thinks I shall have something to leave Hugh, but I told her only yesterday that I should leave little or nothing."

"My dear Mama, I can assure you that my secretary—my secretary," John repeated with as much pomposity as might impress the old lady, "is not at all dazzled by the glamour of your wealth or James' wealth or George's wealth or anybody's wealth for that matter."

He might have said that the donkey's ears were the only recognizable feature of Midas in the Touchwood family had there been the least chance of his mother's understanding the classical allusion.

"I don't mean to hint that she's *only* after Hugh's money. I've no doubt at all that she's excessively in love with him."

"Really?" John exclaimed with such a scornfully ironical intonation that his mother asked anxiously if he had a sore throat.

"You might take a little honey and borax, my dear boy," she advised, and immediately continued her estimate of the emotional situation. "Yes, as I say, excessively in love! But there can't be many young women who resist Hugh. Why, even as a boy he had his little love affairs. Dear me, how poor papa used to laugh about them. 'He's going to break a lot of hearts,' poor papa used to say."

"I don't know about hearts," John commented, gruffly. "But he's broken everything else, including himself. However, I can assure you, Mama, that Miss Hamilton's heart is not made of pie-crust, and that she is more than capable of looking after herself."

"Then you agree with me that she has a selfish disposition. I *am* glad you agree with me. I didn't trust her from the beginning; but I thought you seemed so wrapped up in her cleverness—though when I was young women didn't think it necessary to be clever—that you were quite blind to her selfishness. But I *am* glad you agree with me. There's nobody who has more sympathy for true love than I have. But though I always said that love makes the world go round, I've never been partial to vulgar flirtations. Indeed, if it had to be, I'd rather they got engaged properly, even if it did mean a long engagement—but leading poor Hughie on like this—well, I must speak plainly, Johnnie, for, after all, I am your mother, though I know it's the fashion now to think that children know more than their parents, and, in my opinion, you ought to put your foot down. There! I've said what I've been wanting to say for a week, and if you jump down my throat, well, then you must, and that's all there is to it."

Now, although John thought his mother fondly stupid and was perfectly convinced when he asked himself the question that Miss Hamilton was as remote from admiring Hugh as he was himself, he was nevertheless unable to resist observing Hugh henceforth with a little of the jealousy that most men of forty-two feel for juniors of twenty-seven. He was not prepared to acknowledge that his opinion of Miss Hamilton was colored by any personal emotion beyond the unqualified respect he gave to her practical qualities, and he was sure that the only reason for anxiety about possible developments between her and Hugh was the loss to himself of her valuable services.

"I've reached an age," he told his reflection, whose crow's-feet were seeming more conspicuous than usual in the clear wintry weather, "when a man becomes selfish in small matters. Let me be frank with myself. Let me admit that I do dislike the idea of an entanglement with Hugh, because I *have* found in Miss Hamilton a perfect secretary whom I should be extremely sorry to lose. Is that surprising? No, it is quite natural. Curious! I noticed to-day that Hugh's hair is getting very thin on top. Mine, however, shows no sign of baldness, though fair men nearly always go bald before dark men. But I'm inclined to fancy that few observers would give me fifteen years more than Hugh."

If John had really been conscious of a rival in his youngest brother, he might have derived much encouragement from the attitude of all the other members of the family, none of whom seemed to think that Hugh had a look in. But, since he firmly declined to admit his secretary's potentiality for anything except efficient clerical work, he was only irritated by it.

"Are you going to marry Miss Hamilton?" Harold actually wanted to know one evening. He had recently been snubbed for asking the company what was the difference between gestation and digestion, and was determined to produce a conundrum that could not be evaded by telling him that he would not understand the answer. John's solution was to look at his watch and say it was time for him and Bertram to be in bed, hoping that Bertram would take it out of his cousin for calling attention to their existence. One of Bertram's first measures at Ambles had been to muffle, impede, disorganize and finally destroy the striking of the drawing-room clock. When this had been accomplished he could count every night on a few precious minutes snatched from the annihilation of bed during which he sat mute as a mummy in a kind of cataleptic ecstasy. The betrayer of this profound peace sullenly gathered up the rubbish with which he was wont to litter the room every night, and John saw Bertram's eye flash like a Corsican sharpening the knife of revenge. But whatever was in store for Harold lacked savor when John heard from the group of mothers, aunts, sisters, and sisters-in-law the two words "Children know" dying away in a sibilance of affirmative sighs.

After that it was small consolation to hear a scuffle outside in the hall followed by the crash of Harold's dispersed collections and a wail of protest. For the sake of a childish quarrel Hilda and Eleanor were not going to break up the alliance to which they were now definitely committed.

"It's so nice for poor Harold to have Bertram to play with him," volunteered one mother.

"Yes, and it's nice for Bertram too, because Harold's such a little worker," the other agreed.

Even George's opaque eyes glimmered with an illusion of life when he heard his wife praise her nephew; she had not surprised him so completely since on a wet afternoon, thirteen years ago, she accepted his hand. It was even obvious to Edith that she must begin to think about taking sides; and, having exhausted her intelligence by this discovery, she had not enough wit left to see that now was her opportunity to trade upon John's sentimental affection for herself, but proceeded to sacrifice her own daughter to the success of the hostile alliance.

"I think perhaps it's good for Frida to be teased sometimes," she ventured.

As for Beatrice, she was not going to draw attention to her childlessness by giving one more woman the chance of feeling superior to herself, and her thwarted maternity was placed at the disposal of the three mothers. Indeed it was she who led the first foray, in which she was herself severely wounded, as will be seen.

Among the unnecessary vexations and unsatisfactory pleasures which the human side of John inflicted upon the well-known dramatist, John Touchwood, was the collection of press-cuttings about himself and his work; one of Miss Hamilton's least congenial tasks was to preserve in a scrap-book these tributes to egoism.

"You don't really want me to stick in this paragraph from *High Life?*" she would protest.

"Which one is that?"

"Why, this ridiculous announcement that you've decided to live on the upper slopes of the Andes for the next few months in order to gather material for a tragedy about the Incas."

"Oh, I don't know. It's rather amusing, I think," John would insist, apologetically. Then, rather lamely, he would add, "You see, I subscribe."

Miss Hamilton, with a sigh, would dip her brush in the paste.

"I can understand your keeping the notices of your productions, which I suppose have a certain value, but this sort of childish gossip . . ."

"Gossip keeps my name before the public."

Then he would fancy that he caught a faint mumur about "lack of dignity," and once even he thought she whispered something about "lack of humor."

Therefore, in view of the importance he seemed to attach to the most irrelevant paragraph, Miss Hamilton could not be blamed for drawing his attention to a long article in one of those critical quarterlies or monthlies that are read in club smoking-rooms in the same spirit of desperation in which at railway stations belated travelers read time-tables. This article was entitled *What Is Wrong With Our Drama?* and was signed with some obscurely allusive pseudonym.

"I suppose I am involved in the general condemnation?" said John, with an attempt at a debonair indifference.

Had he been alone he might have refrained from a descent into particulars, but having laid so much stress upon the salvage of worthless flotsam, he could not in Miss Hamilton's presence ignore this large wreck.

"Let us pause now to contemplate the roundest and the rosiest of our romantic cherubs. Ha-ha! I suppose the fellow thinks that will irritate me. As a matter of fact, I think it's rather funny, don't you? Rather clever, I mean. Eh? *But, after all, should we take Mr. Touchwood seriously? He is only an exuberant schoolboy prancing about with a pudding-dish on his head and shouting 'Let's pretend I'm a Knight-at-Arms' to a large and susceptible public. Let us say to Mr. Touchwood in the words of an earlier romantic who was the fount and origin of all this Gothic stucco:*

> '*O what can ail thee, Knight-at-Arms,*
> *So staggered by the critics' tone?*
> *The pit and gallery are full,*
> *And the play has gone.*'

"I don't mind what he says about *me*," John assured his secretary. "But I do resent his parodying Keats. Yes, I do strongly resent that. I wonder who wrote it. I call it rather personal for anonymous criticism."

"Shall I stick it in the book?"

"Certainly," the wounded lion uttered with a roar of disdain. At least that was the way John fancied he said "certainly."

"Do you really want to know who wrote this article?" she asked, seriously, a minute or two later.

"It wasn't James?" the victim exclaimed in a flash of comprehension.

"Well, all I can tell you is that two or three days ago your brother received a copy of the review and a letter from the editorial offices. I was sorting out your letters and noticed the address on the outside. Afterwards at breakfast he opened it and took out a check."

"James would call me a rosy cherub," John muttered. "Moreover, I did tell him about Bertram and the pudding-dish when he was playing at Perseus. And—no, James doesn't admire Keats."

"Poor man," said Miss Hamilton, charitably.

"Yes, I suppose one ought to be sorry for him rather than angry," John agreed, snatching at the implied consolation. "All the same, I think I ought to speak to him about his behavior. Of course, he's quite at liberty to despise my work, but I don't think he should take advantage of our relationship to introduce a note of personal—well, really, I don't think he has any right to call me a round and rosy cherub in print. After all, the public doesn't know what a damned failure James himself is. I shouldn't so mind if it really was a big pot calling the kettle black. I could retaliate then. But as it is I can do nothing."

"Except stick it in your press-cutting book," suggested Miss Hamilton, with a smile.

"And then my mother goes and presents him with all the silver! No, I will not overlook this lapse of taste; I shall speak to him about it this morning. But suppose he asks me how I found out?"

"You must tell him."

"You don't mind?"

"I'm your secretary, aren't I?"

"By Jove, Miss Hamilton, you know, you really are . . ."

John stopped. He wanted to tell her what a balm her generosity was to his wound; but he felt that she would prefer him to be practical.

It was like the critic to welcome with composure the accusation of what John called his duplicity, or rather of what he called duplicity in the privacy of his own thoughts: to James he began by referring to it as exaggerated frankness.

"I said nothing more than I've said a hundred times to your face," his brother pointed out.

"That may be, but you didn't borrow money from me on

the strength of what you said. You told me you had an article on Alfred de Vigny appearing shortly. You didn't tell me that you were raising the money as a post obit on my reputation."

"My dear Johnnie, if you're going to abuse me in metaphors, be just at any rate. Your reputation was a corpse before I dissected it."

"Very well, then," cried John, hotly, "have it your own way and admit that you're a body-snatcher."

"However," James continued, with a laugh that was for him almost apologetic, "though I hate excuses, I must point out that the money I borrowed from you was genuinely on account of Alfred de Vigny and that this was an unexpected windfall. And to show I bear you no ill will, which is more than can be said for most borrowers, here's the check I received. I'm bound to say you deserve it."

"I don't want the money."

"Yet in a way you earned it yourself," the critic chuckled. "But let me be quite clear. Is this a family quarrel? I don't want to quarrel with you personally. I hate your work. I think it false, pretentious and demoralizing. But I like you very much. Do, my dear fellow, let us contract my good taste in literature and bad taste in manners with your bad taste in literature and good taste in manners. Like two pugilists, let's shake hands and walk out of the ring arm-in-arm. Even if I hit you below the belt, you must blame your curves, Johnnie. You're so plump and rosy that . . ."

"That word is becoming an obsession with you. You seem to think it annoys me, but it doesn't annoy me at all."

"Then it is a family quarrel. Come, your young lady has opened her campaign well. I congratulate her. By the way, when am I to congratulate you?"

"This," said John, rising with grave dignity, "is going too far."

He left his brother, armed himself with a brassey, proceeded to the twenty-acre field, and made the longest drive of his experience. At lunch James announced that he and Beatrice must be getting back to town that afternoon, a resolution in which his host acquiesced without even a conventional murmur of protest. Perhaps it was this attitude of John's that stung Beatrice into a challenge, or perhaps she had been egged on by the mothers who, with their children's future to consider, were not anxious to declare open war upon the rich uncle. At any rate, in her commonest voice she said:

"It's plain that Jimmie and I are not wanted here any longer."

The mothers looked down at their plates with what they hoped was a strictly neutral expression. Yet it was impossible not to feel that they were triumphantly digging one another in the ribs with ghostly fingers, such an atmosphere of suppressed elation was discernible above the modest attention they paid to the food before them. Nobody made an effort to cover the awkwardness created by the remark, and John was faced with the alternative of contradicting it or acknowledging its truth; he was certainly not going to be allowed to ignore it in a burst of general conversation.

"I think that is rather a foolish remark, Beatrice," was his comment.

She shrugged her shoulders so emphatically that her stays creaked in the horrid silence that enveloped the table.

"Well, we can't all be as clever as Miss Hamilton, and most of us wouldn't like to be, what's more."

"The dog-cart will be round at three," John replied, coldly.

His sister-in-law, bursting into tears, rushed from the room. James guffawed and helped himself to potatoes. The various mothers reproved their children for breaches of table manners. George looked nervously at his wife as if she was on the point of following the example of Beatrice. Grandmama, who was daily receding further and further into the past, put on her spectacles and told John, reproachfully, that he ought not to tease little Beatrice. Hugh engaged Miss Hamilton in a conversation about Bernard Shaw.

John, forgetting he had already dipped twice in mustard the morsel of beef upon his fork, dipped it again, so that his eyes presently filled with tears, to which the observant Harold called everybody's attention.

"Don't make personal remarks, darling," his mother whispered.

"That's what Johnnie said to me this morning," James chuckled.

When the dog-cart drove off with James and Beatrice at three o'clock to catch the 3:45 train up to town, John retired to his study in full expectation that when the mare came back she would at once turn round for the purpose of driving Miss Hamilton to catch the 5:30 train up to town: no young woman in her position would forgive that vulgar scene at lunch. But when he reached his desk he found his secretary hard at work upon the collection of material for the play as if nothing had happened. In the presence of such well-bred indifference the recollection of Beatrice's behavior abashed him more than ever, and, feeling that any kind of even indirect apology from him would be distasteful to Miss Hamilton, he tried to concentrate upon the grouping of the trial scene with an equal show of indifference to the mean events of family life. He was so far successful that the afternoon passed away without any allusion to Beatrice, and when the gong sounded for tea his equanimity was in order again.

After tea, however, Eleanor managed to get hold of John for what she called a little chat about the future, but which he detected with the mind's nose as an unpleasant rehash of the morning's pasticcio. He always dreaded this sister-in-law when she opened with zoological endearments, and his spirits sank to hear her exclaim boisterously:

"Now, look here, you poor wounded old lion, I'm going to talk to you seriously about Beatrice."

"There's nothing more to be said," John assured her.

"Now don't be an old bear. You've already made one poor aunt cry; don't upset me too."

Anybody less likely to be prostrated by grief than Eleanor at that moment John could not have imagined. She seemed to him the incarnation of a sinister self-assurance.

"Rubbish," he snapped. "In any case, yours would only be stage tears, you old crocodile—if I may copy your manner of speech."

"Isn't he in a nasty, horrid, cross mood?" she demanded, with an affected glance at an imaginary audience. "No, but seriously, John! I do want to give you a little advice. I suppose it's tactless of me to talk about advising the great man, but don't bite my head off."

"In what capacity?" the great man asked. "You've forgotten to specify the precise carnivore that will perform the operation."

"Oh dear, aren't we sarcastic this afternoon?" she asked, opening wide her eyes. "However, you're not going to frighten me, because I'm determined to have it out with you, even if you order the dog-cart before dinner. Johnnie, is it fair to let a complete stranger make mischief among relations?"

John played the break in Eleanor's voice with beautiful ease.

"I will not have Miss Hamilton's name dragged into these sordid family squabbles," he asseverated.

"I'm not going to say a word against Miss Hamilton. I think she's a charming young woman—a little too charming perhaps for you, you susceptible old goose."

"For goodness sake," John begged, "stick to the jungle and leave the farmyard alone."

"Now you're not going to rag me out of what I'm going to say. You know that I'm a real Bohemian who doesn't pay attention to the stupid little conventionalities that, for instance, Hilda or Edith might consider. Therefore I'm sure you won't misunderstand me when I warn you about people talking. Of course, you and I are accustomed to the freedom of the profession, and as far as I'm concerned you might engage half a dozen handsome lady secretaries without my even noticing it. But the others don't understand. *They* think it's funny."

"Good heavens, what are you trying to suggest?" John demanded.

He could manage the break, but this full pitch made him slog wildly.

"*I'm* not trying to suggest anything. I'm simply telling you what other people may think. You see, after all, Hilda and Edith couldn't help noticing that you did allow Miss Hamilton to make mischief between you and your brother. I dare say James was in the wrong; but is it a part of a secretary's duties to manage her employer? And James *is* your brother. The natural deduction for conventional people like Hilda and Edith was that—now, don't be annoyed at what I'm going to say, but I always speak out—I'm famous for my frankness. Well, to put it frankly, they think that Miss Hamilton can twist you round her little finger. Then, of course, they ask themselves why, and for conventional people like Hilda and Edith there's only one explanation. Of course, I told them it was all nonsense and that you were as innocent as an old lamb. I dare say you don't mind people talking. That's your business, but I shouldn't have been a good pal if I hadn't warned you that people will talk, if they aren't talking already."

"You've got the mind of an usher," said John. "I can't say worse than that of anybody. Wasn't it you who suggested a French governess should be given the freedom of Church Row and who laughed at me for being an old beaver or some other prudish animal because I objected? If I can be trusted with a French governess, I can surely be trusted with a confidential secretary. Besides, we're surrounded by an absolute *chevaux de frise* of chaperons, for I suppose that Hilda and Edith may fairly be considered efficient chaperons, even if you are still too youthfully Bohemian for the post."

Eleanor's age was the only vulnerable spot in her self-confidence, and John took advantage of it to bring her little chat to a bitter end.

"My dear Johnnie," she said, tartly, "I'm not talking about the present. I'm warning you about the future. However, you're evidently not in the mood to listen to anybody."

"No, I'm not," he assented, warmly. "I'm as deaf as an old adder."

The next day John, together with Mrs. Worfolk and Maud, left for Hampstead, and his secretary traveled with him up to town.

"Yes," his housekeeper was overheard observing to Elsa in the hall of 36 Church Row, "dog-cart is a good name for an unnatural conveyance, but give me a good old London cab for human beings. Turn again, Whittington, they say, and they're right. They may call London noisy if they like, but it's as quiet as a mouse when you put it alongside of all that baaring and mooing and cockadoodledoing in the country. Well, I mean to say, Elsa, I'm getting too old for the country. And the master's getting too old for the country, in my opinion. I'm in hopes he'll settle down now, and not go wearing himself out any more with the country. Believe me or not as you will, Elsa, when I tell you that the pore fellow had to play at ball like any little kid to keep himself amused."

"Fancy that, Mrs. Worfolk," Elsa murmured with a gentle intake of astonished breath.

"Yes, it used to make me feel all over melancholy to see him. All by himself in a great field. Pore fellow. He's lonely, that's what it is, however . . ."

At this point the conversation born upon whispers and tut-tut passed out of John's hearing toward the basement.

"I suppose my own servants will start gossiping next," he grumbled to himself. "Luckily I've learnt to despise gossip. Hullo, here's another bundle of press-cuttings.

"*It is rumored that John Touchwood's version of Joan of Arc which he is writing for that noble tragedienne, Miss Janet Bond, will exhibit the Maid of Orleans in a new and piquant light. The distinguished dramatist has just returned from France where he has been obtaining some startling scenic effects for what is confidently expected will be the playwright's most successful production. We are sorry to hear that Miss Bond has been suffering from a sharp attack of 'flu, but a visit to Dr. Brighton has—"*

These and many similar paragraphs were all pasted into the album by his secretary the next morning, and John was quite annoyed when she referred to them as worthless gossip.

"You don't know what gossip is," he said, thinking of Eleanor. "I ignore real gossip."

Miss Hamilton smiled to herself.

CHAPTER XIII

AFTER the Christmas party at Ambles John managed to secure a tranquillity that, however brief and deceptive he felt it was like to be, nevertheless encouraged him sufficiently to make considerable progress with the play while it lasted. Perhaps Eleanor's warning had sunk deeper than she might have supposed from the apparent result of that little chat with her brother-in-law about his future; at any rate, he was so firmly determined not to give the most evil mind the least opportunity for malicious exaggeration that in self-defense he devoted to Joan of Arc a more exclusive attention than he had hitherto devoted to any of his dramatic personages. Moreover, in his anxiety to prove how abominably unjust the insinuations of his family were, he imparted to his heroine some of his own temporary remoteness from the ordinary follies and failings of humanity.

"We are too much obsessed by sex nowadays," he announced at the club one afternoon, and was tempted to expatiate upon his romantic shibboleth to several worn out old gentlemen who had assented to this proposition. "After all," he argued, "life is not all sex. I've lately been enormously struck by that in the course of my work. Take Joan of Arc for instance. Do we find any sex obsession in her? None. But is she less psychologically interesting on that account? No. Sex is the particular bane of modern writers. Frankly, I cannot read a novel nowadays. I suppose I'm old-fashioned, but I'd rather be called old-fashioned than asked to appreciate one of these young modern writers. I suppose there's no man more willing than myself to march with the times, but I like the high roads of literature, not the muddy lanes . . ."

"The John Longs and John Lanes that have no turnings," a club wag put in.

"Look at Stevenson," the dramatist continued, without paying any attention to the stupid interruption. "When Stevenson wrote a love scene he used to blush."

"So would any one who had written love scenes as bad as his," sniggered a young man, who seemed oblivious of his very recent election to the club.

The old members looked at him severely, not because he had sneered at Stevenson, but because, without being spoken to, he had volunteered a remark in the club smoking-room at least five years too soon.

"I've got a young brother who thinks like you," said John, with friendly condescension.

"Yes, I know him," the young man casually replied.

John was taken aback; it struck him as monstrous that a friend of Hugh's should have secured election to *his* club. The sanctity of the retreat had been violated, and he could not understand what the world was coming to.

"How is Hugh?" the young man went on, without apparently being the least conscious of any difference between the two brothers. "Down at your place in Hampshire, isn't he? Lucky chap; though they tell me you haven't got many pheasants."

"I beg your pardon?"

"You don't preserve?"

"No, I do not preserve." John would have liked to add "except the decencies of intercourse between old and young in a club smoking-room"; but he refrained.

"Perhaps you're right," said the young man. "These are tough times for landed proprietors. Well, give my love to Hugh when you see him," he added, aud turning on his heel disappeared into the haze of a more remote portion of the smoking-room.

"Who is that youth?" John demanded.

The old members shook their heads helplessly, and one of the waiters was called up to be interrogated.

"Mr. Winnington-Carr, I believe, sir," he informed them.

"How long has he been a member?"

"About a week, I believe, sir."

John looked daggers of exclamation at the other members.

"We shall have perambulators waiting in the lobby before we know where we are," he said, bitterly.

Everybody agreed that these ill-considered elections were a scandal to a famous club, and John, relinquishing the obsession of sex as a topic, took up the obsession of youth, which he most convincingly proved to be the curse of modern life.

It was probably Mr. Winnington-Carr's election that brought home to John the necessity of occupying himself immediately with his brother's future; at this rate he should find Hugh himself a member of his club before he knew where he was.

"I'm worrying about my young brother," he told Miss Hamilton next day, and looked at her sharply to watch the effect of this remark.

"Why, has he been misbehaving himself again?"

"No, not exactly misbehaving; but a friend of his has just been elected to my club, and I don't think it's good for Hugh to be hanging about in idleness. I do wish I could find the address of that man Raikes from British Honduras."

"Where is it likely to be?"

"It was a visiting-card. It might be anywhere."

"If it was a visiting-card, the most likely place to find it is in one of your waistcoat-pockets."

John regarded his secretary with the admiration that such a practical suggestion justified, and rang the bell.

"Maud, please bring down all my waistcoats," he told his valeting parlor-maid, who presently appeared in the library bowed down by a heap of clothes as a laborer is bowed down by a truss of hay.

In the twenty-seventh waistcoat that was examined the card was found:

Mr. Sydney Ricketts.

14 Lyonesse Road,	Belize,
Balam, S.W.,	British Honduras.

"I thought his name was Raikes," John muttered, indignantly.

" Never mind. A rose by any other name . . ." Miss Hamilton began.

John might almost have been said to interrupt what she was going to say with an angry glare; but she only laughed merrily at his fierce expression.

"Oh, I beg your pardon—I'd forgotten your objection to roses."

Mr. Ricketts, who was fortunately still in London, accepted John's invitation to come and see him at Church Row on business. He was a lantern-jawed man with a tremendous capacity for cocktails, a sinewy neck, and a sentimental affection for his native suburb. At the same time, he would not hear a word against British Honduras.

"I reckon our regatta at Belize is the prettiest little regatta in the world."

"But the future of logwood and mahogany?" John insisted.

"Great," the visitor assured him. "Why don't *you* come out to us? You'd lose a lot of weight if you worked for a few months up the Zucara river. Here's a photograph of some of our boys loading logwood."

"They look very hot," said John, politely.

"They are very hot," said Mr. Ricketts. "You can't expect to grow logwood in Iceland."

"No, of course not. I understand that."

In the end it was decided that John should invest £2000 in the logwood and mahogany business and that sometime in February Hugh should be ready to sail with Mr. Ricketts to Central America.

"Of course he'll want to learn something about the conditions of the trade at first. Yes, I reckon your brother will stay in Belize at first," said the planter, scratching his throat so significantly that John made haste to fill up his glass, thinking to himself that, if the cocktails at the Belize Yacht Club were as good as Mr. Ricketts boasted, Hugh would be unlikely ever to see much more of mahogany than he saw of it at present cut and rounded and polished to the shape of a solid dining-room table. However, the more attractive Belize, the less attractive England.

"I think you told me this was your first visit home in fifteen years?" he asked.

"That's right. Fifteen years in B.H."

"B.H.?" repeated the new speculator, nervously.

"British Honduras."

"Oh, I beg your pardon. The initials associated themselves in my mind for the moment with another place. B.H. you call it. Very appropriate I should think. I suppose you found many changes in Balham on your return?"

"Wouldn't have known it again," said Mr. Ricketts. "For one thing they'd changed all the lamp-posts along our road. That's the kind of thing to teach a man he's growing old."

Perhaps Hugh wouldn't recognize Hampstead after fifteen years, John thought, gleefully; he might even pass his nearest relations in the street without a salute when like a Rip van Winkle of the tropics he returned to his native country after fifteen years.

"I suppose the usual outfit for hot climates will be necessary?"

Mr. Ricketts nodded; and John began to envisage himself equipping Hugh from the Army and Navy Stores.

"I always think there is something extraordinarily romantic about a tropical outfit," he ventured.

"It's extraordinarily expensive," said Mr. Ricketts. "But everything's going up. And mahogany's going up when I get back to B.H., or my name isn't Sydney Ricketts."

"There's nothing you particularly recommend?"

"No, they'll tell you everything you want at the Stores and a bit over, except—oh, yes, by the way, don't let him forget his shaker."

"Is that some special kind of porous overcoat?"

Mr. Ricketts laughed delightedly.

"Well, if that isn't the best thing I've heard since I was home. Porous overcoat! No, no, a shaker is for mixing drinks."

"Humph!" John grunted. "From what I know of my brother, he won't require any special instrument for doing that. Good-by, Mr. Ricketts; my solicitor will write to you about the business side. Good-by."

When John went back to his work he was humming.

"Satisfactory?" his secretary inquired.

"Extremely satisfactory. I think Hugh is very lucky. Ricketts assures me that in another fifteen years—that is about the time Hugh will be wanting to visit England again—there is no reason why he shouldn't be making at least £500 a year. Besides, he won't be lonely, because I shall send Harold out to British Honduras in another five years. It must be a fascinating place if you're fond of natural history, B.H.—as the denizens apparently call it among themselves," he added, pensively.

It could not be claimed that Hugh was enraptured by the prospect of leaving England in February, and John who was really looking forward to the job of getting together his outfit was disappointed by his brother's lack of enthusiasm. He simply could not understand anybody's failure to be thrilled by snake-proof blankets and fever-proof filters, by medicine-chests and pith helmets and double-fly tents and all the paraphernalia of adventure in foreign parts. Finally he delivered an ultimatum to Hugh, which was accepted albeit with ill grace, and hardening his heart against the crossed letters of protest that arrived daily from his mother and burying himself in an Army and Navy Stores' catalogue, he was able to intrench himself in the opinion that he was doing the best that could be done for the scapegrace. The worst of putting Hugh on his feet again was the resentment such a brotherly action aroused among his other relations. After the quarrel with James he had hardly expected to hear from him for a long time; but no sooner had the news about British Honduras gone the round of the family than his eldest brother wrote to ask him for a loan of £1000 to invest in a projected critical weekly of which he was to be the editor. James added that John could hardly grudge him as much as that for log-rolling at home when he was prepared to spend double that amount on Hugh to roll logs abroad.

"I can't say I feel inclined to help James after that article about my work," John observed to Miss Hamilton. "Besides, I hate critical weeklies."

It happened that the post next morning brought a large check from his agent for royalties on various dramas that in various theaters all over the world were playing to big business; confronted by that bright-hued token of prosperity he could not bring himself to sit down and pen a flat refusal to his brother's demand. Instead of doing that he merely delayed for a few hours the birth of a new critical weekly by making an appointment to talk the matter over, and it was only a fleeting pleasure that he obtained from adding a postscript begging James not to bring his dog with him when he called at Church Row.

"For if that wretched animal goes snorting round the room all the time we're talking," he assured his secretary, "I shall agree to anything in order to get rid of it. I shall find all my available capital invested in critical weeklies just to save the carpet from being eaten."

James seemed to have entirely forgotten that his brother had any reason to feel sore with him; he also seemed entirely unconscious of there being the least likelihood of his refusing to finance the new venture. John remembering how angry James had been when on a former occasion he had reminded him that Hugh's career was still before him, was careful to avoid the least suggestion of throwing cold water upon the scheme. Therefore in the circumstances James' unusual optimism, which lent his sallow cheeks some of the playwright's roses, was not surprising, and before the conversation had lasted many minutes John had half promised a thousand pounds. Having done this, he did try to retrieve the situation by advising James to invest it in railway-stock and argued strongly against the necessity of another journal.

"What are you going to call this further unnecessary burden upon our powers of assimilation?"

"*I* thought *The New Broom* would be a good title."

"Yes, I was positive you'd call it The New-Something-or-other. Why not The New Way to pay Old Scores? I'll back you to do that, even if you can't pay your old debts. However, listen to me. I'll lend the money to you personally. But I will not invest it in the paper. For security —or perhaps compensation would be a better word—you shall hand over to me the family portraits and the family silver."

"I'd rather it was a business proposition," James objected.

"My dear fellow, a new critical weekly can never be a business proposition. How many people read your books?"

"About a dozen," James calculated.

"Well, why should more people read your paper? No, you can have the money, but it must be regarded as a personal loan, and I must have the portraits and the silver."

"I don't see why you should have them."

"I don't see why you should start a new critical weekly."

John could not help enjoying the power that his brother's ambition had put in his hands and he insisted firmly upon the surrender of the heritage.

"All right, Jacob, I suppose I must sell my birthright for a mess of pottage."

"A printer's pie would describe it better," said John.

"Though why you want a few bad pictures and a dozen or so forks and spoons, I can't conceive."

"Why do you want them?" John countered.

"Because they're mine."

"And the money is mine."

James went away with a check for a thousand pounds in his pocket; but he went away less cheerful than he arrived. John, on the other hand, was much impressed by the manner in which he had dealt with his eldest brother; it was worth while losing a thousand pounds to have been able to demonstrate clearly to James once for all that his taste in literature was at the mercy of the romanticism he so utterly despised. And while he felt that he had displayed a nice dignity in forcing James to surrender the portraits and the silver, he was also pleasantly aware of an equally nice magnanimity in being willing to overlook that insulting article. But Miss Hamilton was at his elbow to correct the slightest tendency to be too well pleased with himself.

"After all I couldn't disappoint poor old James," he said, fishing for an encomium and dangling his own good heart as the bait. His secretary, however, ignored the tempting morsel and swam away into the deeps of romantic drama where his munificence seemed less showy somehow.

"You know best what you *want* to do," she said, curtly. "And now, have you decided upon this soliloquy for Joan in her dungeon?"

"What do you feel about it?"

She held forth upon the advantages of a quiet front scene before the trial, and the author took her advice. He wished that she were as willing to discant upon his treatment of James, but he consoled himself for her lack of interest by supposing that she was diffident about giving the least color to any suggestion that she might be influencing him to her own advantage.

Hugh came up to town in order to go more fully into the question of his future, and John regarding Miss Hamilton's attitude towards him tried to feel perfectly sure that she was going out of her way to be pleasant to Hugh solely with an idea of accentuating the strictly professional side of her association with himself. If this were not the case, he should be justified in thinking that she did really like Hugh very much, which would be an uncomfortable state of affairs. Still, explain it away as he might, John did feel a little uneasy, and once when he heard of a visit to the theater preceded by dinner he was upon the verge of pointing out to Hugh that until he was definitely established in mahogany and logwood he must be extremely careful about raising false hopes. He managed to refrain from approaching Hugh on the subject, because he knew that if he betrayed the least anxiety in that direction Hugh was capable of making it a matter of public jest. He decided instead to sound Miss Hamilton upon her views.

"You've never had any longing for the tropics?" he asked, as casually as he was able.

"Not particularly, though of course I should enjoy any fresh experience."

"I was noticing the other day that you seemed to dislike spiders; and, of course, the spiders in hot countries are terrible. I remember reading of some that snare birds, and I'm not sure that in parts of South America they don't even attack human beings. Many people of course do not mind them. For instance, my brother-in-law Daniel Curtis wrote a very moving account of a spider as large as a bat, with whom he fraternized on the banks of the Orinoco. It's quite a little classic in its way."

John noted with the warmest satisfaction that Miss Hamilton shuddered.

"Your poor brother," she murmured.

"Oh, he'll be all right," said John, hurriedly. "I'm equipping him with every kind of protection against insects. Only yesterday I discovered a most ingenious box which is guaranteed to keep one's tobacco from being devoured by cockroaches, and I thought Hugh looked very well in his pith helmet, didn't you?"

"I'm afraid I really didn't notice," Miss Hamilton replied, indifferently.

Soon after this conversation James' birthright was formally surrendered and John gave up contemplating himself upon a peak in Darien in order to contemplate himself as the head of an ancient and distinguished family. While the portraits were being hung in the library he discoursed upon the romance of lineage so volubly that he had a sudden dread of Miss Hamilton taking him for a snob, which he tried to counteract by putting into the mouth of Joan of Arc sentiments of the purest demophilism.

"I shall aim at getting all the material for the play complete by April 1st—my birthday, by the way. Yes, I shall be forty-three. And then I thought we might go into retreat and aim at finishing entirely by the end of June. That would enable Miss Bond to produce in September without hurrying the rehearsals. *Lucretia* will be produced over here in April. I think it would be rather jolly to finish off the play in France. Domrèmy, Bourges, Chinon, Orleans, Compiègne, Rouen—a delightful tour. You could have an aluminum typewriter . . ."

John's dreams of literature and life in France were interrupted by Mrs. Worfolk, who entered the room with a mystery upon her lips.

"There's the Reverend Armitage waiting to see you in the hall, sir. But he was looking so queer that I was in two minds if I ought to admit him or not. It was Elsa who happened to open the door. Well, I mean to say, Maud's upstairs doing her rooms, and Elsa was a bit frightened when she saw him, through her being engaged to a policeman and so her mind running on murders and such like. Of course as soon as I saw it was the Reverend Armitage I quieted her down. But he really does look most peculiar, if you'll pardon the obsivation on Mrs. Armitage's husband. I don't think he's actually barmy *yet;* but you know, he gives any one the idea he will be soon, and I thought you ought to be told before he started to rave up and down the house. He's got a funny look in his eye, the same as what a man once had who sat opposite me in a bus and five minutes afterwards jumped off on Hammersmith Bridge and threw himself into the river. Quite a sensation it created, I remember, and we all had to alight, so as the conductor could give what information he had to a policeman who'd only heard the splash."

Mrs. Worfolk had been too garrulous; before she had time to ascertain her master's views on the subject of admitting Laurence there was a tap at the door, and Laurence himself stalked into the room. Unquestionably, even to one who had not known him as a clergyman, he did present an odd appearance with his fur-lined cloak of voluminous black, his long hair, his bundle of manuscript and theatrical newspapers, and his tragic eye; the only article of attire that had survived his loss of faith was the clergyman's hat; but even that had lost its former meekness and now gave the effect of a farouche sombrero.

"Well met," he intoned, advancing solemnly into the room and gripping his brother-in-law's hand with dramatic effect. "I would converse with you, John."

"That's a blank verse line," said John. There really was not much else that he could have said to such an affected greeting.

"Probably, probably," Laurence muttered, shaking his head. "It's difficult for me to talk in prose nowadays. But I have news for you, John, good news. *Thomas* is finished."

"You needn't wait, Mrs. Worfolk," said John.

His housekeeper was standing by the door with a face wreathed in notes of interrogation and seemed unwilling to retire.

"You needn't wait, Mrs. Worfolk," he repeated, irritably.

"I thought you might have been wanting somebody fetched, sir."

John made an impatient gesture and Mrs. Worfolk vanished.

"You know Miss Hamilton, Laurence," said John, severely.

"Ah, Miss Hamilton! Forgive my abstraction. How d'ye do? But—ah—I was anxious to have a few words in private."

"Miss Hamilton is my confidential secretary."

"I bow to your domestic arrangements," said Laurence. "But—ah—my business is of an extremely private nature. It bears in fact directly upon my future."

John was determined to keep his secretary in the room.

He had a feeling that money was going to be asked for, and he hoped that her presence would encourage him to hold out against agreeing to lend it.

"If you have anything to say to me, Laurence, you must say it in front of my secretary. I cannot be continually shooing her from the room like a troublesome cat."

The ex-vicar looked awkward for a moment; but his natural conceit reasserted itself and flinging back his cloak he laid upon the table a manuscript.

"Fresh from Miss Quirk's typewriting office here is *Thomas*," he announced. "And now, my dear fellow, I require a little good advice." There was flowing into his voice the professional unction of the clergyman with a north transept to restore. "Who was it that first said 'Charity begins at home'? Yes, a little good advice about my play. In deference to the Lord Chamberlain while reserving to my conscience the right to execrate his despotism I have expunged from my scenes the *central* figures of the gospel story, and I venture to think that there is now no reason why *Thomas* should not be—ah—produced."

"I'm afraid I can't invite you to read it to me just at present, Laurence," said John, hurriedly. "No, not just at present, I'm afraid. When I'm working myself I'm always chary of being exposed to outside influences. *You* wouldn't like and *I* shouldn't like to find in *Joan of Arc* echoes of *Thomas*. Miss Hamilton, however, who is thoroughly conversant with my point of view, would perhaps . . ."

"I confess," Laurence interrupted, loftily, "that I do not set much store by its being read. No, no. You will acquit me of undue self-esteem, my dear fellow, if I say at once in all modesty that I am satisfied with my labors, though you may be a little alarmed when I confide in you my opinion that it is probably a classic. Still, such is my deliberate conviction. Moreover, I have already allowed our little party at Ambles to hear it. Yes, we spent a memorable evening before the manuscript was dispatched to Miss Quirk. Some of the scenes, indeed, proved almost too dramatic. Edith was quite exhausted by her emotion and scarcely slept all night. As for Hilda, I've never seen her so overcome by anything. She couldn't say anything when I finished. No, no, I sha'n't read it to you. In fact, to be—ah—blunt, I could scarcely endure the strain a second time. No, what I want you to do, my dear fellow, is to—ah—back it. The phrase is Hugh's. We have all been thrilled down at Ambles by rumors of your generosity, and I know you'll be glad of another medium for exercising it. Am I unduly proud of my work if I say that it seems to me a more worthy medium than British Honduras or weekly papers?"

John had been gazing at Miss Hamilton with a mute appeal to save him while his brother-in-law was talking; she, however, bending lower every moment to hide her mirth made no attempt to show him a way of escape and John had to rely upon his own efforts.

"Wouldn't it be better," he suggested, mildly, "to submit your play to a manager before we—before you try to put it on yourself? I have never invested any money in my own plays, and really I . . ."

"My dear John, far be it from me to appear to cast the least slur—to speak in the faintest way at all slightingly of your plays, but I do not quite see the point of the comparison. Your plays—excellent as they are, most excellent—are essentially commercial transactions. My play is not a commercial transaction."

"Then why should I be invited to lose my money over it?"

Laurence smiled compassionately.

"I thought you would be glad of the opportunity to show a disinterested appreciation of art. In years to come you will be proud to think that you were one of the first to give practical evidence of your belief in *Thomas.*"

"But perhaps I'm just as skeptical as your hero was. I may not believe in your play's immortality."

Laurence frowned.

"Come, my dear fellow, this is being petty. We are all counting on you. You wouldn't like to hear it said that out of jealousy you had tried to suppress a rival dramatist. But I must not let my indignation run away with me, and you must forgive my heat. I am overstrained. The magnitude of the subject has almost been too much for me. Besides, I should have explained at once that I intended to invest in *Thomas* all that is left of my own little capital. Yes, I am even ready to do that. Then I shall spend a year as an actor, after which I shall indulge my more worldly self by writing a few frankly commercial plays before I begin my next great tragedy entitled *Paul*."

John decided that his brother-in-law had gone mad; unable to think of any action more effective at such a crisis, he rang the bell. But when Maud came to inquire his need he could not devise anything to tell her except that Mr. Armitage was staying to lunch.

It was a most uncomfortable meal, because Miss Hamilton in order to keep herself from laughing aloud had to be preternaturally grave, and John himself was in a continuous state of nervous irritation at Laurence, who would let everything on his plate grow cold while he droned on without a pause about the simplicity of the best art. It was more than tantalizing to watch him gradually build up a mouthful upon his fork, still talking; slowly raise it to his lips, still talking; and wave the overloaded fork to and fro before him, still talking. But it was an agony to watch the carefully accumulated mouthful drop back bit by bit upon his plate, until at last very slowly and still talking he would insert one cold and tiny morsel into his patient mouth, so tiny a morsel that the mastication of it did not prevent him from still talking.

"I'm afraid you're not enjoying your lunch," his host said.

"Don't wait for me, my dear fellow; when I am interested in something else I cannot gobble my food. Though in any case," he added in a resigned voice, "I shall have indigestion. One cannot write plays like *Thomas* without exposing oneself to the ills that flesh is heir to."

After lunch, much to John's relief, his brother-in-law announced that he had an appointment with Eleanor and would therefore be unable to stay even long enough to smoke a cigar.

"Yes," he said. "Eleanor and I are going to interview one or two of her theatrical friends. No doubt I shall soon be able to proclaim myself a rogue and a vagabond. Yes, yes, poor Edith was quite distressed this morning when I told her that jestingly. However, she will be happy to hear to-night when I get back that her brother has been so large"

"Eh?"

"Not that Edith expected him to be otherwise. No, no, my dear fellow, Edith has a most exalted opinion of you, which indeed I share, if I may be permitted so to do. Good-by, John, and many thanks. Who knows? Our little lunch may become a red-letter day in the calendar of English dramatic art. Let me see, the tube-station is on the left as I go out? Good-by, John; I wish I could stay the night with you, but I have a cheap day-ticket which forbids any extension of my plans."

When John got back to the library he turned in bewilderment to his secretary.

"Look here. I surely never gave him the least idea that I was going to back his confounded play, did I?"

"On the contrary, you made it perfectly clear that you were not."

"I'm glad to hear you say so, because he has gone away from here apparently under the delusion that I am. He'll brag about it to Eleanor this afternoon, and before I know where I am she will be asking me to set George up with a racing-stable."

Eleanor did not go as far as that, but she did write to John and point out that the present seemed a suitable moment to deal with the question of George's health by sending him on a voyage round the world. She added that for herself she asked nothing; but John had an uneasy impression that it was only in the belief that he who asks not to him shall it be given.

"Take down two letters, please, Miss Hamilton," he said, grimly.

DEAR LAURENCE,—I am afraid that you went away yesterday afternoon under a misapprehension. I do *not* see my way to offer any financial contribution toward the production of your play. I myself passed a long apprenticeship before I was able to get one of my plays acted, and I do not think that you can expect to do otherwise. Do not imagine that I am casting any doubts upon the excellence of *Thomas*. If it is as good as you claim, you will have your reward without any help from me. Your idea of getting acquainted with the practical side of the stage is a good one. If you are not already engaged in the autumn, I think I can offer you one of the minor bishops in *Joan of Arc*.
     Your affectionate brother-in-law,
      JOHN TOUCHWOOD.

DEAR ELEANOR,—I must say decidedly that I do not perceive any likelihood of George's health deriving much benefit from a voyage round the world. If he is threatened with sleeping sickness, it would be rash to expose him to a tropical climate. If he is suffering from a sluggish liver, he will get no benefit from lolling about in smoking-saloons, whatever the latitude and longitude. I have repeatedly helped George with his schemes to earn a living for himself and he has never failed to squander my money upon capricious racehorses. You know that I am always willing to come forward on behalf of Bertram and Viola; but their father must show signs of helping himself before I do anything more for him. I am sorry that I cannot offer you a good part in *Joan of Arc;* there is really nothing to suit you for I presume you would not care to accept the part of Joan's mother. However, it has now been decided to produce *Lucretia* in

April and I shall do my best to persuade Grohmann to offer you a part in that.

Your affectionate brother-in-law,
JOHN TOUCHWOOD.

John did not receive an answer to either of these letters, and out of an atmosphere of pained silence he managed to conjure optimistically an idea that Laurence and Eleanor had realized the justice of his point of view.

"You do agree with me that they were going too far?" he asked Miss Hamilton; but she declined to express an opinion.

"What's the good of having a confidential secretary, if I can't ask her advice about confidential matters?" he grumbled.

"Are you dissatisfied with me?"

"No, no, no. I'm not dissatisfied. What an exaggeration of my remark! I'm simply a little puzzled by your attitude. It seems to me—I may be wrong—that instead of . . . well, at first you were always perfectly ready to talk about my relations and about me, whereas now you won't talk about anything except Joan of Arc. I'm really getting quite bored with Joan of Arc."

"I was only an amateur when I began," she laughed. "Now I'm beginning to be professional."

"I think it's a great mistake," said John, decidedly. "Suppose I insist upon having your advice?"

"You'd find that dictation bears two meanings in English, to only one of which are you entitled under the terms of our contract."

"Look here, have I done anything to offend you?" he asked, pathetically.

But she would not be moved and held her pencil so conspicuously ready that the author was impaled upon it before he could escape and was soon hard at work dictating his first arrangement of the final scene in a kind of indignant absent-mindedness.

Soon after this John received a note from Sir Percy Mortimer, asking if he could spare time to visit the great actor-manager some evening in the course of the current week. Between nine-thirty and ten was indicated as a suitable time, inasmuch as Sir Percy would then be in his dressing-room gathering the necessary momentum to knock down all the emotional fabric carefully built up in the first two acts by the most cunning of contemporary dramatists. Sir Percy Mortimer, whose name was once Albert Snell, could command anybody, so it ought not to have been remarkable that John rather flustered by the invitation made haste to obey. Yet, he must have been aware of an implied criticism in Miss Hamilton's smile, which flashed across her still deep eyes like a sunny wind, for he murmured, apologetically:

"We poor writers of plays must always wait upon our masters."

He tried to convey that Sir Percy was only a mortal like himself, but he failed somehow to eliminate the deep-rooted respect, almost it might be called awe of the actor that was perceptible under the assumed carelessness of the author.

"You see, it may be that he is anxious to hear some of my plans for the near future," he added.

If Sir Percy Mortimer was impressive in the smoking-room of the Garrick Club as himself, he was dumbfounding in his dressing-room as Lord Claridge, the ambassador, about to enter Princess Thingumabobski's salon and with diplomatic wiles and smiles to settle the future of several couples, incidentally secure for himself the heart and hand of a young heiress. His evening-dress had achieved an immaculation that even Ouida never dreamed of; he wore the Grand Cross of the Victorian Order with as easy an assurance as his father had worn the insignia of a local friendly society in Birmingham; he was the quintessential diplomat of girlish dreams, and it was not surprising that women were ready to remove even their hats to see him perform at matinees.

"Ah, it's very good of you to look me up, my dear fellow. I have just a quarter-of-an-hour. Godfrey!" He turned to address his valet, who might have been a cardinal driven by an ecclesiastical crisis like the spread of Modernism into attendance upon an actor.

"Sir Percy?"

"I do not wish to be disturbed until I am called for the third act."

"Very good, Sir Percy."

"And Godfrey!"

"Sir Percy?"

"The whisky and soda for Mr. Touchwood. Oh, and Godfrey!"

"Sir Percy?"

"If the Duke of Shropshire comes behind, tell His Grace that I am unavoidably prevented from seeing him until after the third act. I will *not* be interrupted."

"No, Sir Percy. I quite understand, Sir Percy."

The valet set the decanter at John's elbow and vanished like the ghost of a king.

"It's just this, my dear fellow," the actor-manager began, when John who had been trying to decide whether he should suggest Peter the Great or Augustus the Strong as the next part for his host was inclining towards Augustus. "It's just this. I believe that Miss Cartright, a former member of my company, is *also* a relation of yours."

"She is my sister-in-law," admitted John, swallowing both Peter and Augustus in a disappointed gulp.

"In fact, I believe that in private life she is Mrs. George Touchwood. Correct me if I am wrong in my names."

Sir Percy waited, but John did not avail himself of the offer, and he went on.

"Well, my dear fellow, she has approached me upon a matter which I confess I have found somewhat embarrassing, referring as it does to another man's private affairs; but as one of the—as—how shall I describe myself?—" He fingered the ribbon of the Victorian Order for inspiration. "As an actor-manager of some standing, I felt that you would prefer me to hear what she had to say in order that I might thereby adjudicate—yes, I think that is the word—without any—no, forgive me—adjudicate is *not* the word. Adjudicate is too strong. What is the word for outsiders of standing who are called in to assist at the settlement of a trade dispute? Whatever the word is, that is the word I want. I understand from Miss Cartright—Mrs. George Touchwood in private life—that her husband is in a very grave state of health and entirely without means." Sir Percy looked at himself in the glass and dabbed his face with the powder-puff. "Miss Cartright asked me to use my influence with you to take some steps to mitigate this unpleasant situation upon which, it appears, people are beginning to comment rather unfavorably. Now, you and I, my dear fellow, are members of the same club. You and I have high positions in our respective professions. Is it wise? There may of course be a thousand reasons for leaving your brother to starve with an incurable disease. But is it wise? As a man of the world, I think not." He touched his cheeks with the hare's-foot and gave them a richer bloom. "Don't allow me to make any suggestion that even borders upon the impertinent, but if you care to accept my mediation—*that* is the word I couldn't remember." In his enthusiasm Sir Percy smacked his leg, which caused him a momentary anxiety for the perfection of his trousers. "Mediation! Of course, that's it—if you care, as I say, to accept my mediation I am willing to mediate."

John stared at the actor-manager in angry amazement. Then he let himself go:

"My brother is not starving—he eats more than any human being I know. Nor is he suffering from anything incurable except laziness. I do not wish to discuss with you or anybody else the affairs of my relations, which I regret to say are in most cases only too much my own affairs."

"Then there is nothing for me to do," Sir Percy sighed, deriving what consolation he could from being unable to find a single detail of his dress that could be improved.

"Nothing whatever," John agreed, emphatically.

"But what shall I say to Miss Cartright, who you *must* remember is a former member of my company, as well as your sister-in-law?"

"I leave that to you."

"It's very awkward," Sir Percy murmured. "I thought you would be sure to see that it is always better to settle these unpleasant matters—out of court, if I may use the expression. I'm so afraid that Miss Cartright will air her grievance."

"She can wash as much dirty linen as she likes and air it every day in your theater," said John, fiercely. "But my brother George shall *not* go on a voyage round the world. You've nothing else to ask me? Nothing about my plans for the near future?"

"No, no. I've a success, as you know, and I don't expect I shall want another play for months. You've seen my performance, of course?"

"No," said John, curtly, "I've not."

And when he left the actor-manager's dressing-room he knew that he had wounded him more deeply by that simple negative than by all the mighty insults imaginable.

However, notwithstanding his successful revenge John left the theater in a rage and went off to his club with the hope of finding a sympathetic listener into whose ears he could pour the tale of Sir Percy's megalomania; but by ill luck there was nobody suitable in the smoking-room that night. To be sure, Sir Philip Cranbourne was snoring in an armchair, and Sir Philip Cranbourne was perhaps a bigger man in the profession than Sir Percy Mortimer. Yet, he was not so much bigger but that he would have welcomed a tale against the younger theatrical knight whose promotion to equal rank with himself he had resented very much. Sir Philip, however, was fast asleep, and John doubted if he hated Sir Percy sufficiently to welcome being woken up to hear a story against him—particularly a story by a playwright, one of that miserable class for which Sir Philip as an actor had naturally a very profound contempt. Moreover, thinking the matter over, John came to the conclusion that the story, while it would tell against Sir Percy would also tell against himself, and he decided to say nothing about it. When he was leaving the club he ran into Mr. Winnington-Carr, who greeted him airily.

"Evening, Touchwood!"

"Good evening."

"What's this I hear about Hugh going to Sierra Leone? Bit tough, isn't it, sending him over to a plague spot like that? You saw that paragraph in *The Penguin?* Things we should like to know, don't you know? Why John Touchwood's brother is taking up a post in the tropics and whether John himself is really sorry to see him go."

"No, I did not see that paragraph," said John, icily.

Next morning a bundle of press-cuttings arrived.

"There is nothing here but stupid gossip," said John to his secretary, flinging the packet into the fire. "Nothing that is worth preserving in the album, I mean to say."

Miss Hamilton smiled to herself.

CHAPTER XIV

THE buzz of gossip, the sting of scandalous paragraph, even the blundering impertinence of the actor-knight were all forgotten the following afternoon when a telegram arrived from Hampshire to say that old Mrs. Touchwood was dying. John left London immediately; but when he reached Ambles he found that his mother was already dead.

"She passed away at five o'clock," Edith sobbed.

Perhaps it was to stop his wife's crying that Laurence abandoned at any rate temporarily his unbelief and proclaimed as solemnly as if he were still Vicar of Newton Candover that the old lady was waiting for them all above. Hilda seemed chiefly worried by the fact that she had never warned James of their mother's grave condition.

"I did telegraph Eleanor, who hasn't come; and how I came to overlook James and Beatrice I can't think. They'll be so hurt. But Mama didn't fret for anybody in particular. No, Hugh sat beside the bed and held her hand, which seemed to give her a little pleasure, and I was kept occupied with changing the hot-water bottles."

In the dining-room George was knitting lugubriously.

"You mustn't worry yourself, old chap," he said to John with his usual partiality for seductive advice. "You can't do anything now. None of us can do anything till the funeral, though I've written to Eleanor to bring my top-hat with her when she comes."

The embarrassment of death's presence hung heavily over the household. The various members sat down to supper with apologetic glances at one another, and nobody took a second helping of any dish. The children were only corrected in whispers for their manners, but they were given to understand by reproachful head-shakes that for a child to put his elbows on the table or crumble his bread or drink with his mouth full was at such a time a cruel exhibition of levity. John could not help contrasting the treatment of children at a death with their treatment at a birth. Had a baby arrived upstairs, they would have been hustled out of sight and sound of the unclean event; but over death they were expected to gloat, and their curiosity was encouraged as the fit expression of filial piety.

"Yes, Frida, darling, dear Grandmama will have lots and lots of lovely white flowers. Don't kick the table, sweetheart. Think of dear Grandmama looking down at you from Heaven, and don't kick the table-leg, my precious," said Edith in tremulous accents, gently smoothing back her daughter's indefinite hair.

"Can people only see from Heaven or can they hear?" asked Harold.

"Hush, my boy," his Uncle Laurence interposed. "These are mysteries into which God does not permit us to inquire too deeply. Let it suffice that our lightest actions are known. We cannot escape the omniscient eye."

"I wasn't speaking about God," Harold objected. "I was asking about Grandmama. Does she hear Frida kicking the table, or does she only see her?"

"At this solemn moment, Harold, when we should all of us be dumb with grief, you should not persist. Your poor grandmother would be pained to hear you being persistent like this."

Harold seemed to think he had tricked his uncle into answering the question, for he relapsed into a satisfied silence; Edith's eyes flashed gladly through her tears to welcome the return of her husband's truant orthodoxy. All managed to abstain while they were eating from any more conspicuous intrusion of the flesh than was inevitable; but there was a painful scene after supper, because Frida insisted that she was frightened to sleep alone, and refused to be comforted by the offer of Viola for company. The terrible increase of Grandmama's powers of hearing and seeing might extend to new powers of locomotion in the middle of the night, in which case Viola would be no protection.

"But Grandmama is in Heaven, darling," her mother urged.

"I want to sleep with you. I'm frightened. I want to sleep with you," she wailed.

"Laurence!" murmured Edith, appealingly.

"Death is a great leveler," he intoned. Grateful to the chance of being able to make this observation, he agreed to occupy his daughter's room and thereby allow her to sleep with her mother.

"You're looking sad, Bertram," John observed, kindly, to his favorite nephew. "You mustn't take this too much to heart."

"No, Uncle John, I'm not. Only I keep wishing Grandmama had lived a little longer."

"We all wish that, old man."

"Yes, but I only meant a very little longer, so that I needn't have gone back for the first week of term."

John nervously hurried his nephew up to bed beyond the scorching of Laurence's rekindled flames of belief. Downstairs, he tried to extract from the attitude of the grown-up members of the family the attitude he would have liked to detect in himself. If a few months ago John had been told that his mother's death would affect him so little he would have been horrified by the suggestion; even now he was seriously shocked at himself. Yet, try as he might, he could not achieve the apotheosis of the old lady that he would have been so content to achieve. Undoubtedly a few months ago he would have been able without being conscious of self-deception to pretend that he believed not only in the reality of his own grief, but also in that of the others. He would have taken his part in the utterance of platitudes about life and death, separation and reunion. His own platitudes would have been disguised with poetic tropes, and he might have thought to himself how well such and such a phrase was put; but he would quickly have assured himself that it was well put because it was the just expression of a deep emotion. Now he could not make a single contribution to the woeful reflections of those round him. He believed neither in himself nor in them. He knew that George was faintly anxious about his top-hat, that Hilda was agitated at the prospect of having to explain to James and Beatrice her unintentional slight, that Laurence was unable to resist the opportunity of taking the lead at this sorrowful time by reverting to his priestly office. And Hugh, for whom the old lady had always possessed a fond unreasoning affection, did his countenance express more than a hardly concealed relief that it was all over? Did he not give the impression that he was stretching his legs after sitting still in one position for too long? Edith, to be sure, was feeling some kind of emotion that required an endless flow of tears, but it seemed to John that she was weeping more for the coming of death than for the going of her mother. And the children, how could they be expected to feel the loss of the old lady? There under the lamp like a cenotaph recording the slow hours of age stood her patience-cards in their red morocco case; there they would be allowed to stand for a while to satisfy the brief craving for reverence, and then one of the children realizing that Grandmama had no more need of playing would take possession of them; they would become grubby and dog-eared in younger hands; they would disappear one by one, and the memory of that placid presence would hardly outlive them.

"It's so nice to think that her little annuity died with her," sighed Edith. She spoke of the annuity as if it were a favorite pug that had died out of sympathy with its mistress. "I should hate to feel I was benefiting from the death of somebody I loved," she explained presently.

John shivered; that remark of his sister's was like a ghostly footstep upon his own grave, and from a few years hence, perhaps much less, he seemed to hear the family lawyer cough before he settled himself down to read the last will and testament of John Touchwood.

"Of course, poor Mama had been dreadfully worried these last weeks," Hilda said. "She felt very much the prospect of Hugh's going abroad—and other things."

John regarded his elder sister, and was on the point of asking what she meant to insinuate by other things, when a lament from upstairs startled the assembled family.

"Come to bed, mother, come to bed, I want you," Frida was shrieking over the balustrade. "The door of Grandmama's room made a noise just now."

"You had better go," said Laurence in answer to his wife's unvoiced appeal; and Edith went off gratefully.

"It will always be a consolation to me," said Laurence, "that Mama was able to hear *Thomas* read to her. Yes, yes, she was so well upon that memorable evening. So very well. By the way, John, I shall arrange with the Vicar to read the burial service myself. It will add the last touch to the intimacy of our common grief."

In his own room that night John tried hard not to criticize anybody except himself. It was he who was cynical, he who was hard, he who was unnatural, not they. He tried to evoke from the past early memories of his mother, but he could not recall one that might bring a tear to his eye. He remembered that once she had smacked him for something George had done, that she had never realized what a success he had made of his life's work, that she was—but he tore the unfilial thoughts from his brain and reminded himself how much of her personality endured in his own. George, Edith, and himself resembled her: James, Hilda, and Hugh resembled their father. John's brothers and sisters haunted the darkness; and he knew that deep down in himself he blamed his father and mother for bringing them all into the world; he could not help feeling that he ought to have been an only child.

"I do resent their existence," John thought. "I'm a heartless egotist. And Miss Hamilton thinks I'm an egotist. Her manner towards me lately has been distant, even contemptuous. Could that suggestion of Hilda's have had any truth in it? Was Mama worried to death by Hugh's going abroad? Did James complain to her about my taking the portraits and the silver? Is it from any standpoint conceivable that my own behavior did hasten her end?"

John's self-reproaches were magnified in the darkness, and he spent a restless and unhappy night, trying to think that the family was more important than the individual.

"You feel it terribly, don't you, dear Johnnie?" Edith asked him next morning with an affectionate pressure upon his arm. "You're looking quite worn out."

"We all feel it terribly," he sighed.

During the three days before the funeral John managed to work himself up into a condition of sentimentality which he flattered himself was outwardly at any rate affecting. Continuous reminders of his mother's existence culminating in the arrival of a new cap she had ordered just before her last swift illness seemed to induce in him the illusion of sorrow; and without the least idea of what he intended to do with them afterwards he collected a quantity of small relics like spectacle-cases and caps and mittens, which he arranged upon his dressing-table and brooded over with brimming eyes. He indulged Harold's theories about the psychical state of his grandmother; he practiced swinging a golf club, but he never once took out a ball; he treated everybody to magnificent wreaths, and presented the servants as well as his nephews and nieces with mourning; he ordered black-edged note-paper; he composed an epitaph in the manner of Sir Thomas Browne with cadences and subtle alliterations Then came the funeral, which ruined the last few romantic notions of grief that he had been able to preserve.

To begin with, Beatrice arrived in what could only be described as a towering rage: no less commonplace epithet would have done justice to the vulgarity of her indignation. That James the eldest son and she his wife should not have been notified of the dangerous condition of Mama, but should have been summoned to the obsequies like mere friends of the family had outraged her soul, or, as Beatrice herself put it, had knocked her down like a feather. Oh yes, she had always been considered beneath the Touchwood standard of gentility, but poor Mama had not thought the worse of her for that; poor Mama had many times gone out of her way to be specially gracious towards her; poor Mama must have "laid" there wondering why her eldest daughter-in-law did not come to give her the last and longest farewell. She had not been lucky enough to be blessed with children, but poor Mama had sometimes congratulated her upon that fact; poor Mama had realized only too well that children were not always a source of happiness. She knew that the undeserved poverty which had always dogged poor old Jimmie's footsteps had lately caused to be exacted from him the family portraits and the family silver pressed upon him by poor Mama herself; but was that a reason for excluding him from his mother's death-bed? She would not say whom she blamed, but she had her own ideas, and though Hilda might protest it was her fault, she knew better; Hilda was incapable of such barbarity. No, she would *not* walk beside James as wife of the chief mourner; she would follow in the rear of the funeral procession and hope that at any rate she was not grudged that humble place. If some people resented her having bought the largest wreath from a very expensive flower-shop, she was not too proud to carry the wreath herself; she had carried it all the way from town first-class to avoid its being crushed by heedless third-class passengers.

"And when I die," sobbed Beatrice, "I hope that James will remember we weren't allowed to see poor Mama before she went to Heaven, and will let me die quite alone. I'm sure I don't want my death to interfere with other people's amusements."

The funeral party gathered round the open grave; Laurence read the service so slowly and the wind was so raw that grief was depicted upon every countenance; the sniffing of many noses, above which rose Beatrice's sobs of mortification and rage, mingled with the sighing of the yews and the sexton's asthma in a suitably lachrymose symphony.

"Now that poor Mama has gone," said Hilda to her brother that afternoon, "I dare say you're anxious for me to be gone too."

"I really don't think you are entitled to ascribe to me such unnatural sentiments," John expostulated. "Why should I want you to die?"

He could indeed ask this, for such an event would inevitably connote his adoption of Harold.

"I didn't mean you wanted me to die," said Hilda, crossly. "I meant you would like me to leave Ambles."

"Not at all. I'm delighted for you to stay here so long as it suits your convenience. And that applies equally to Edith. Also I may say to George," he added with a glance at Eleanor, who had taken the opportunity of mourning to equip herself with a new set of black bearskin furs. Eleanor shook herself like a large animal emerging from the stream.

"And to me?" she asked with a challenge in her eyes.

"You must judge for yourself, Eleanor, how far my hospitality is likely to be extended willingly to you after last week," replied John, coldly. He had not yet spoken to his sister-in-law about the interference of Sir Percy Mortimer with his private affairs, and he now awaited her excuses of reproaches with a curiosity that was very faintly tinged with apprehension.

"Oh, I'm not at all ashamed of what I did," she declared. "George can't speak up for himself, and it was my duty to do all I could to help him in a matter of life and death."

John's cheeks flushed with stormy rose like a menacing down, and he was about to break over his sister-in-law in thunder and lightning when Laurence, entering the room at the moment and only hearing imperfectly her last speech, nodded and sighed:

"Yes, yes. Eleanor is indeed right. Yes, yes. In the midst of life. . . ."

Everybody hurried to take advantage of the diversion;

a hum of platitudes rose and fell upon the funereal air. John in a convulsion of irritability ordered the dog-cart to drive him to the station. He was determined to travel back to town alone; he feared that if he stayed any longer at Ambles his brother-in-law would revive the discussion about his play; he was afraid of Hugh's taking advantage of his mother's death to dodge British Honduras and of James' trading upon his filial piety to recover the silver and the family portraits.

When John got back to Church Row he found a note from Miss Hamilton to say she had influenza and was unlikely to be back at work for at least a week—if indeed, she added, she was able to come back at all. This unpleasant prospect filled him with genuine gloom, and it was with great difficulty that he refrained from driving immediately to Camera Square in order to remonstrate with her in person. His despondency was not lightened by Mrs. Worfolk's graveside manner and her assumption of a black satin dress hung with jet bugles that was usually reserved to mark the more cheerful festivals of the calendar. Worn thus out of season hung it about the rooms like a fog, and its numerous rustlings coupled with the housekeeper's sighs of commiseration added to the lugubrious atmosphere a sensation of damp which gave the final touch to John's depression. Next morning the weather was really abominable; the view over London from his library window showed nothing but great cobwebs of rain that seemed to be actually attached to a sky as gray and solid as a dusty ceiling. Action offered the only hope of alleviating life upon such a day, and John made up his mind to drive over to Chelsea and inquire about his secretary's health. He found that she was better, though still in bed; being anxious to learn more about her threatened desertion he accepted the maid's invitation to come in and speak to Mrs. Hamilton. The old lady looked more like a clown than ever in the forenoon while the rice-powder was still fresh upon her cheeks, and John found her humor as irritating as he would have found the humor of a real clown in similar circumstances. Her manner towards him was that of a person who is aware of, but on certain terms is willing to overlook a grave indiscretion, and she managed most successfully to make him feel that he was on his defense.

"Yes, poor Doris has been very seedy. And her illness has unluckily coincided with mine."

"Oh, I'm sorry . . ." he began.

"Thank you. I'm used to being ill. I am always ill. At least, as luck will have it, I usually feel ill when Doris has anything the matter with her."

This John was ready to believe, but he tried to look at once shocked and sympathetic.

"Do not let us discuss my health," Mrs. Hamilton went on scorching her eyebrows in the aureole of martyrdom she wore. "Of what importance is my health? Poor Doris has had a very sharp attack, a very sharp attack indeed."

"I'm afraid that the weather . . ."

"It's not the weather, Mr. Touchwood. It is overwork." And before John could say a word she was off. "You must remember that Doris is not used to hard work. She has spent all her life with me, and you can easily imagine that with a mother always at hand she has been spared the least hardship. I would have done anything for her. Ever since my husband died, my life has been one long buffer between Doris and the world. You know how obstinately she has refused to let me do all I wanted. I refer to my brother-in-law, Mr. Hamilton of Glencockie. And this is the result. Nervous prostration, influenza, a high temperature—and sharp pains, which between ourselves I'm inclined to think are perhaps not so bad as she imagines. People who are not accustomed to pains," said the old lady, jealously, "are always apt to be unduly alarmed and to attribute to them a severity that is a leetle exaggerated. I suffer so much myself that I cannot take these pains quite as seriously as Doris does. However, the poor child really has a good deal to put up with, and of course I've insisted that she must never attempt such hard work again. I don't suppose you meant to be inconsiderate, Mr. Touchwood. I don't accuse you of deliberate callousness. Please do not suppose that I am suggesting that the least cruelty in your behavior; but you *have* overworked her. Moreover, she has been worried. One or two of our friends have suggested more in joke than in earnest that she might be compromised by her association with you. No doubt this was said in joke, but Doris lacks her mother's sense of humor, and I'm afraid she has fretted over this. Still, a stitch in time saves nine, and her illness must serve as an excuse for what with a curiously youthful self-importance she calls 'leaving you in the lurch.' As I said to her, 'Do not, my dear child, worry about Mr. Touchwood. He can find as many secretaries as he wants. Probably he thought he was doing you a good turn, and you've overstrained yourself in trying to cope with duties to which you have not been accustomed. You cannot expect to fly before you can walk.'"

The old lady paused to fan back her breath, and John seized the conversation.

"Does Miss Hamilton herself wish to leave me like this, or is it only you who think that she ought to leave me?"

"I will be frank with you," the old lady panted. "Doris has not yet made up her mind."

"As long as she is allowed to make up her own mind," said John, "I have nothing to say. But I hope you are not going to overpersuade her. After all she is old enough to know what she wants to do."

"She is not as old as her mother."

He shook his head impatiently.

"Could I see her?"

"See her?" the old lady answered in amazement. "See her, Mr. Touchwood? Didn't I explain that she was in bed?"

"I beg your pardon. I'd forgotten."

"Men are apt to forget somewhat easily. Come, come, do not let us get bitter. I took a great fancy to you when I met you first, and though I have been a little disappointed by the way in which you have taken advantage of Doris's eagerness for new experiences I don't really bear you any deep grudge. I don't believe you meant to be selfish. It is only a mother who can pierce a daughter's motives. You with your recent loss should be able to appreciate that particularly now. Poor Doris! I wish she were more like me."

"If you really think I have overworked her," said John, "I'm extremely sorry. I dare say her enthusiasm carried me away. But I cannot relinquish her services without a struggle. She has been, and she *is* invaluable," he added, warmly.

"Yes, but we must think of her health. I'm sorry to seem so *intransigente,* but I am only thinking of her."

John was not at all taken in by the old lady's altruism, but he was entirely at a loss how to argue in favor of her daughter's continuing to work for him. His perplexity was increased by the fact that she herself had written to express her doubtfulness about returning; it might conceivably be that she did not want to return and that he was misjudging Mrs. Hamilton's sincerity. Yet when he looked at the old lady he could not discover anything but a cold egotism in every fold of those flabby cheeks where the powder lay like drifted snow in the ruts of a sunless lane. It was surely impossible that Doris should willingly have surrendered the liberty she enjoyed with him; she must have written under the depressing effects of influenza.

While John was pondering his line of action Mrs. Hamilton had fanned herself into a renewed volubility; finding that it was impossible to cross the torrent of words that she was now pouring forth, he sat down by the edge of it, confused and deafened, and sometimes gasping a faint protest when he was splashed by some particularly outrageous argument.

"Well, I'll write to her," he said at last.

"I beg you will do nothing of the kind. In the present feeble state of her health a letter will only agitate her. I hope to persuade her to come with me to Glencockie where her uncle will, I know, once more suggest adopting her as his heiress...."

The old lady flowed on with schemes for the future of Doris in which there was so much talk of Scotland that in the end his secretary appeared to John like an advertisement for whisky. He saw her rosy-cheeked and tam-o-shantered, smiling beneath a fir-tree while mockingly she quaffed a glass to the health of her late employer. He saw her as a kind of cross between Flora Macdonald and Highland Mary by the banks of Loch Lomond. He saw her in every guise except that in which he desired to see her—bending with that elusive and ironical smile over the typewriter they had purchased together. Damn!

John made hurried adieus and fled to his taxi from the little house in Camera Square. The interview with Mrs. Hamilton had cost him half-a-crown and his peace of mind: it had cost the driver one halfpenny for the early edition of the *Star*. How much happier was the life of a taxi-driver than the life of a playwright!

"I wouldn't say as how Benedictine mightn't win at Kempton this afternoon," the driver observed to John when he alighted. "I reckon I'll have half-a-dollar on, any old way. It's Bolmondeley's horse and bound to run straight."

Benedictine did win that afternoon at six to one: indubitably the life of a taxi-driver was superior to his own, John thought as he turned with a shudder from the virgin foolscap upon his writing-desk and with a late edition of the *Star* sank into a deep armchair.

"A bachelor's life is a very lonely one," he sighed. For some reason Maud had neglected to draw the curtains after tea, and the black yawning window where the rain glistened drearily weighed upon his heart with a sense of utter abandonment. Ordinarily he would have rung the bell and pointed reproachfully to the omission; but this afternoon, he felt incapable of stirring from his chair to ring a bell. He could not even muster enough energy to poke the fire, which would soon show as little life as himself. He listened vainly for the footsteps of Maud or Mrs. Worfolk that he might call out and be rescued from this lethargy of despair; but not a sound was audible except the dripping rain outside and the consumptive coughs of the moribund fire.

"Perhaps I'm feeling my mother's death," said John, hopefully.

He made an effort to concentrate his mind upon an affectionate retrospect of family life. He tried to convince himself that the death of his mother would involve a change in the attitude of his relations. Technically he might not be the eldest son, and while his mother had been alive he had never assumed too definitely the rights of an eldest son. Practically, however, that was his status, and his acquisition of the family portraits and family silver could well be taken as the visible sign of that status; with his mother's death he might surely consider himself in the eyes of the world the head of the family. Did he want such an honor? It would be an expensive, troublesome, and ungrateful post like the Lord-Lieutenancy of Ireland. Why didn't Maud come and draw those curtains? A thankless job, and it would be more congenial to have a family of his own. That meant marriage. And why shouldn't he get married? Several palmists had assured him he would be married one day: most of them indeed had assured him he was married already.

"If I get married I can no longer be expected to bother about my relations. Of course in that case I should give back the portraits and the silver. My son would be junior to Bertram. My son would occupy an altogether inconspicuous position in the family, though he would always take precedence of Harold. But if my son had a child, Harold would become an uncle. No, he wouldn't. Harold would be a first cousin once removed. Harold cannot become an uncle unless Hilda marries again and has another child who has another child. Luckily, it's all very improbable. I'm glad Harold is never likely to be an uncle: he would bring the relationship into an even greater disrepute. Still, even now an uncle is disreputable enough.

The wicked uncle! It's proverbial, of course. We never hear of the wicked cousin or the nefarious aunt. No, uncles share with stepmothers the opprobrium and with mothers-in-law the ridicule of the mob. Unquestionably, if I do marry, I shall still be an uncle, but the status may perhaps be merged in paternity. Suppose I marry and never have any children? My wife will be pitied by Hilda, Edith, and Eleanor and condoled with by Beatrice. She would find her position intolerable. My wife? I wish to goodness Maud would come in and draw those curtains. My wife? That's the question. At this stage the problem of her personality is more important than theoretical speculation about future children. Should I enjoy a woman's bobbing in and out of my room all the time? Suppose I were married at this moment, it would be my wife's duty to correct Maud for not having drawn those curtains. If I were married at this moment I should say, 'My dear, Maud does not seem to have drawn the curtains. I wonder why.' And my wife would of course ring the bell and remonstrate with Maud. But suppose my wife were upstairs? She might be trying on a new hat. Apparently wives spend a great deal of time with hats. In that case I should be no better off than I am at present. I should still have to get out of this chair and ring for Maud. And I should have to complain twice over. Once to Maud herself and afterwards all over again to my wife about Maud. Then my wife would have to rebuke Maud. Oh, it would be a terribly complicated business. Perhaps I'm better off as a bachelor. It's an odd thing that with my pictorial temperament I should never yet have visualized myself as a husband. My imagination is quite untrammeled in most directions. Were I to decide to-morrow that I would write a play about Adam and Eve, I should see myself as Adam and Eve and the Serpent and almost as the Forbidden Fruit itself without any difficulty. Why can't I see myself as a husband? When I think of the number of people and things I've been in imagination it really does seem extraordinary I should never have thought of being a husband. Apparently Maud has completely forgotten about the curtains. It looks as if I should have to give up all hope now of her coming in to draw them of her own accord. Poor Miss Hamilton! I do trust that horrible old clown of a mother isn't turning somersaults round her room at this moment and sending up her temperature to three figures. Of course, she must come back to me. She is indispensable. I miss her very much. I've accustomed myself to a secretary's assistance, and naturally I'm lost without her. These morbid thoughts about matrimony are due to my not having done a stroke of work all day. I will count seventeen and rise from this chair."

John counted seventeen, but when he came to the fatal number he found that his will to move was still paralyzed, and he went on to forty-nine—the next fatal number in his private cabbala. When he reached it he tightened every nerve in his body and leapt to his feet. Inertia was succeeded by the bustle of activity: he rang for Maud; he poked the fire; he brushed the tobacco-ash from his waistcoat; he blew his nose; he sat down at his desk.

My dear Miss Hamilton, [he wrote,] I cannot say how distressed I was to hear the news of your illness and still more to learn from your mother that you were seriously thinking of resigning your post. I'm also extremely distressed to hear from her that there are symptoms of overwork. If I've been inconsiderate I must beg your forgiveness and ask you to attribute it to your own good-will. The fact is your example has inspired me. With your encouragement I undoubtedly do work much harder than formerly. To-day, without you, I have not written a single word, and I feel dreadfully depressed at the prospect of your desertion. Do let me plead for your services when you are well again, at any rate until I've finished Joan of Arc, for I really don't think I shall ever finish that play without them. I have felt the death of my poor mother very much, but I do not ascribe my present disinclination for work to that. No, on the contrary, I came back from the funeral with a determination to bury myself—that might be expressed better—to plunge myself into hard work. Your note telling me of your illness was a great shock, and your mother's uncompromising attitude this morning has added to my dejection. I feel that I am growing old and view with horror the approach of age. I've been sitting by the fire indulging myself in very morbid thoughts. You will laugh when I tell you that amongst them was the idea—I might call it the chimera of marriage. Do please get well soon and rescue me from myself.

Yours very sincerely,

JOHN TOUCHWOOD.

I do not, of course, wish to disturb the relationship between yourself and your mother, but my own recent loss has reminded me that mothers do not live forever.

CHAPTER XV

JOHN waited in considerable anxiety for Miss Hamilton's reply to his letter, and when a few days later she answered his appeal in person by presenting herself for work as usual he could not express in words the intensity of his satisfaction, but could only prance round her as if he had been a dumb domestic animal instead of a celebrated romantic playwright.

"And what have you done since I've been away?" she asked, without alluding to her illness or to her mother or to her threat of being obliged to leave him.

John looked abashed.

"Not very much, I'm afraid."

"How much?"

"Well, to be quite honest, nothing at all."

She referred sympathetically to the death of Mrs. Touchwood, and, without the ghost of a blush, he availed himself of that excuse for idleness.

"But now you're back," he added, "I'm going to work harder than ever. Oh, but I forgot. I mustn't overwork you."

"Nonsense," said Miss Hamilton, sharply. "I don't think the amount you write every day will ever do me much harm."

John busied himself with paper, pens, ink, and notebooks, and was soon as deep in the fourth act as if there had never been an intermission. For a month he worked in perfect tranquillity, and went so far as to calculate that if Miss Hamilton was willing to remain forever in his employ there was no reason why he should not produce three plays a year until he was seventy. Then one morning in mid-February Mr. Ricketts arrived in a state of perturbation to say that he had been unable to obtain any reply to several letters and telegrams informing Hugh when their steamer would leave. Now here they were with only a day before departure, and he was still without news of the young man. John looked guilty. The fact was that he had decided not to open any letters from his relations throughout this month, alleging to himself the interruption they caused to his work and trusting to the old superstition that if left unanswered long enough all letters, even the most disagreeable, answered themselves.

"I was wondering why your correspondence had dwindled so," said Miss Hamilton, severely.

"But that is no excuse for my brother," John declared. "Because I don't write to him, that is no reason why he shouldn't write to Mr. Ricketts."

"Well, we're off to-morrow," said the mahogany-planter.

An indignant telegram was sent to Hugh; but the prepaid answer came back from Hilda to say that he had gone off with a friend a fortnight ago without leaving any address. Mr. Ricketts, who had been telephoned for in the morning, arrived about noon in a taxi loaded with exotic luggage.

"I can't wait," he assured John. "The lad must come on by the next boat. I shan't go up country for a week or so. Good-by, Mr. Touchwood; I'm sorry not to have your brother's company. I was going to put him wise to the job on the trip across."

"But look here, can't you . . ." John began, despairingly.

"Can't wait. I shall miss the boat. West India Docks," he shouted to the driver, "and stop at the last decent pub in the city on the way through."

The tax buzzed off.

Two days later Hugh appeared at Church Row, mentioned casually that he was sorry he had missed the boat, but that he had been doing a little architectural job for a friend of his.

"Very good bridge," he commented, approvingly.

"Over what?" John demanded.

"Over very good whisky," said Hugh. "It was up in the North. Capital fun. I was designing a smoking-room for a man I know who's just come into money. I've had a ripping time. Good hands every evening and a very decent fee. In fact, I don't see why I shouldn't start an office of my own."

"And what about mahogany?"

"Look here, I never liked that idea of yours, Johnnie. Everybody agrees that British Honduras is a rotten climate, and if you want to help me, you can help me much more effectively by setting me up on my own as an architect."

"I do not want to help you. I've invested £2,000 in mahogany and logwood, and I insist on getting as much interest on my money as your absence from England will bring me in."

"Yes, that's all very well, old chap. But why do you want me to leave England?"

John embarked upon a justification of his attitude, in the course of which he pointed out the dangers of idleness, reminded Hugh of the forgery, tried to inspire him with hopes of independence, hinted at moral obligations, and rhapsodized about colonial enterprise. As a mountain of forensic art the speech was wonderful: clothed on the lower slopes with a rich and varied vegetation of example and precept, it gradually ascended to the hard rocks of necessity, honor, and duty until it culminated in a peak of snow where John's singleness of motive glittered immaculately and inviolably to heaven. It was therefore discouraging for the orator when he paused and walked slowly up stage to give the culprit an opportunity to make a suitably penitent reply, after which the curtain was to come down upon a final outburst of magnanimous eloquence from himself, that Hugh should merely growl the contemptuous monosyllable "rot."

"Rot?" repeated John in amazement.

"Yes. Rot. I'm not going to reason with you . . ."

"Ah, indeed?" John interrupted, sarcastically.

"Because reason would be lost on you. I simply repeat 'Rot!' If I don't want to go to British Honduras, I won't go. Why, to hear you talk anybody would suppose that I hadn't had the same opportunities as yourself. If you chose to blur your intelligence by writing romantic tushery, you must remember that by doing so you yielded to temptation just as much as I did when I forged Stevie's name. Do you think I would write plays like yours? Never!" he proclaimed, proudly.

"It seems to me that the conversation is indeed going outside the limits of reason," said John, trying hard to restrain himself.

"My dear old chap, it has never been inside the limits. No, no, you collared me when I was down over that check. Well, here's what you paid to get me out of the mess." He threw a bundle of notes on the table. "So long, Johnnie, and don't be too resentful of my having demonstrated that when I *am* left for a while on my own I can earn money as well as you. I'm going to stay in town for a bit before I go North again, so I shall see you from time to time. By the way, you might send me the receipt to Carlington Road. I'm staying with Aubrey as usual."

When his brother had gone, John counted the notes in a stupor. It would be too much to say that he was annoyed at being paid back; but he was not sufficiently pleased to mention the fact to Miss Hamilton for two days

"Oh, I am so glad," she exclaimed when at last he did bring himself to tell her.

"Yes, it's very encouraging," John agreed, doubtfully. "I'm still suffering slightly from the shock, which has been a very novel sensation. To be perfectly honest, I never realized before how much less satisfactory it is to be paid back than one thinks beforehand it is going to be."

In spite of the disturbing effect of Hugh's honesty, John soon settled down again to the play, and became so much wrapped up in its daily progress that one afternoon he was able without a tremor to deny admittance to Laurence, who having written to warn him that he was taking advantage of a further reduction in the price on day-tickets, had paid another visit to London. Laurence took with ill grace his brother-in-law's message that he was too busy on his own work to talk about anybody's else at present.

"I confess I was pained," he wrote from Ambles on John's own note-paper, "by the harsh reception of my friendly little visit. I confess that Edith and I had hoped you would welcome the accession of a relative to the ranks of contemporary playwrights. We feel that in the circumstances we cannot stay any longer in your house. Indeed, Edith is even as I pen these lines packing Frida's little trunk. She is being very brave, but her tear-stained face tells its own tale, and I confess that I myself am writing with a heavy heart. Eleanor has been most kind, and in addition to giving me several more introductions to her thespian friends has arranged with the proprietress of Halma House for a large double room with dressing-room attached on terms which I can only describe as absurdly moderate. Do not think we are angry. We are only pained, bitterly pained that our happy family life should suddenly collapse like this. However, excelsior, as the poet said, or as another poet even greater said, 'sic itur ad astra.' You will perhaps be able to spare a moment from the absorption of your own affairs to read with a fleeting interest that Sir Percy Mortimer has offered me the part of the butler in a comedy of modern manners which he hopes to stage—you see I am already up to the hilt in the jargon of the profession—next autumn. Eleanor considers this to be an excellent opening, as indeed so do I. Edith and little Frida laugh heartily when they are not too sad for such simple fun when I enter the room and assume the characteristic mannerisms of a butler. All agree I have a natural propensity for droll impersonation. Who knows? I may make a great hit, although Sir Percy warns me that the part is but a slight one. Eleanor, however, reminds me that deportment is always an asset for an actor. Have I not read somewhere that the great Edmund Kean did not disdain to play the tail end of a dragon erstwhile? I wish you all good luck in your own work, my dear John. People are interested when they hear you are my brother-in-law, and I have told them many tales of the way you are wont to consult me over the little technical details of religion in which I as a former clergyman have been able to afford you my humble assistance."

"What a pompous ass the man is," said John to his secretary. He had read her the letter, which made her laugh.

"I believe you're really quite annoyed that *he's* showing an independent spirit now."

"Not at all. I'm delighted to be rid of him," John contradicted. "I suppose he'll share George's aquarium at Halma House."

"You don't mind my laughing? Because it is very funny, you know."

"Yes, it's funny in a way," John admitted. "But even if it weren't, I shouldn't mind your laughing. You have, if I may say so, a peculiarly musical laugh."

"Are you going to have Joan's scaffold right center or left center?" she asked, quickly.

"Eh? What? Oh, put it where you like. By the way, has your mother been girding at you lately?"

Miss Hamilton shrugged her shoulders.

"She isn't yet reconciled to my being a secretary, if that's what you mean."

"I'm sorry," John murmured. "Confound all relations!" he burst out. "I suppose she'd object to your going to France with me to finish off the play?"

"She would object violently. But you mustn't forget that I've a will of my own."

"Of course you have," said John, admiringly. "And you will go, eh?"

"I'll see—I won't promise. Look here, Mr. Touchwood, I don't want to seem—what shall I call it—timid, but if I did go to France with you, I suppose you realize my mother would make such a fuss about it that people would end by really talking? Forgive my putting such an unpleasant idea into your innocent head; being your confidential secretary, I feel I oughtn't to let you run any risks. I don't suppose you care a bit how much people talk, and I'm sure I don't; at the same time I shouldn't like you to turn round on me and say I ought to have warned you."

"Talk!" John exclaimed. "The idea is preposterous. Talk! Good gracious me, can't I take my secretary abroad without being accused of ulterior motives?"

"Now, don't work yourself into a state of wrath, or you won't be able to think of this terribly important last scene. Anyway, we sha'n't be going to France yet, and we can discuss the project more fully when the time comes."

John thought vaguely how well Miss Hamilton knew how to keep him unruffled, and with a grateful look—or what was meant to be a grateful look, though she blushed unaccountably when he gave it—he concentrated upon the site of his heroine's scaffold.

During March the weather was so bright and exhilarating that John and his secretary took many walks together on Hampstead Heath; they also often went to town, and John derived much pleasure from discussing various business affairs with her clerical support; he found that it helped considerably when dealing with the manager of a film company to be able to say "Will you make a note of that, please, Miss Hamilton?" The only place, in fact, to which John did not take her was his club, and that was only because he was not allowed to introduce ladies there.

"A rather mediæval restriction," he observed one day to a group assembled in the smoking-room.

"There was a time, Touchwood, when you used to take refuge here from your leading ladies," a bachelor member chuckled.

"But nowadays Touchwood has followed Adam with the rest of us," put in another.

"What's that?" said John, sharply.

There was a general burst of merriment and headshaking and wagging of fingers, from which and a succession of almost ribald comment John began to wonder if his private life was beginning to be a subject for club gossip. He managed to prevent himself from saying that he thought such chaff in bad taste, because he did not wish to give point to it by taking it too much in earnest. Nevertheless, he was seriously annoyed and avoided the smoking-room for a week.

One night, after the first performance of a friend's play, he turned in to the club for supper, and, being disinclined for sleep, because although it was a friend's play it had been a tremendous success, which always made him feel anxious about his own future he lingered on until the smoking-room was nearly deserted. Towards three o'clock he was sitting pensively in a quiet corner when he heard his name mentioned by two members, who had taken seats close by without perceiving his presence. They were both strangers to him, and he was about to rise from his chair and walk severely out of the room, when he heard one say to the other:

"Yes, they tell me his brother-in-law writes his plays for him."

John found this so delightfully diverting an idea that he could not resist keeping quiet to hear more.

"Oh, I don't believe that," said the second unknown member.

"Fact, I assure you. I was told so by a man who knows Eleanor Cartright."

"The actress?"

"Yes, she's a sister-in-law of his."

"Really, I never knew that."

"Oh yes. Well, this man met her with a fellow called Armitage, an ex-monk who broke his vows in order to marry Touchwood's sister."

John pressed himself deeper into his armchair.

"Really? But I never knew monks could marry," objected number two.

"I tell you, he broke his vows."

"Oh, I see," murmured number two, who was evidently no wiser, but was anxious to appear so.

"Well, it seems that this fellow Armitage is a thundering fine poet, but without much experience of the stage. Of course, he wouldn't have had much as a monk."

"Of course not," agreed number two, decidedly.

"So, what does Johnnie Touchwood do—"

"Damned impudence calling me Johnnie," thought the subject of the duologue.

"But make a contract with his brother-in-law to stay out of the way down in Devonshire or Dorsetshire—I forget which—but, anyway, down in the depths of the country somewhere, and write all the best speeches in old Johnnie's plays. Now, it seems there's been a family row, and they tell me that Armitage is going to sue Johnnie."

"What was the row about?"

"Well, apparently Johnnie is a bit close. Most of these successful writers are, of course," said number one with the nod of an expert.

"Of course," agreed his companion, with an air of equally profound comprehension.

"And took advantage of his position as the fellow with money to lord it over the rest of his family. There's another brother—an awful clever beggar—James, I think his name is—a real first-class scientist, original research man and all that, who's spent the whole of his fortune on some great discovery or other. Well, will you believe it, but the other day when he was absolutely starving, Johnnie Touchwood offered to lend him some trifling sum if he would break the entail."

"I didn't know the Touchwoods were landed proprietors. I always understood the father was a dentist," said number two.

"Oh, no, no. Very old family. Wonderful old house down in Devonshire or Dorset—I wish I could remember just where it is. Anyway, it seems that the eldest brother clung on to this like anything. Of course, he would."

"Of course," number two agreed.

"But Johnnie, who's hard as flint, insisted on breaking

the entail in his own favor, and now I hear he's practically turned the whole family into the street, including James' boy, who in the ordinary course of events would have inherited."

"Did Eleanor Cartright tell your friend this?" asked number two.

"Oh no, I've heard that from lots of people. It seems that old Mrs. Touchwood died of grief over the way Johnnie carried on. It's really a very grim story when you hear the details; unfortunately, I can't remember all of them. My memory's getting awfully bad nowadays."

Number two muttered an expression of sympathy, and the other continued:

"But one detail I do remember is that another brother—"

"It's a large family, then?"

"Oh, very large. As I was saying, the old lady was terribly upset not only about breaking the entail, but also over her youngest son, who had some incurable disease. It seems that he was forced by Johnnie to go out to the Gold Coast—I think it was—in order to see about some money that Johnnie had invested in rubber or something. As I say, I can't remember the exact details. However, cherchez la femme, I needn't add the reasons for all this."

"A woman?"

"Exactly," said number one. "Some people say it's a married woman, and others say it's a young girl of sixteen. Anyway, Johnnie's completely lost his head over her, and they tell me . . ."

The two members put their heads together so that John could not hear what was said: but it must have been pretty bad, because when they put them apart again number two was clicking his tongue in shocked amazement.

"By Jove, that will cause a terrific scandal, eh?"

John decided he had heard enough. Assuming an expression of intense superiority, the sort of expression a man might assume who was standing on the top of Mount Everest, he rose from his chair, eyed the two gossips with disdain, and strode out of the smoking-room. Just as he reached the door, he heard number one exclaim:

"Hulloa, see who that was? That was old Percy Mortimer."

"Oh, of course," said number two, as sapiently as ever, "I didn't recognize him for a moment. He's beginning to show his age, eh?"

On the way back to Hampstead John tried to assure himself that the conversation he had just overheard did not represent anything more important than the vaporings of an exceptionally idiotic pair of men about town; but the more he meditated upon the tales about himself evidently now in general circulation, the more he was appalled at the recklessness of calumny.

"One has joked about it. One has laughed at Sheridan's *School for Scandal*. One has admitted that human beings are capable of almost incredible exaggeration. But—no, really this is too much. I've gossiped sometimes myself about my friends, but never like that about a stranger—a man in the public eye."

John nearly stopped the taxi to ask the driver if *he* had heard any stories about John Touchwood; but he decided it would not be wise to run risk of discovery that he enjoyed less publicity than he was beginning to imagine, and he kept his indignation to himself.

"After all, it is a sign of—well, yes, I think it might fairly be called fame—a sign of fame to be talked about like that by a couple of ignorant chatterboxes. It is, I suppose, a tribute to my position. But Laurence! That's what annoyed me most. Laurence to be the author of my plays! I begin to understand this ridiculous Bacon and Shakespeare legend now. The rest of the gossip was malicious, but that was—really, I think it was actionable. I shall take it up with the committee. The idea of that pompous nincompoop writing Lucretia's soliloquy before she poisons her lips! Laurence! Good heavens! And fancy Laurence writing Nebuchadnezzar's meditation upon grass! By Jove, an audience would have some cause to titter then! And Laurence writing Joan's defense to the Bishop of Beauvais! Why, the bombastic pedant couldn't even write a satisfactory letter to the Bishop of Silchester to keep himself from being ignominiously chucked out of his living."

The infuriated author bounced up and down on the cushions of the taxi in his rage.

"Shall I give you an arm up the steps, sir?" the driver offered, genially, when John, having alighted at his front door, had excessively overpaid him under the impression from which he was still smarting of being called a skinflint.

"No, thank you."

"Beg pardon, sir. I thought you was a little bit tiddly. You seemed a bit lively inside on the way up."

"I suppose the next thing is that I shall get the reputation of being a dipsomaniac," said John to himself, as he flung open his door and marched immediately, with a slightly accentuated rigidity of bearing, upstairs to bed.

But he could not sleep. The legend of his behavior that was obviously common gossip in London oppressed him with its injustice. Every accusation took on a new and fantastic form, while he turned over and over in an attempt to reach oblivion. He began to worry now more about what had been implied in his association with Miss Hamilton than about the other stories. He felt that it would only be a very short time before she would hear of the tale in some monstrous shape and leave him forever in righteous disgust. Ought he, indeed, to make her aware to-morrow morning of what was being suggested? And even if he did not say anything about the past, ought he to compromise her more deeply in the future?

It was six o'clock before John fell asleep, and it was with a violent headache that he faced his secretary after breakfast. Luckily there was a letter from Janet Bond asking him to come and see her that morning upon a matter of importance. He seized the excuse to postpone any discussion of last night's revelation, and, telling Miss Hamilton he should be back for lunch, he decided to walk down to the Parthenon Theater in the hope of arriving there with a clearer and saner view of life. He nearly told her to go home; but, reflecting that he might come back in quite a different mood, he asked her instead to occupy herself with the collation of some scattered notes upon Joan of Arc that were not yet incorporated into the scheme of the play. He remembered, too, that it would be his birthday in three days' time, and he asked her to send out notes of invitation to his family for the annual celebration, at which the various members liked to delude themselves with the idea that by presenting him with a number of useless accessories to the smoking-table they were repaying him in full for all his kindness. He determined that his birthday speech on this occasion should be made the vehicle for administering a stern rebuke to malicious gossip. He would dam once for all this muddy stream of scandal, and he would make Laurence write a letter to the press disclaiming the authorship of his plays. Burning with reformative zeal and fast losing his headache, John swung down Fitzjohn's Avenue in the spangled March sunlight to the wicked city below.

The Parthenon Theater had for its acropolis the heights of the Adelphi, where, viewed from the embankment gardens below, it seemed to be looking condescendingly down upon the efforts of the London County Council to intellectualize the musical taste of the generation. In the lobby—it had been called the propylæum until it was found that such a long name had discouraged the public from booking seats beforehand through fear of mispronunciation—a bust of Janet Bond represented the famous statue Pallas Athene on the original acropolis, and the programme-girls, dressed as caryatides, supplied another charming touch of antiquity. The proprietress herself was the outstanding instance in modern times of the exploitation of virginity—it must have been a very profitable exploitation, because the Parthenon Theater itself had been built and paid for by her unsuccessful admirers. Each year made Janet Bond's position as virgin and actress more secure, and at the rate her reputation was growing it was probable that she would soon be at liberty to produce the most immodest plays. At present, however, she still applied the same standard of her conduct to her plays as to herself. Nor did she confine herself to that. She was also very strict about the private lives of her performers, and many a young actress had been seen to leave the stage door in tears because Miss Bond had observed her in unsuitable company at supper. Mothers wrote from all over England to beg Miss Bond to charge herself with the care of their stage-struck daughters; the result was a conventional tone among the supernumeraries slightly flavored with militant suffragism and the higher mathematics. Nor was art neglected; indeed some critics hinted that in the Parthenon Theater art was cultivated at the expense of life, though none of them attempted to gainsay that Miss Bond had learned how to make virtue pay without selling it.

In appearance the great tragedienne was somewhat rounder in outline than might have been expected, and more matronly than virginal, perhaps because she was in her own words a mother to all her girls. Her voice was rich and deep with as much variety as a cunningly sounded gong. She never made up for the stage, and she wore hygienic corsets: this intimate fact was allowed to escape through the indiscretion of a widespread advertisement, but its publication helped her reputation for decorum, and clergymen who read their wives' *Queen* or *Lady* commented favorably on the contrast between Miss Bond and the numerous open-mouthed actresses who preferred to advertise toothpaste. England was proud of Miss Bond, feeling that America had no longer any right to vaunt a monopoly of virtuous actresses; and John, when he rang the bell of Miss Bond's flat that existed cleverly in the roof of the theater, was proud of his association with her. He did not have to wait long in her austere study; indeed he had barely time to admire the fluted calyx of a white trumpet daffodil that in chaste symbolism was the only occupant of a blue china bowl before Miss Bond herself came in.

"I'm so hating what I'm going to have to say to you," she boomed.

This was a jolly way to begin an interview, John thought, especially in his present mood. He tried to look attentive, faintly surprised, dignified, and withal deferential; but, not being a great actor, he failed to express all these states of mind at a go, and only succeeded in dropping his gloves.

"Hating it," the actress cried. "Oh, hating it!"

"Well, if you'd rather postpone it," John began.

"No, no. It must be said now. It's just this!" She paused and fixed the author more intensely than a snake fixes a rabbit or a woman in a bus tries to see if the woman opposite has blacked her eyelashes. "Can I produce *Joan of Arc?*"

"I think that question is answered by our contract," replied John, who was used to leading ladies, and when they started like this always fell back at once in good order on business.

"Yes, but what about my unwritten contract with the public?" she demanded.

"I don't know anything about that," said the author. "Moreover, I don't see how an unwritten contract can interfere with our written contract."

"John Touchwood, I'm going to be frank with you, fiercely frank. I can't afford to produce a play by you about a heroine like Joan of Arc unless you take steps to put things right."

"If you want me to cut that scene . . ."

"Oh, I'm not talking about scenes, John Touchwood. I'm talking about these terrible stories that everybody is whispering about you. I don't mind myself what you do. Good gracious me, I'm a broad-minded modern woman; but my public looks for something special at the Parthenon. The knowledge that I am going to play the Maid of Orleans has moved them indescribably; I was fully prepared to give you the success of your career, but . . . these stories! This girl! You know what people are saying? You must have heard. How can I put your name on my programme as the author of *Joan of Arc?* How can I, John Touchwood?"

If John had not overheard that conversation at his club the night before, he would have supposed that Miss Bond had gone mad.

"May I inquire exactly what you have heard about me and my private life?" he inquired, as judicially as he could.

"Please spare me from repeating the stories. I can honestly assure you that I don't believe them. But you as a man of the world know very well how unimportant it is whether a story is true or not. If you were a writer of realistic drama, these stories, however bad they were, wouldn't matter. If your next play was going to be produced at the Court Theater, these stories would, if anything, be in favor of success . . . but at the Parthenon . . ."

"You are talking nonsense, Miss Bond," interrupted John, angrily. "You are more in a condition to play Ophelia than Joan of Arc. Moreover, you sha'n't play Joan of Arc now. I've really been regretting for some weeks now that you were going to play her, and I'm delighted to have this opportunity of preventing you from playing her. I don't know to what tittle-tattle you've been listening. I don't care. Your opinion of your own virtue may be completely justified, but your judgment of other people's is vulgar and—however, let me recommend you to produce a play by my brother-in-law, the Reverend Laurence Armitage. Even your insatiable ambition may be gratified by the part of the Virgin Mary, who is one of the chief characters. Good morning, Miss Bond. I shall communicate with you more precisely through my agent."

John marched out of the theater, and on the pavement outside ran into Miss Ida Merritt.

"Ah, you're a sensible woman," he spluttered, much to her astonishment. "For goodness' sake, come and have lunch with me, and let's talk over everything."

John, in his relief at meeting Miss Merritt, had taken her arm in a cordial fashion, and steered her across the Strand to Romano's without waiting to choose a less conspicuously theatrical restaurant. Indeed in his anxiety to clear his reputation he forgot everything, and it was only when he saw various people at the little tables nudging one another and bobbing their heads together that he realized he was holding Miss Merritt's arm. He dropped it like a hot coal, and plunged down at a table marked "reserved." The head waiter hurried across to apprise him of the mistake, and John, who was by now horribly self-conscious, fancied that the slight incident had created a stir throughout the restaurant. No doubt it would be all over town by evening that he and his companion in guilt had been refused service at every restaurant in London.

"Look here," said John, when at last they were accommodated at a table painfully near the grill, the spitting and hissing from which seemed to symbolize the attitude of a hostile society. "Look here, what stories have you heard about me? You're a journalist. You write chatty paragraphs. For heaven's sake, tell me the worst."

"Oh, I haven't heard anything that's printable," Miss Merritt assured him, with a laugh.

John put his head between his hands and groaned; the waiter thought he was going to dip his hair into the hors d'œuvres and hurriedly removed the dishes.

"No, seriously, I beg you to tell me if you've heard my name connected in any unpleasant way with Miss Hamilton."

"No, the only thing I've heard about Doris is that your brother, Hugh, is always pestering her with his attentions."

"What?" John shouted.

"Coming, sir," cried the waiter, skipping round the table like a monkey.

John waved him away, and begged Miss Merritt to be more explicit.

"Why didn't she complain to me?" he asked when he had heard her story.

"She probably thought she could look after herself. Besides, wasn't he going to British Guiana?"

"He was," replied John. "At least he was going to some tropical colony. I've heard so many mentioned that I'm beginning myself to forget which it was now. So that's why he didn't go. But he shall go. If I have to have him kidnaped and spend all my savings on chartering a private yacht for the purpose, by Heaven, he shall go. If he shrivels up like a burnt sausage the moment he puts his foot on the beach he shall be left there to shrivel. The rascal! When does he pester her? Where?"

"Don't get so excited. Doris is perfectly capable of looking after herself. Besides, I think she rather likes him in a way."

"Never," John cried.

"Liver is finished, sair," said the officious waiter, dancing in again between John and Miss Merritt.

John shook his fist at him and leant earnestly over the table with one elbow in the butter.

"You don't seriously suggest that she is in love with him?" he asked.

"No, I don't think so. But I met him myself once and took rather a fancy to him. No, she just likes him as a friend. It's he who's in love with her."

"Under my very eyes," John ejaculated. "Why, it's overwhelming."

A sudden thought struck him that even at this moment while he was calmly eating lunch with Miss Merritt, as he somewhat loosely qualified the verb, Hugh might be making love to Miss Hamilton in his own house.

"Look here," he cried, "have you nearly finished? Because I've suddenly remembered an important appointment at Hampstead."

"I don't want any more," said Miss Merritt, obligingly.

"Waiter, the bill! Quick! You don't mind if I rush off and leave you to finish your cheese alone?"

His guest shook her head and John hurried out of the restaurant.

No taxi he had traveled in had ever seemed so slow, and he kept putting his head out of the window to urge the driver to greater speed, until the man goaded to rudeness by John's exhortations and the trams in Tottenham Court Road asked if his fare thought he was a blinking bullet.

"I'm not bullying you. I'm only asking you to drive a little faster," John shouted back.

The driver threw his eyes heavenward in a gesture of despair for John's sanity but he was pacified at Church Row by half-a-sovereign and even went so far as to explain that he had not accused John of bullying him, but merely of confusing his capacity for speed with that of a bullet's. John thought he was asking for more money, gave him half-a-crown and waving his arm, half in benediction, half in protest, he hurried into the hall.

"They've nearly finished lunch, sir," murmured Maud who was just coming from the dining-room. "Would you like Elsa to hot you up something?"

John without a word pounced into the dining-room, where he caught Hugh with a stick of celery half-way to his mouth and Miss Hamilton with a glass of water half-way down from hers in the other direction.

"Oh, I'm so sorry we began without you," said the culprits simultaneously.

John murmured something about a trying interview with Janet Bond, lit a cigar, realized it was rude to light cigars when people were still eating, threw the cigar away, and sat down with an appearance of exhaustion in one of those dining-room armchairs that stand and wait all their lives to serve a moment like this.

"I'm sorry, but I must ask you to go off as soon as you've

finished your lunch, Hugh. I've a lot of important business to transact with Miss Hamilton."

"Oh, but I've finished already," she exclaimed, jumping up from the table.

It was the first pleasant moment in John's day, and he smiled, gratefully. He felt he could even afford to be generous to this intrusive brother, and before he left the room with Miss Hamilton he invited him to have some more celery.

"And you'll find a cigar in the sideboard," he added. "But Maud will look after you. Maud, look after Mr. Hugh, please, and if anybody calls this afternoon, I'm not at home."

CHAPTER XVI

JOHN'S first impulse had been to pour out in Miss Hamilton's ears the tale of his wrongs, and afterward, when he had sufficiently impressed her with the danger of the position in which the world was trying to place them, to ask her to marry him as the only way to escape from it. On second thoughts, he decided that she might be offended by the suggestion of having been compromised by him and that she might resent the notion of their marriage's being no more than a sop to public opinion. He therefore abandoned the idea of enlarging upon the scandal their association had apparently created and proposed to substitute the trite but always popular scene of the prosperous middle-aged man's renunciation of love and happiness in favor of a young and penurious rival. He recalled how many last acts in how many sentimental comedies had owed their success to this situation, which never failed with an audience. But then the average audience was middle-aged. Thinking of the many audiences on which from private boxes he had looked down, John was sure that bald heads always predominated in the auditorium; and naturally those bald heads had been only too ready to nod approval of a heroine who rejected the dashing jeune premier to fling herself into the arms of the elderly actor-manager. It was impossible to think of any infirmity severe enough to thwart an actor-manager. Yet a play was make-believe: in real life events would probably turn out quite differently. It would be very depressing, if he offered to make Doris and Hugh happy together by settling upon them a handsome income, to find Doris jumping at the prospect. Perhaps it would be more prudent not to suggest any possibility of a marriage between them. It might even be more prudent not to mention the subject of marriage at all.

John looked at his secretary with what surely must have been a very eloquent glance indeed, because she dropped her pencil, blushed, and took his hand.

"How much simpler life is than art," John murmured. He would never have dared to allow one of his heroes in a moment of supreme emotion like this to crane his neck across a wide table in order to kiss the heroine. Any audience would have laughed at such an awkward gesture; yet, though he only managed to reach her lips with half an inch to spare, the kiss was not at all funny somehow. No, it ranked with Paolo's or Anthony's or any other famous lover's kiss.

"And now of course I can't be your secretary any longer," she sighed.

"Why? Do you disapprove of wives' helping their husbands?"

"I don't think you really want to get married, do you?"

"My dear, I'm absolutely dying to get married."

"Truly?"

"Doris, look at me."

And surely she looked at him with more admiration than he had ever looked at himself in a glass.

"What a time I shall have with mother," she gasped with the gurgling triumphant laugh of a child who has unexpectedly found the way to open the store-cupboard.

"Oh, no, you won't," John prophesied, confidently. "I'm not going to have such an excellent last scene spoilt by unnecessary talk. We'll get married first and tell everybody afterwards. I've lately discovered what an amazing capacity ordinary human nature has for invention. It really frightens me for the future of novelists, who I cannot believe will be wanted much longer. Oh no, Doris, I'm not going to run the risk of hearing any preliminary gossip about our marriage. Neither your mother nor my relations nor the general public are going to have any share in it before or after. In fact to be brief I propose to elope. Notwithstanding my romantic plays I have spent a private life of utter dullness. This is my last opportunity to do anything unusual. Please, my dearest girl, let me experience the joys of an actual elopement before I relapse into eternal humdrummery."

"A horrid description of marriage!" she protested.

"Comparative humdrummery, I should have said, comparative, that is to say, with the excesses attributed to me by rumor. I've often wanted to write a play about Tiberius, and I feel well equipped to do so now. But I'm serious about the elopment. I really do want to avoid my relations' tongues."

"I believe you're afraid of them."

"I am. I'm not ashamed to admit that I'm in terror of them," he said.

"But where are we going to elope to?"

John picked up the *Times*.

"If only the *Murmania*," he began. "And by Jove, she will too," he cried. "Yes, she's due to sail from Liverpool on April 1st."

"But that's your birthday," she objected.

"Exactly."

"And I've already sent out those invitations."

"Exactly. For some years my relations have made an April fool of me by dining at my expense on that day. I have two corner-cupboards overflowing with their gifts—the most remarkable exhibition of cheapness and ingenuity ever known. This year I am going to make April fools of them."

"By marrying me?" she laughed.

"Well, of course it's no use pretending that they'll be delighted by that joke, though I intend to play another still more elaborately unpleasant. At the back of all their minds exists one anxiety—the dispositions of my last will and testament. Very well. I am going to cure that worry forever by leaving them Ambles. I can't imagine anything more irritating than to be left a house in common with a number of people whom you hate. Oh, it's an exquisite revenge. Darling secretary, take down for dictation as your last task the following:

"'I, John Touchwood, playwright, of 36 Church Row,

Hampstead, N.W., and Ambles, Wrottesford, Hants, do hereby will and bequeathe.'"

"I don't understand," she said. "Are you really making a will? or are you only playing a joke?"

"Both."

"But is this really to take effect when you're dead? Oh dear, I wish you wouldn't talk about death when I've just said I'll marry you."

John paused thoughtfully:

"It does seem rather a challenge to fate," he agreed. "I know what I'll do. I'll make over Ambles to them at once. After all, I am dead to them, for I'll never have anything more to do with any of them. Cross out what you took down. I'll alter the form. Begin as for a letter:

"'My dear relations,

"'When you read this I shall be far away.' . . . I think that's the correct formula?" he asked.

"It sounds familiar from many books," she assured him.

"'Far away on my honeymoon with Miss Doris Hamilton.' Perhaps that sounds a little ambiguous. Cross out the maiden name and substitute ' with Mrs. John Touchwood, my former secretary. Since you have attributed to us every link except that of matrimony you will no doubt be glad of this opportunity to contradict the outrageous tales you have most of you' . . . I say most of you," John explained, "because I don't really think the children started any scandal . . . 'you have most of you been at such pains to invent and circulate. Realizing that this announcement will come as a sad blow, I am going to soften it as far as I can by making you a present of my country house in Hampshire, and I am instructing my solicitors to effect the conveyance in due form. From now onwards therefore one fifth of Ambles will belong to James and Beatrice, one fifth to George, Eleanor, Bertram, and Viola, and one fifth to Hilda and Harold, one fifth to Edith, Laurence, and Frida, and one fifth to Hugh.' . . . I feel that Hugh is entitled .o a proportionately larger share," he said with his eyes on the ceiling, "because I understand that I've robbed him of you."

"Who on earth told you that?" she demanded, putting down her pencil.

"Never mind," said John, humming gayly his exultation. "Continue please, Miss Hamilton! 'I shall make no attempt to say which fifth of the house shall belong to whom. Possibly Laurence and Hilda will argue that out between them, and if any structural alterations are required no doubt Hugh will charge himself with them. The twenty-acre field is included in the gift, so that there will be plenty of ground for any alterations or extensions deemed necessary by the future owners.'"

"How ridiculous you are . . . John," she laughed. "It all sounds so absurdly practical—as if you really meant it."

"My dear girl, I do mean it. Continue please, Miss Hamilton! 'I have long felt that the collection of humming-birds made by Daniel Curtis in the Brazils should be suitably housed, and I propose that a portion of the stables should be put in order for their reception together with what is left of the collection of British dragon-flies made by James. My solicitors will supply a sum of £50 for this purpose and Harold can act as curator of what will be known as the Touchwood Museum. With regard to Harold's future, the family knows that I have invested £2000 in the mahogany plantations of Mr. Sydney Ricketts in British Honduras, and if Hugh does not take up his post within three months I shall ask Mr. Ricketts to accept Harold as a pupil in five years' time. He had better begin to study Hondurasian or whatever the language is called at once. Until Harold is called upon to make his decision I shall instruct Mr. Ricketts to put the interest with the capital. While on the subject of nephews and nieces, I may as well say that the family pictures and family silver will be sent back to Ambles to be held in trust for Bertram upon his coming of age. Furthermore, I am prepared to pay for the education of Bertram,

Harold, Frida, and Viola at good boarding-schools. Viola can practice her dancing in the holidays. Bertram's future I will provide for when the time comes. I do not wish George to have any excuse for remaining at Halma House—and I have no doubt that a private sitting-room will be awarded to him at Ambles. In the event of undue congestion his knitting would not disturb Laurence's poetic composition, and his system of backing second favorites in imagination can be carried on as easily at Ambles as in London. If he still hankers for a sea voyage, the river with Harold and himself in a Canadian canoe will give him all the nautical adventure he requires. My solicitors have been instructed to place a canoe at his disposal. To James who has so often reproved me for my optimism I would say once more "Beware of new critical weeklies" and remind him that a bird in the hand is worth two in the bush. In other words, he has got a thousand pounds out of me, and he won't get another penny. Eleanor has shown herself so well able to look after herself that I am not going to insult her by offering to look after her. Hilda with her fifth of the house and her small private income will have nothing to do but fuss about the proportionate expenses of the various members of the family who choose to inhabit Ambles. I am affording her an unique opportunity for being disagreeable, of which I'm sure she will take the fullest advantage. I may say that no financial allowance will be made to those who prefer to live elsewhere. As for Laurence, his theatrical future under the patronage of Sir Percy Mortimer is no doubt secure. However, if he grows tired of playing butlers, I hope that his muse will welcome him back to Ambles as affectionately as his wife.

"'I don't think I have anything more to say, my dear relations, except that I hope the presents you are bringing me for my birthday will come in useful as knick-knacks for your delightful house. You can now circulate as many stories about me as you like. You can even say that I have founded a lunatic asylum at Ambles. I am so happy in the prospect of my marriage that I cannot feel very hardly towards you all, and so I wish you good luck.

"'Your affectionate brother, brother-in-law, and uncle,
"'JOHN TOUCHWOOD.'

"Type that out, please, Miss Hamilton, while I drive down to Doctors Commons to see about the license and book our passage in the *Murmania.*"

John had never tasted any success so sweet as the success of these two days before his forty-third birthday; and he was glad to find that Doris having once made up her mind about getting married showed no signs of imperilling the adventure by confiding her intention to her mother.

"Dear John," she said, "I bolted to America with Ida Merritt last year without a word to Mother until I sent her a wireless from on board. Surely I may elope with you . . . and explain afterwards."

"You don't think it will kill her," suggested John a little anxiously. "People are apparently quite ready to accuse one of breaking a maternal heart as lightly as they would accuse one of breaking an appointment."

"Dear John, when we're married she'll be delighted."

"Not too delighted, eh, darling? I mean not so delighted that she'll want to come and gloat over us all day. You see, when the honeymoon's over, I shall have to get to work again on that last act, and your mother does talk a good deal. I know it's very intelligent talk, but it would be rather an interruption."

The only person they took into their confidence about the wedding, except the clergyman, the verger, and a crossing-sweeper brought in to witness the signing of the register was Mrs. Worfolk.

"Well, that's highly satisfactory! You couldn't have chosen a nicer young lady. Well, I mean to say, I've known her so long and all. And you expect to be back in June? Oh well, I shall have everything nice and tidy you may be sure. And this letter you want handed to Mr. James to be read to the family on your birthday? And I'm to give them their dinners the same as if you were here yourself? I see. And how many bottles of champagne shall I open? Oh, not to stint them? No, I quite understand. Of course, they would want to drink your healths. Certainly. And so they ought! Well, I'm bound to say I wish Mr. Worfolk could have been alive. It makes me quite aggravated to think he shouldn't be here. Well, I mean to say, he being a family carpenter had helped at so many weddings."

The scene on the *Murmania* did not differ much from the scene on board the same ship six months ago. John had insisted that Doris should wear her misty green suit of Harris tweed; but he himself had bought at the Burlington Arcade a traveling cap that showed plainly the sobering effects of matrimony. In the barber's saloon he invested in a pair of rope-soled shoes; he wanted to be sure of being able to support his wife even upon a heeling deck. Before dinner they went forward to watch the stars come out in the twilight—stars that were scarcely as yet more luminous in the green April sky than daisies in a meadow. They stood silent listening to the splash of the dusky sea against the bows, until the shore lamps began to wink astern.

"How savage the night looks coming after us," said John. "It's jolly to think that in the middle of all that blackness James is reading my birthday welcome to the family."

"Poor dears!"

"Oh, they deserve all they've got," he said, fiercely. "And to think that only six months ago I was fool enough to read their letters of congratulation quite seriously in this very ship. It was you with your remark about poor relations that put your foot through my picture."

"You're very much married already, aren't you, John?"

"Am I?"

"Yes, for you're already blaming me for everything."

"I suppose this is what James would call one of my confounded sentimental endings," John murmured.

"Whatever he called it, he couldn't invent a better ending himself," she murmured back. "You know, critics are very like disappointed old maids."

The great ship trembled faintly in the deeper motion, and John holding Doris to him felt that she too trembled faintly in unison. They stood like this in renewed silence until the stars shone clearly, and the shore lamps were turning to a gold blur. John may be excused for thinking that the bugle for dinner sounded like a flourish from *Lohengrin*. He had reason to feel romantic now.

THE END

BIBLIOLIFE

Old Books Deserve a New Life
www.bibliolife.com

Did you know that you can get most of our titles in our trademark **EasyScript**™ print format? **EasyScript**™ provides readers with a larger than average typeface, for a reading experience that's easier on the eyes.

Did you know that we have an ever-growing collection of books in many languages?

Order online:
www.bibliolife.com/store

Or to exclusively browse our **EasyScript**™ collection:
www.bibliogrande.com

At BiblioLife, we aim to make knowledge more accessible by making thousands of titles available to you – quickly and affordably.

Contact us:
BiblioLife
PO Box 21206
Charleston, SC 29413

Printed in Great Britain by
Amazon.co.uk, Ltd.,
Marston Gate.